ANCHORED IN VIETNAM

THE MAKING OF A SERVANT

SAM JAMES

ARCHWAY
PUBLISHING

Archway Publishing books may be ordered through booksellers or by contacting:

Archway Publishing
1663 Liberty Drive
Bloomington, IN 47403
www.archwaypublishing.com
1 (888) 242-5904

Scriptures taken from the King James Bible.

Scripture quotations marked (NIV) are taken from the Holy Bible, New
International Version®, NIV®. Copyright © 1973, 1978, 1984, 2011 by Biblica,
Inc.™ Used by permission of Zondervan. All rights reserved worldwide. www.
zondervan.com The "NIV" and "New International Version" are trademarks
registered in the United States Patent and Trademark Office by Biblica, Inc.™

ISBN: 978-1-4808-6250-0 (sc)
ISBN: 978-1-4808-6248-7 (hc)
ISBN: 978-1-4808-6249-4 (e)

Library of Congress Control Number: 2017919675

Print information available on the last page.

Archway Publishing rev. date: 4/26/2018

CONTENTS

PART I: PREPARING THE CLAY IN THE POTTER'S HANDS

PART II: FORMING THE VESSEL

PART III: FILLING THE VESSEL

PART IV: BREAKING, REMAKING, REFILLING THE VESSEL

ACKNOWLEDGMENTS

Rachel Kerr James has been my inseparable partner throughout our service together for sixty years. She is my greatest supporter, my insightful critic, and the love of my life. Without her, this book could not be written. Deborah, Stephen, Philip, and Michael, each totally committed to our Lord, are not only daughter and sons but also partners in ministry in all we have done.

My Vietnamese students not only taught me to become Vietnamese in my heart but also accepted me as a teacher, colleague, and friend.

My dear friend John McGill, encourager to many Christian authors, has inspired me in all my writings.

David Cornelius, effective pastor, missionary, and Christian friend, gave important advice on the writing of African American relationships and experiences.

Each of the individuals, American and Vietnamese, entered my life at crucial points to shape me into the vessel God would use throughout these years.

I owe a debt of gratitude to Dan Allen, Erich Bridges, Marty Croll, Wendy Norvelle, Van Payne, Deborah James Winans, and Ana Winans for their reviews, advice, and counsel.

The word *thanks* is hardly sufficient to express my gratitude for Ann Lovell, who edited my manuscript and gave significant advice and counsel.

FOREWORD

In 2012, I had the privilege of introducing Dr. Sam James to our congregation at The Summit Church. Most didn't know who he was or that he had planted our church in 1962. I couldn't blame them because up until just a few years ago, I hadn't been aware of the connection either.

I was asked to speak to the staff of the International Mission Board at IMB headquarters in Richmond, Va. It was an incredible honor, because I had been trained at these very headquarters nearly a decade before when I was sent out to Southeast Asia to serve as a missionary. As I walked into the training center, I noticed the building bore the honorific, "The Sam James Educational Center." I knew that I had heard that name before, and when I inquired about him, I found out it was because Sam James had planted our church as "The Homestead Heights Baptist Mission" in 1962.

Dr. James hadn't intended on planting a church in North Carolina, but en route to Vietnam, where he believed God had called him, he was delayed by some family health concerns. While waiting for medical clearance, he worked with 5 motivated laymen in North Durham who had a dream of planting a church there.

Dr. James worked with that core group of 5 men for a year, and left the day it officially launched. He told me he only preached one official sermon for the new church, on that launch Sunday. He chose Isaiah 54 for the text, William Carey's famous missionary text, because he believed it best embodied the hopes and dreams he had for this church.

2"Enlarge the place of your tent,
   stretch your tent curtains wide,
   do not hold back;
   lengthen your cords,
   strengthen your stakes.
3 For you will spread out to the right and to the left;
   your descendants will dispossess nations
   and settle in their desolate cities.[1]

He preached the sermon that morning, and left that afternoon for Vietnam, where he would serve as God's messenger for the next 40 years. God graciously has enabled our church to fulfill his vision, with more than 200 of our members currently serving on church planting teams overseas. It is no exaggeration to say that what we are experiencing goes back to the seeds of faith planted by Dr. Sam James more than 50 years ago.

"Do not hold back!" Sam repeated those words to our church on that Sunday he visited us in 2012, and they still ring in my ears. How can we hold back with so urgent a gospel and so willing and powerful a God behind it?

Dr. James's life is a picture of what it looks like to not hold back. He has, in the words of William Carey, expected great things of God and attempted great things for God. And his life shows the amazing results of what happens when you live that way.

The book you hold in your hand is a chronicling of the miraculous and faithful ways God uses those who expect great things of him and attempt great things for him. His stories will motivate, instruct, and inspire you. His faith has literally shaped our church and continues to inspire our vision and ignite our passion.

Since 2012, we have enjoyed having Dr. James back several times to preach to our church and teach our leaders. We are always humbled by the grace, love, joy, and humility he displays. We are

---

[1] Isaiah 54:2-3, NIV

also greatly enriched by the depth of wisdom and experience from which he speaks. In his first letter to the Corinthians, Paul made what I always found to be an audacious statement. "Follow my example as I follow Christ." In my life, I have only known a few men and women who have set such an example of what Christ-honoring, faith-filled, gospel-rich discipleship looks like. Our church seeks to continue to follow Dr. James as he follows Jesus, and I hope this book will inspire you to do the same. We will turn the world upside-down if we do.

J. D. Greear, PhD

Author of several books including "Gaining by Losing: Why the future belongs to churches that send;" and "Gospel: Recovering the power that made Christianity revolutionary."

Professor, Southeastern Baptist Theological Seminary

Pastor, The Summit Church, Durham, North Carolina, a church with more than 10,000 people in attendance regularly in five worship services weekly on Saturday and Sunday, 200 international missionaries serving in teams overseas through the International Mission Board, SBC, and planted 250 churches in the United States and world-wide with a goal of 1,000 church plants in this generation.

INTRODUCTION

This book is about one man's life and his struggle to become what God created him to be. The question is: "What makes a man and his wife pick up their family and move to another country, not knowing the language and the culture or any person in that country, and spend most of his life there?" A second question often asked is: "Why would a man take his family into a country that erupts into a major war and continue to live there until the resolution of the conflict over thirteen years later?" Another question is: "What makes a person decide to serve the Lord overseas and remain in that service fifty-four years?"

Some would say such a life is not normal. Some would say it is foolhardy. Some say such a commitment—leaving father and mother, siblings and friends to serve the Lord far away—is too great a sacrifice. "We need ministers here at home!" they say.

Many of us struggle intensely trying to find that right direction we should take to find peace, joy, and meaning in life. Faced with so many choices, how do we find that pathway?

I am reminded of the story of Alice in Wonderland.[1] One day Alice came to a fork in the road and saw a Cheshire cat in a tree:

> "Would you tell me, please, which way I ought to
> go from here?" she asked.
>   "That depends a good deal on where you want
> to get to," said the Cat.
>   "I don't much care where," said Alice.

"Then it doesn't matter which way you go—," said the Cat.

"The matter" is important because it means either spending one's life in meaning, joy, contentment, and fulfillment or spending one's life always wondering with regret, "What if I had only taken the other fork in the road?"

Many influences all along the pathway of life help us with our direction. We are born with gifts and talents, which, when used, bring fulfillment. Opportunities for training and education either rule out a direction or set us on the path we desire. I have often said, "We have spent more money helping our kids find out what they didn't want to do in life than what they did want to do!"

From the earliest moments of our life, experiences influence the inevitable choices we make in the direction of our life. When confronted with forks in the road, even later in life, consciously or unconsciously, past experiences nudge us in the direction we take. Relationships with people are powerful in determining who we are and what we do.

John Ortberg, in his book, *Everybody's Normal Till You Get To Know Them*[2] tells of a friend's first trip down South. At breakfast in a Toddle House in South Carolina, he saw something on the menu called "grits." Not knowing what grits were, he asked the waitress, "What is a grit?" She replied, "Honey, they don't come by themselves!" The truth is, none of us comes here by ourselves!

We are born in the midst of people and events, always interacting, influencing others, and being influenced. We never cease "becoming." It is through the cruxes of life that we realize our need to become something we are not.

Many of us go through long periods of restlessness, questioning, seeking answers, and hungering for significant meaning. Saint Augustine of Hippo in his *Confessions* writes to God, "Thou hast made us for Thyself, O Lord, and our heart is restless until it finds rest in Thee."³ Trials and turmoil reveal our restlessness and form the basis for our self-discovery and growth.

When things happen and we are shocked, we often ask, "Why? Why is this happening to me?" The truth is we seldom get an answer to that question. A long time ago, I changed the question to, "Lord, what can I learn from this experience?" It is this restlessness and seeking that sets us on a path to discover who we are in a world that is trying to form us into something we don't want to be.

It is our Creator, the Lord, our God, who gives us our "being" and leads us in our "becoming." It is our trust in Him that inspires obedience to Him. Through that trust and obedience, He shapes us into the vessel He wants us to be as His servants in a world that needs Him so desperately. Through my fifty-four years in the mission field, He has never asked me to do something He has not already prepared and gifted me to do. I am inspired by Jeremiah 18:3–6 (NIV):

> So I went down to the potter's house, and I saw him working at the wheel.
> But the pot he was shaping from the clay was marred in his hands; so the potter formed it into another pot, shaping it as seemed best to him.

Then the word of the LORD came to me.

> He said, "Can I not do with you, Israel, as this potter does?" declares the LORD. "Like clay in the hand of the potter, so are you in my hand." Jeremiah 18:3-6 (NIV)

This passage reflects a process of preparing, of molding and then the breaking and remolding us for life and service in changing circumstances. At times the process is unexpected and painful, and at times, it is exhilarating and joyful. But we are always moving forward. It is in the experiences of life, as we process and understand them, that we find ourselves growing, maturing, moving into the future, and hearing God's call to service. In the New Testament, the apostle Paul continues this metaphor, "We have this treasure in jars of clay to show that this all-surpassing power is from God and not from us" II Corinthians 4:7 (NIV).

The statement "this all-surpassing power is from God and not from us," is significant. However imperfect and temporary this body is, it holds the very presence of God in His great love, majesty, and power. As we become transparent, people are able to look at and experience that power in us, rather than focus on the external features of skin, bones, our educational achievements, our wealth, and worldly power. Our desire is that whatever direction we take, whatever our accomplishments, these clay vessels we are will reflect the very glory and majesty of our Living God.

You are encouraged to look back at those experiences that helped shape who you are today and who you are becoming. You will enjoy the thrill of discovering how the Lord has been preparing you for what He wants you to be and do in this world. God's formation and shaping of us as a vessel is always spiritual and internal!

PART I
PREPARING THE CLAY IN THE POTTER'S HANDS

CHAPTER 1

A LIFE-ALTERING CRISIS

I was shaken to the core of my being. It was a cold December night two days before Christmas 1952; I was a quartermaster on board the USS *Sitkoh Bay* (CVE-86) bound for Yokosuka, Japan.

I went to bed early, anticipating getting up for my midnight watch on the bridge. About eleven that night, a deafening crunching sound woke me up. Simultaneously I was thrown to the deck, water washing all around me. The lights flickered several times, and then I was plunged into darkness.

In a flash, my feelings moved from disorientation to confusion to terror—and then to action. I knew I had to move fast. Training and drills for emergency situations kicked in. We always placed our clothing and shoes in the same place so that, in an emergency, we could find them and dress quickly. I had no idea where the water was coming from or what had happened, but it was a desperate situation. Within moments, I was climbing the ladder and running toward my emergency station on the ship's bridge. As I emerged from below deck, there in front of me, almost within an arm's reach, loomed a large merchant ship just off the port side, evidently dead in the water. This merchant vessel had plowed into the side of our heavily loaded aircraft carrier.

The officer of the deck was establishing order and instituting emergency procedures. The ship's captain arrived on the bridge.

"Okay, what's the situation?" the captain asked.

I listened to the report from the officer of the deck. "Sir, a merchant ship has collided with us, hitting us just forward of midships on the port side extending below the waterline. We have stopped all engines. We don't know yet how extensive the damaged area is, but we are taking on a sizable amount of water. Emergency power is on. The damage control crew is assessing the damage and will report posthaste. No message has gone out anywhere yet regarding our situation. We are waiting for word from you. The sick bay is alerted and preparing for any casualties, but none have been reported yet."

The captain ordered the ship turned so the damaged side would be on the lee side, protected from the wind and waves. Very quickly, he turned his attention to the other ship.

"Do we know anything about the freighter?"

"No, sir. No contact has been made. It appears she has cut her engines and is adrift right now."

"Quartermaster, contact that ship and find out what their situation is. Find out if there are any casualties and how we can help," the captain ordered.

"Aye, aye, sir," I said. Immediately I turned to our signal light and began contacting the other ship but to no avail. I switched to a much larger light but still no response. "Captain, I cannot get a response from them."

"Check the wind and sea conditions and report back immediately," the captain ordered.

It was a dark night. I could hardly see the water below. I contacted the ship's meteorologist. "There is a moderate wind and sea, but the wind is rapidly increasing," I reported to the captain.

Since we could not contact the other ship, the captain ordered an emergency crew to board the captain's gig immediately, go to the other ship, and assess the situation.

Within minutes the emergency crew, including me as visual communicator, was lowered to the sea. On the way down, we passed the gaping hole in the side of the ship just above and extending below the waterline. It was much larger than we had imagined. Every wave was washing huge amounts of water into the gaping hole. There was already a slight list toward the port side. Immediately, our small boat was moving through what appeared to be an increasing wave height. The coxswain at the helm spoke ominously directly into my ear over the sound of the engine, wind, and waves: "If we continue to take on water at this rate, our ship will list too far." I could barely make out the worried look on his face in the darkness. He added, "It will be impossible to hoist us back onto the ship."

I nodded. The situation seemed grim.

Waves were much higher than anticipated, so at times we were totally obscured from sight as we drew farther away. By now the two ships were very far apart. It took around forty-five minutes to approach. We circled the bow. I directed the light toward the damaged area. It looked to be above the waterline and not extensive. I trained my portable light, requesting permission to board. There was no answer, but immediately, netting appeared over the side. A desperate fear gripped me as I tried to launch myself from a wildly heaving small boat to the loosely dangling netting. The danger of falling into that surging ocean between our boat and the ship was terrifying. With every ounce of strength, we climbed up and over the ship's side.

The ship was a freighter hauling coal from the United States to Japan. They were operating with a minimal crew. At the time of the collision, the ship was on automatic pilot. The entire crew was below deck watching a movie. One man was slightly injured. Our ship's corpsman treated his wound. Such carelessness filled me with disgust. For that, we were going through what appeared to be a catastrophic situation!

One look around revealed the disarray on deck. Nothing seemed to be in its appropriate place. This kind of mess was not caused by a collision. It was simply neglect and poor seamanship. As I walked from one area to another, I had to step over boxes and all kinds of equipment. Should they run into a storm, seamen could be seriously injured. I could only shake my head at the chaos this carelessness had caused.

I prepared a brief report to send back to our ship. Sending a message visually at such a distance on two heavily rolling ships was nearly impossible. Soon, a very brief visual message came for us to return immediately.

By now the sea was much rougher and the two ships farther apart. It took well over an hour to return. As we drew near, it was evident our ship was listing rather heavily to the port side. With planes filling the flight deck, we were in a desperate situation. The waves were higher. Our small boat was almost uncontrollable as we tried to move alongside. With the angle of the ship leaning to the left and a rough sea, it was going to be impossible for the hoisting apparatus to be attached to our boat to lift us back into place. I received a visual communication from the captain ordering us to remain close and wait for conditions to change. We had no way of knowing the progress of repairs on the ship or even whether or not it could be saved.

These small escort aircraft carriers were often called "Kaiser's coffins." At the beginning of World War II, Kaiser Shipyards in Washington State took regular oceangoing freighters and completely remodeled them. They built a flight deck and an operations bridge on top. During World War II, these freighters carried one or more squadrons of fighter planes to protect convoys. These freighters were not built for that much weight on top of a much lighter hull. This made them less seaworthy than most naval ships. This was one reason our ship was so devastated by this collision. In recent years, these ships ferried planes from one area to another. The *Sitkoh Bay* was ferrying various types of planes from the United States to be used in the Korean War. It also brought damaged planes back to the United States for repair or disposal.

It was a difficult night. We were constantly pressured away from our ship by the rough sea and wind. The air was cold, the sea was cold, and we were wet to the core. A couple of men were seasick from the rolling and tossing of the small captain's gig on a rough sea. At times, we completely lost sight of our ship in the trough of high waves. It was always a comfort to reach the crest of a wave and see the masthead light in the distance. It was rather dim since the ship was using emergency lighting. Of necessity, we kept our bow pointed toward the light to keep our bearings.

I often look back on that night. We kept the light in sight to avoid being lost in the expansive ocean. When the seas of life are violent and my direction and meaning in life are obscured, I have a light that keeps me steadily moving in the right direction. There is an old hymn that reads, "Let the lower lights be burning, send the gleam across the wave. Some poor fainting, struggling seaman you may rescue, you may save."[4] That hymn will always have special meaning for me!

As we sat silently and were being tossed about by a rough sea, one thing that happened just a few weeks before came to my mind. I had rented a bicycle and was riding through the countryside outside of Yokosuka, Japan. I saw a small cottage with a sign, which had the picture of the palm of a person's hand with large lines. Evidently this was a Japanese palm reader. Out of curiosity, I stopped and spoke to him. He waved me in, served tea, and took hold of my palm. He only spoke Japanese, so I could not understand. He reached in his pocket and pulled out a paper with two columns of numbered sentences. In one column was a sentence in Japanese. In the corresponding column was a sentence in English. He would point to a line on my palm and indicate a sentence in Japanese. I would then read the English translation. The first sentences he pointed to were true. Soon he pointed to a final sentence that read, "You will lead a short but happy life."

I confess I never believed in fortune-telling of any kind. However, this sentence bothered me in spite of my doubt. I was a sailor serving in the midst of the Korean War. I was at sea constantly. I did not want to hear anything about living a short life, happy or otherwise!

For days and weeks after that I kept telling myself, "This is pure nonsense. No human being can know the fate of another human being. It is impossible." But, I couldn't get it out of my mind. Sitting in the boat that night, tossed violently by the sea, cold and wet, near my ship that could well be sinking, this experience rushed back into my mind with a vengeance. I promised myself, "If I live through this experience, I will tell every person to stay away from fortune-tellers." They could plant seeds in your mind, which were totally untrue. Your mind knew they were unfounded, but they could affect your sense of well-being for years to come.

We sat silently huddled against the wind and the sting of the sea spray. No one wanted to talk, but neither could anyone sleep. My mind drifted back to my childhood and various experiences. My experiences as an Eagle Scout learning to survive under harsh conditions were a comfort to me, giving assurance that I could and I would survive.

I reflected on my feelings of restlessness and loneliness. I was obsessed with questions about the direction of my life. There was no question I loved my hometown, but from my earliest memories I'd never felt my future was going to lie there. I was always looking at the horizon and wanting to see what was beyond. I felt there was something missing from my life keeping me from being at peace with myself. That night, I determined I was going to have to find whatever I was missing.

I was awakened from these thoughts by the coxswain, asking if I could steer the boat for a while so he could rest his arms. He had been fighting the waves for at least three hours. As I took the helm, I sensed this night had changed my life. Some serious questions needed to have answers, like, "How do I find the peace of mind I have longed for so long?" "Where is all of this leading me?" "How am I going to get to wherever it is I really belong?" "How can I find out what and who I am supposed to be?"

At dawn, the sea began to calm. We could see the ship was no longer listing to one side. The ship's pumps had successfully pumped out hundreds of gallons of water. Electricity was restored throughout the ship. We were now able to be hoisted into place. We were back "home."

Lying on my bunk after that difficult night, I thought again how my life was like a puzzle. One piece was missing, and I didn't know what or where it might be. I resolved from that point, "I am going to discover what is missing. I will know it when I see it."

National Aviation Museum Photograph Collection

CHAPTER 2

FORMED BY BEGINNINGS

I was seven years into my life. It was 1939, in the small town of Liberty, North Carolina. I lay in bed, cozy against the chill on my face, tucked beneath a heavy cover of quilt and blankets. It was not yet dawn when I woke up. Outside my bedroom window was a thickening blanket of snow, brightening the air with a soft, white glow. I listened as the wind growled and whistled in rhythm around the corners and underneath the floors of our poorly insulated wooden house with no underpinning to protect from the wind. When the snow fell with winds howling, the small snow crystals would sometimes be pressed under the eaves of our tin roof, into the attic. Then at times they would filter through the thin ceiling onto my bed. My brother, Vernon, three years older, was responsible each morning for lighting a fire in the woodstove near our kitchen. I would need to take the top cover out on the back porch and shake the snow off before it melted into the covers. The half-drunk glass of water I had placed on a low table by my bed was now a frozen chunk of ice. Every morning during those cold winter months, it took all of my willpower to get out of bed and step on the cold, linoleum floor! That dread was slightly ameliorated by the realization there would be no school today!

Our family was poorer than most. My father grew up on a farm and learned to be a butcher by trade. He managed a small grocery and meat market on the highway just out of town and was the only employee in that store. He went to work every morning except

Sunday at 6:00 a.m. to open the store and returned home after the 9:00 p.m. closing time. My mother taught every little girl in and around Liberty to play the piano. In addition, she walked all over town taking Avon orders and delivering them to her customers. Mother was a city girl from Winston-Salem, North Carolina. Her mother was a South Carolina genteel southerner. Her mother taught her father to read and write after they were married. Her father was an artist and ultimately owned his own paint shop, where he painted all sorts of horse-drawn carriages and buggies. As soon as the automobile was invented, he converted his shop to painting automobiles and school buses.

My own mother and father were an interesting combination of a city girl and a country boy. From the city girl, I received my love of and hunger for education and desire to achieve. From my father, I received my strong work ethic and desire for adventure. My mother and father were not "touchy-feely" people. It was difficult for them to show their love physically for their boys. I was aware, though, of love and compassion that showed in unspoken ways from time to time. Their hard life due to the Great Depression had made them somewhat stoical. They kept their emotions bottled up inside. Every afternoon after football practice I walked the two miles down the highway to help my dad in the grocery store. One cold night, I was outside drawing kerosene into a can for a customer. Trying to get the cap off of the container, I banged my knuckles painfully on the cold cement. I muttered aloud, "I can't get the d ... cap off." I did not notice my father standing behind me. He didn't say a word, but as I looked around, I saw a pained look on his face as he turned and went into the store.

The next morning, my mother asked, "Son, did you use a curse word last night?"

"Yes," I replied.

"After you went to bed last night, your father sat by the fire, and I saw tears in his eyes. I asked him, 'Why?' He said, 'Last night, for the first time, I heard Sammy utter a curse word. I feel so bad that, at such a young age, he has to work around the store and hear all the cursing and lurid conversations of men hanging around the store.'"

Hearing that, I have never uttered a curse word again, even to this day. He did not have to say anything to me. I felt the hurt and care of someone who loved me very much.

On the other hand, when I needed punishment, he never had to strike me. All he had to do was focus those dark brown eyes on me with a look that struck fear in my heart and sent a shiver of deep regret for my actions.

I felt sorry for my father. Like so many men during those hard years, the problems of the Great Depression era and our poverty weighed heavily on him. These circumstances resulted in depression which he sought to escape by drinking alcohol.

During this decade of the Great Depression, President Franklin Roosevelt defined a certain amount of income as the "poverty level." The combined income of my father and mother never rose anywhere near the poverty level, so the government labeled us "poverty people." This greatly incensed my father, who had far too much pride to admit we lived in poverty. He always said that, as long as he had strength and health, he would have a job and would work with his own hands to support his family. He would never become dependent on the government for our livelihood!

It was my parents' dream to someday move out of rental housing into our own house. They were able to buy a small, old house on a red dirt street for five hundred dollars and promised to pay ten dollars a week until it was paid off. Gradually as he was able to save a little money, he began making necessary improvements. Our water came from a small, hand-operated pump just off of our back porch. We pumped water and carried it into the house for all of our needs. It was a great day when a bathroom, complete with a sink, commode, and shower, was installed in a small room built on the back porch. I felt like cheering when a truck hauled away the outhouse that sat on the back corner of our yard. I never complained about having to go out on the cold back porch to get to the new bathroom because that was so much better than going thirty yards across the backyard to the outhouse! My only regret was the beautiful damson plum trees surrounding the outhouse no longer produced large, delicious plums as it had done in previous years.

Though we lived in the city limits with fourteen hundred other citizens, it was like we lived in the country. I could walk downtown to school in fifteen minutes, and I could be in deep woods in half that time! These thick woods became like a second home to me. It was there I learned to shoot a .22 caliber rifle and to hunt rabbit and squirrel for food. I earned most of my merit badges for my Eagle Scout award in those woods. I also retreated there when I needed to calm down, lick my wounds, and deal with my problems. Being the middle child of three boys, I quite often felt somewhat left out. My father depended on my brother Vernon for many things. My mother devoted herself to taking care of Jimmy, my brother who was five years younger than me.

On one occasion when I was about nine years old, I was feeling quite ignored, unloved, and overdisciplined. I decided to run away. I put two apples and a banana in a paper sack and went to the woods. All afternoon I remained there nursing my strong, negative feelings. As it grew dark, I thought of my family and how they must be worried about me. "They probably have already alerted the entire community to form search parties to look for me," I thought to myself. I had eaten my apples and banana and realized it was almost dinnertime. I decided to go home.

Creeping in the darkness to the window of our kitchen and dining area, I peered in. Mom was preparing dinner. My older brother was doing his homework. I opened the back door and walked into the kitchen, expecting my mother would be in tears and tightly hug her lost son. Instead, she simply said, "Wash your hands. We're ready to eat." So much for running away!

One lazy Sunday afternoon, I looked longingly at the woods. I had wondered where the woods ended. I decided to ignore my mother's frequent warnings not to go too deep into the woods. She said, "You don't know what creatures and things are lurking there. It could be dangerous for you." My tenth birthday had just passed, and I was feeling confident in my new maturity.

I plunged into the depths of briars, shrub bushes, and undergrowth of all kinds to find a path or opening leading through the woods. I soon discovered years had passed since anyone walked through those woods. Suddenly, after a long struggle, I stepped out onto a fallow cornfield and, at that moment, heard the most beautiful music I had ever heard. Just across the cornfield beside a narrow dirt road was a small, white church. The sign read "Edwards Grove Baptist Church." The Sunday afternoon worship service was just beginning. Seeing the people arriving, I realized this was an African American church. I crawled across the cornfield to get as close as possible without being seen.

There was a beehive of activity as the congregants arrived. Little children played outside under supervision, and a number of children my age entered the church with their parents. I sat there in a ditch beside the dirt road all afternoon, entranced by music I had never heard before. The pastor preached as though he was singing his message. The congregation, from time to time, burst into music right in the middle of his sermon. I could hear rhythmic clapping and feet pounding the floor like dancing. It was nearly impossible to listen without moving, my body controlled by the rhythm of the music. There was excitement and joy like I had never heard or felt. I could not tear myself away.

The service ended, and people began to exit the church. Hoping I would not be seen, I crawled back across the cornfield, slipped into the woods, and began moving toward home.

This experience started me on a lifelong journey that shaped my life into what it is today. It sparked an interest in the realm of spiritual things that only increased with the passing of time. I was suddenly awakened to a different culture that existed all around me but that I had never noticed or touched. Until the day I graduated from high school, practically every Sunday afternoon, I made my way through the woods to sit on the side of that dirt road. My heart longed to go inside and be a part of something I was learning to deeply appreciate. Why couldn't I go inside? What kept me from sharing that experience with a people I did not know but longed to be with? The answer to that question lay in the community in which I grew up. As I grew, I seldom touched or had interaction with the African American community.

The all-white Liberty School was the center of activity for our town. Elementary, middle, and high school facilities and auditorium were all on the same property and formed the location for all kinds of interaction. There were special occasions when the main streets were blocked off on Saturday nights for community square dances. On those evenings, there was no distinction made between bankers and farmers, managers and workers, teachers and pupils, rich and poor, adults and children. All danced together and were one as a community.

Another center of community life was the church. Inside the city limits for the fourteen hundred citizens were six churches belonging to six different denominations. In addition, several churches were open to the black community. The countryside around Liberty was filled with churches of all kinds. Most everyone was a member of one of those churches, though not everyone attended with the same faithfulness. While there were often teasing and jokes between Baptists, Methodists, Lutherans, or Holiness groups, there was never hostility or competition between them. Joint services were held on special occasions. My two brothers and I, when we were small, went to every church's Vacation Bible School in the summer. My mother played the organ for the Lutheran church. My father's mother and father were faithful members of the Sandy Creek Primitive Baptist Church, just a few miles south of Liberty, one of the oldest churches in the South. My father never attended any church until very late in life, when he joined the Lutheran Church.

We planted a garden in a vacant lot next to our house and canned the vegetables to eat during the winter. The canned vegetables were stored in my bedroom. One autumn night, my brother and I were awakened by a series of explosions and a horrible smell. The corn my mother had canned in glass jars had not sealed properly. It had fermented and gradually built up air inside until the glass jars exploded all over our bedroom. It was weeks before the smell of bad corn disappeared from our room.

The only help my mother and father were ever able to give toward our education was encouragement and inspiration. They taught us to be independent and self-sufficient. This was not a contrived strategy in which they withheld their resources from us to encourage us to be self-sufficient. It was a necessity because they had no resources to give. We knew that, if we wanted new clothes, we needed to get a job and buy what we could afford. We also knew we needed to take care of what we had because our resources were scarce and hard-earned.

During those early years, college did not cost as much as it does today, but there was little to no scholarship or government assistance available. My older brother, Vernon, joined the Air Force ROTC at the University of North Carolina and, before he retired, became a colonel in the US Air Force as a medical doctor. My younger brother, Jimmy, joined the Naval ROTC program at the University of North Carolina and became a lieutenant commander flight surgeon. Among his duties, he flew from the deck of an aircraft carrier on downed pilot rescue missions in Vietnam during the war. I was able to go to college on the G.I. Bill after my naval service in the Korean War. In spite of our economic background, all three of us received our doctoral degrees in our professional fields.

I got one of my first jobs on December 7, 1941, when Pearl Harbor was bombed. In those days, there was no television. News on the radio was often hard to get. My older brother and I heard the *Greensboro Daily News* wanted help selling "extras" on the streets of Liberty to report Pearl Harbor and the beginning of World War II. We were the first to apply. At the age of nine, I was walking all over town yelling, "Extra, extra." People came out of their homes to buy this special edition paper.

From the time I was ten until I was thirteen years old, I had a seven-mile paper route. I delivered the *Greensboro Daily News* every morning, seven days a week, on my bicycle. During the summer, all three of us worked for my grandfather on his tobacco farm. When I was fourteen, I began working for my father in the grocery store and worked there until I graduated from high school. Football practice usually ended around 5:00 p.m. After practice, I walked two miles down the highway to the grocery store and worked until 9:00 p.m.

There was a large number of bootleggers who ran liquor stills in the woods surrounding Liberty. On Saturday nights, they drove their speedy 1940 Fords to the back of the store for supplies. I spent every Saturday night loading sugar and fruit jars for making the next supply of whiskey. These cars were equipped with extra-strong springs in the back so, when they were loaded, the sheriff would not suspect they were carrying supplies or their load of "white lightning." Rumor has it that many of the stock car race drivers got their start driving these fast cars on the back roads of Randolph County eluding the sheriff's deputies!

The result of this kind of upbringing was that we developed a strong work ethic, which remained a part of our lives through the years. Since our money came from hard work, we learned to use it carefully and save for our clothes and other needs.

Liberty was very much a one-culture town. Most people spoke with the same basic North Carolina accent. Seldom did I meet anyone from another state. I cannot remember from birth to graduation from high school ever meeting a person from another country.

A family from a much larger city in another state bought the local furniture store. On their first Sunday in town, they joined the First Baptist Church. Every Sunday, the mother wore elegant clothes topped with a huge wide-brimmed "picture hat," as it was called in those days. It was not long before every seat in the church behind her was empty nearly to the back of the auditorium. No one could see over or around that hat! She was perfectly stylish for the large city, but in Liberty, a hat, any hat, was quite strange. People were too polite to complain, so everyone just moved his or her seat in order to see past the hat. People could hardly wait to see her grand entrance each Sunday and what clothes she would be wearing. Through the years, she never changed her stylish appearance and never ceased to be the entire town's object of attention. I often wondered what it would be like to be the unenviable object of attention of a whole town of people!

Spending much of my childhood playing and exploring the woods stimulated a consuming interest first in the Cub Scouts and later in the Boy Scouts. To achieve various ranks in the Scouts, a person had to earn merit badges. Each of these badges represented a specific skill. As I was pursuing my Eagle Scout rank, the highest rank in scouting, I became aware of a bugle merit badge. Since I had some skill in music, I decided to learn to play the bugle. This decision resulted in another of the life-shaping events in my childhood.

I taught myself to play the bugle. I learned all the various bugle calls used by the military and usually played for Boy Scout meetings and camporees. In late 1945 and 1946, soon after World War II ended, bodies of men who died in the war began to be brought back to the States for burial. The American Legion had a large responsibility for arranging military burials. A search was made in Randolph County for someone who could play "Taps" for these funerals. After much searching, they discovered I was the only one in the area who could play. For the next two years, I was called upon over and over again to play "Taps" for military funerals and even excused from school from time to time.

At the young age of thirteen, I was at first fascinated by graveside services and then deeply moved emotionally by the reverence and solemnity with which the military honor guard conducted themselves. The very first service I participated in changed my life forever.

The honor guard marched into the cemetery and positioned themselves near the grave. The pastor led some formalities and a spiritual emphasis. Then the young marine officer dressed in carefully pressed marine dress uniform stepped forward. Carefully he opened a paper and began to read. He read a historical account of the deceased soldier. This soldier grew up on a farm not far from Liberty. He was a top student in his high school class. On the very afternoon of graduation from high school, he went directly to the United States Marine Corps recruiting office and enlisted. In boot camp, he was a leader and led his platoon before the reviewing stand of high-ranking officers at his graduation ceremony from boot camp. Within months of his enlistment, he was leading a platoon of marines across the beach under heavy fire on an island in the South Pacific. The man next to him fell, gravely wounded. This young man reached down and, at great danger to himself, grabbed the fallen marine and dragged him across the beach to a sheltered area. He gave medical care until a corpsman could arrive. He immediately returned to battle with his group of men. Days later as they charged up a hill after hours of fierce combat, he again dragged a fellow marine to safety and was returning to his position when he was fatally struck by an enemy bullet and died almost instantly. He was decorated posthumously for his bravery. He was buried among many killed on that island. Finally, he was being returned home to his family.

Immediately after the reading of this moving story, the marines slowly removed the American flag from the coffin. So carefully and reverently they folded the flag. The young officer presented it to the mother of this fallen marine. The only sounds I could hear throughout this part of the service were the soft sobs of a grieving mother, brothers, and sisters as the words were read and the flag presented. Suddenly, the silence was broken when the marines were ordered to attention and raised their rifles. The clear, loud voice of the officer ordered, "Fire!" Each crack of the rifle gave a strange solemnity and reality to the honoring of this young marine. It was now time for me to play "Taps."

It is difficult to even begin to recall and allow myself to feel again the emotions of that moment. I had just listened to every word read about his young man; I had just been deeply moved by the somber reverence in the care, folding, and presentation of the American flag to a grieving mother. The sound of the gun salutes, so carefully and precisely timed, was almost overwhelming. I had just watched the grieving and heard the soft sobs of the family. They had already experienced the intense grief years ago when they received that dreaded telegram telling of their son's sacrifice for his country. Now I was experiencing their renewed grief at finally saying goodbye to a precious son. All of this kind of emotion was new to a young thirteen-year-old boy, who now was expected to raise the bugle to his lips and play music. How I did it, I will never know. I was grateful I had moved a good distance from the graveside to play because, as soon as I finished, all the emotion of the moment came pouring out of me. I hid myself in the shelter of the trees on the edge of the cemetery and let it all out.

I never really adjusted to the trauma of those moments in almost every funeral after that. Each time I had to get control of myself to be able to play "Taps." At thirteen, I had never really shed tears except when I was injured or angry. These were new emotions for me. These were a different kind of tears coming from deep in my soul. In a sense, I was learning empathy, compassion, and the meaning of grief. Most especially, I was learning patriotism.

As I look back on these experiences, I am conscious of a new depth of feeling and pride that pervaded my thinking and feelings regarding my country. I learned about the honor of military service and the significance of the defense of the liberty we hold dear. In years to come, every time I saw an American flag, I was filled with pride and thanksgiving that I was an American. Again and again at each funeral, I heard of the bravery and the sacrifice of these men.

I also experienced the sacrifice of the families who gave their sons and daughters to fight and to die for our freedom. I sensed these families would never be the same again. They uniquely understand the high cost of freedom.

Sometimes after one of those military funerals, I would lie on my bed at night and wonder, If another war should come, would I be willing to go and give my life for my country? I always ended those thoughts with the conclusion that I would be among the first to volunteer if called upon.

For a young boy of thirteen years old to experience this over and over again was a rare honor, and it had a powerful impact on my thinking. In a way I had never thought before, I also began to realize the brevity of life.

This experience birthed in my young thirteen-year-old mind new questions I had never before considered. Questions such as the meaning of giving one's life for a greater cause, life after death, dealing with grief, the meaning of sacrifice, making a commitment more important than preservation of life, and a myriad of others gave me a new kind of seriousness and maturity.

I began attending the First Baptist Church with my friends. This church had a strong youth program. They dealt with many of the questions about life I was dealing with. In a very real sense, this was a deepening of my quest for spiritual meaning that started with my exposure to the African American worship services when I was ten years old, and the quest intensified during the military funerals.

On Mother's Day, just before my fourteenth birthday, I responded to Pastor Woodrow Hill's invitation to walk down the aisle and join the First Baptist Church of Liberty. In September 1946, I was baptized. I know I was serious about that decision, but I also know I did not really understand.

From my Lutheran background, I knew more about joining the church than what it meant to follow Jesus. It was not that I had a remarkable repentance and salvation experience. Instead, it was a collection of feelings. I sincerely thought that joining the church was what I needed to do at that point in my life. I also knew people in the church were accepting and affirming of me, and I needed that very much. The adult choir knew I loved music, and they invited me as a young fourteen-year-old to join the adult choir. As I look back on that experience, I am certain my feelings about the plight of people who experience segregation and isolation, and especially the military funeral experiences, were strong influences that caused me to see joining the church as a part of my spiritual quest. All of the events in my young life informed my decision to be baptized. Perhaps I did not understand and embrace all that Jesus would come to mean to me, but it was a step in the right direction.

In my diary, which I kept rather meticulously during the years from 1945 to 1948, I recently found a brief entry dated December 27, 1947, written at eleven o'clock at night. It reads, "Got a Bible today. I am troubled. Something I think wants me to be a preacher." Following that entry and throughout my diary, no other mention is made of this. Nor do I elaborate on the idea. I don't know what was troubling me. Was it related to the Bible I had just gotten? Was it related to the military funerals? What was that "something" that wanted me to be a preacher? Was it all the experiences I'd had leading up to this? I have no memory of ever sharing this with anyone or processing it further. I do know it persisted in the recesses of my mind for many years.

Upon my arrival at school one morning, my teacher handed me a note asking me to come to the school principal's office. This was such a rare experience I broke into a cold sweat! I gingerly knocked on the door and heard the stern voice, "Come in!" As I entered, I clumsily tripped over the threshold of the doorway and almost fell into the principal's office. He grinned and invited me to sit down. He immediately began talking.

"The Rotary Club has invited you and one other student to participate in the annual Boy's State on the campus of the University of North Carolina. They will pay your expenses of course. Would you like to accept this invitation?"

Even though I had never heard of this before, I responded immediately, "Yes, sir!"

He explained, "This program focuses on leadership and the organization and working of government. You and other participants will run for office, conduct political campaigns, and hold an election. You will organize a government patterned on our own national government and debate appropriate issues during the week."

Then, with a stern look, he said, "Son, I want you to realize what an honor this is to get to participate in this. You will learn so much about the way America governs itself."

This experience was exciting for a young boy raised in a small town in rural Randolph County. Participating with boys from all over the state, who were far more "urbanized" and aware of political trends and issues, energized me. My eyes were lifted to a broader world.

Every year the American Legion conducted an oratorical contest for high school students all over America. Contestants wrote a speech and delivered it before a group of judges. I decided to enter. No one from my school had ever entered a contest like this. I wrote a speech on the Preamble to the United States Constitution. It was a ten-minute speech. Since no one else from Liberty entered the contest, I was declared the winner from Liberty. I was then invited to compete in the Randolph County competition. When I arrived, I was informed I was the only entry from the county. A special dinner was served, and afterward, I gave my speech. I was declared the winner for Randolph County. I was somewhat embarrassed because I really did not win anything! It was anticlimactic not even to have an opponent. I decided it would be best to keep it a secret back in Liberty.

The first thing on Monday morning, a class member rose to announce to the entire class that I had won the Randolph County Oratorical Contest. The class broke into applause and made me stand up. This was utterly embarrassing. I would now have to tell them the truth.

Nervously I looked down at the floor and almost whispered, "I gave my speech and was declared the winner because no one competed against me. I really did not win anything!"

At first, there was silence. Then, before anyone could react, a fellow student, Barbara Jones, addressed me in front of everyone: "Sammy!" I still remember her exact words. "It isn't important whether you won or were simply declared the winner. What is important is that you entered the contest and did your best when no one else even tried!" I will be forever grateful for that moment.

From there, I was invited to the North Carolina State Finals to be held in a large high school auditorium in Raleigh, the state capital. The date was set for March 25, 1948, just before my sixteenth birthday. In those days, just a visit to see the state capital was a huge affair for a young person from Liberty. After all, there were only twenty-seven students in my entire junior class! To stand before a huge auditorium of people in the state capital of North Carolina and deliver a speech was about the height of sheer terror!

Mr. Don Kessler, principle of Liberty High School, escorted me to the contest. There were ten contestants from all over the state. The officials explained we were to wait in a back room while each contestant gave his speech. Following the end of this part of the competition, each of us would be called upon to deliver an extemporaneous speech on an assigned topic with no prior preparation. The subject for this extemporaneous speech was the American Bill of Rights. This was a complete surprise to all of the contestants. We were given a copy of the American Bill of Rights and told to give a five-minute speech on one of the ten articles as assigned to each of us. We were to remain as a group in the back room and wait for our name to be called to take the podium and deliver our extemporaneous speech. In those days, just after World War II, everyone in my school studied civics as a required course. Careful attention was given to all of the documents of the founding fathers of our nation. My civics teacher demanded we memorize at least the first sentence of each article of the Bill of Rights and be prepared to explain what each meant. I will never forget the terror of standing on the podium speaking before that large audience on the importance of the American Bill of Rights and my assigned topic, the third article of the Bill of Rights.

This article reads, "No soldier shall in time of peace be quartered in any house, without the consent of the owner, nor in time of war, but in a manner to be described by Law." I was grateful my civics teacher had required me to memorize this article and explain it in class. However, to me, it was the hardest of all to explain in today's world.

On the way home, neither the principal nor I spoke for a long distance. Finally, he broke the silence: "How do you think you did?"

"Honestly, I think I was probably last or next to last."

He pulled the car over to the side of the road and stopped. He looked at me with a rather severe stare. "What did you learn from this experience?"

"Mr. Keesler, I think I learned I am not a very good public speaker."

"Sammy, look at me. Do you know where the officials rated you? They rated you in third place! I was sorry they did not announce it, so I asked them. Let me speak honestly with you. I hope you learned you are a capable young man who is able to overcome all obstacles in your way. You can do anything you set your mind to! Hear me! I think you have a low concept of yourself, and unless you learn to overcome, you will always think you are in last place! In reality, I know you will never come in last in anything."

We continued our journey in silence. I was in deep thought about what he had said. I had never heard the concept of self-esteem. When I arrived home, I researched everything I could learn about self-esteem.

As I think through this experience, I cannot really define why I entered the contest when so few students statewide were even interested. I know I was introverted as a child. I spent most of my young life in the woods, alone in the great outdoors. I was greatly lacking in self-confidence in the presence of people and the least likely in my entire school to attempt this kind of competition. Something within me compelled me to participate, and what I learned about myself has impacted me throughout life.

From the earliest moments of life, we have experiences that inform and influence the decisions we make. It is possible to ignore these experiences and let them fade away from memory, but they have a way of returning at the most unexpected times. As I look back, I know God was preparing me for the task He would give me to do. These childhood experiences were of tremendous value in years to come when He called me to serve Him. Everything that happened in my childhood seems to be some kind of preparation for life leading to a future commitment. I was clay in the Potter's hands, being prepared to become a vessel that the Potter could use. All of these experiences lifted my eyes toward a new horizon, but I still had hard lessons to learn.

CHAPTER 3

FORMED BY AN AWARENESS OF CULTURES

I was covered in black—my face, arms, and hands thoroughly smeared. Like others in the school play, we were promoting our Saturday afternoon and evening performances. I sat on the hood of a 1942 Ford, my legs dangling over the front fender, holding a poster advertising our play. The entire town watched as the parade passed by.

I was playing the part of a Negro handyman, and a classmate was playing a Negro housemaid. She sat on the other side of the hood, like me her exposed skin completely blackened. She wore a maid's dress and apron; I was in bib overalls. Waving and smiling, I felt the car making its turn onto Main Street. Since it was Saturday, the whole town and those from the countryside were in town shopping for the week. I looked out to see both sides of the street crowded with people, watching the parade. Suddenly, I was horrified! I wanted to cover my face, jump off of the car, and run away as fast as I could. Why didn't I think earlier about what I was doing?

An entire section of Main Street was lined with African Americans! My heart was pounding, and my face flushed in a rush of tingly heat: "They're going to think I am making fun of them." Those Sunday afternoons listening to the worship service in the African American church rushed into my mind. I suddenly felt ugly and cruel. "The white people will laugh and think it's amusing, but it looks like I am mocking the black folks. How will they feel when they see us made up this way?"

Since blacks wouldn't be allowed into our school auditorium, they would never understand the context of our play. "Who will explain to them so they will understand I don't mean any harm or disrespect? This morning, I won't be able to explain that."

Sometimes we can be insensitive and not even realize others are hurt. I vowed at that moment to never do anything again that could be interpreted as insensitive or harmful, especially to people of a different cultural background.

A large African American family lived and worked on my grandfather's farm. At harvest time, when work in the fields was the most consuming, my grandmother cooked lunch for all the workers. A bell in the backyard called everyone to eat. My grandfather would lead in a prayer of blessing. We all ate the meal together, blacks and whites. There was always good-natured bantering among all of us together, but even then the black workers ate on one end of the tables and white workers on the other. This was a way of life in that period of history.

When we planned the promotion of our school play, I never considered how it could affect African Americans in our town. The almost total separation of the races was common in all of our North Carolina cities and towns. In our town, like others, black people lived in one part of town, and white people lived in other parts of town. Everyone had jobs working together, but there was little, if any, social involvement between the races.

The local cinema was a good example. Liberty had only one theater. Blacks could sit in the small balcony, but the rest of the theater was for whites. There were two water fountains, one for whites and one for blacks. There was one restroom for white men and one for white women—but none for the blacks.

Perhaps most significant, blacks had their own schools. I saw the Negro school for the first time as a high school student on my bike delivering special delivery letters for the post office. When I saw it, I immediately stopped and stared for a long time.

It was clean, but it was small, glaringly small, to handle all the students from kindergarten to high school. All of these kids crowded into that building would have little to no opportunity to compete in sports with other schools. No doubt there was limited equipment for academics and sports. Tears came to my eyes. I realized how much I took for granted. Suddenly, I was overwhelmed by the lack of fairness. These were children and young people no different from me. The only difference between us was a fraction of a centimeter of skin, which happened to be black. But there was a vast difference when it came to opportunities to learn, to develop themselves, and to become all they yearned to become.

Repeatedly as I spent these early years in rural North Carolina in the days of segregation, I faced the injustice of it all. It would become a powerful influence on my thinking and my future.

Often, in town on Saturday nights, fights broke out. The sheriff arrested folks, especially at dances where "bootleg whiskey" was consumed. The sheriff had to break up the fights and take those he deemed wrong to jail. After the offenders had spent a night in the county seat jail in Asheboro, the sheriff brought them to my grandfather's home early Sunday morning before church. My grandfather, James Samuel James, was the local justice of the peace. He would pass judgment—he would let them go home, order them to pay a fine, or sentence them to additional jail time. The front porch became the courtroom. I spent many early Sunday mornings on the front steps of my grandparents' home watching the legal proceedings. Usually my grandmother would take a wounded man, white or black, into her living room. She cleaned and bound up the wounds.

Even as a young child, I felt the tenderness of my grandparents as they dealt with African Americans. My grandfather always sent them home to sober up. I never remember him sending anyone back to jail. He must have passed on these values to his son, my father. During the years I worked for my father, I never remember him treating anyone, white or black, rich or poor, any differently or with less respect. Sometimes when waiting on a family he knew to be extremely poor or hungry, he gave me a sly smile and a wink and slipped an extra potato or another ounce or two of hamburger in the package.

My mother and father, who I love and respect with all of my heart, were like most people in that older generation. They expressed love and respect for black people but, at the same time, were evidently committed to keeping them "in their place." I have trouble being too critical of my parents because that was the pervasive worldview throughout their society. From birth until they died, they lived in that perspective.

Still, the love and respect my grandfather, grandmother, and especially my father showed toward African Americans had an indelible influence on me. As I grew toward maturity, I realized it was my culture that separated me from our black citizens or, for that matter, from anyone different from me.

Later, as a senior in high school, I read *Up from Slavery* by Booker T. Washington.[5] I had no idea how reading one single book could impact my life for years to come.

Up from Slavery was one of five most influential, formative books in my early life. Booker T. Washington was born into slavery and wrote this book as a graphic description of his development from a life in slavery to a great American educator. Writing about racial cooperation, he said, "In all things purely social we can be as separate as the fingers, yet one as the hand in all things essential to mutual progress."[6] Washington's philosophy of racial cooperation has never been acceptable to many in the African American community. However, this book opened my eyes to the possibility that any person in the hands of the right potter, from even the poorest, most disadvantaged beginnings, can be transformed from a common piece of clay to become a most beautiful vessel.

I wrote a paper summarizing my reflections on the book, focusing on the potential of every individual to become more than he or she could imagine. I was forming some strong beliefs, and in that paper, I was beginning to express them as my own goals.

"It's absolutely not right," I heard myself saying one day with all the authority a fourteen-year-old boy could muster. I had practiced all day what I would say to this intimidating adult figure. My conscience was burning nonstop within me. In front of me stood Mr. Bill, who owned the complex of businesses on the highway just out of town, including the grocery where my father worked. Besides the grocery store, he owned the gas station, the Pontiac dealership, the auto repair shop, and a café doubling as a beer joint. When the café was busy, I was frequently asked to work there too.

Truck drivers hauling fuel from North Carolina ports to distribution points in Greensboro, just twenty miles north of Liberty, would stop at the café to eat and rest. A white driver would enter the café, choose a booth, eat his food, and rest for a while. A black driver would stand at an outside window on the side of the building, order food, and take it to a suitable spot by a clump of trees where he could sit on the ground to eat (or, in inclement weather, he would eat in his truck). During strong wind, rain, cold, or blazing cloudless sun, no matter what the conditions, a black person was not allowed in the café.

I took a deep breath, fixed my eyes on Mr. Bill, and said, "Black drivers are driving the same trucks as the white drivers, the same number hours, the same distances. You know better than me they must be just as tired and hungry as the white drivers. You should allow them to come inside too."

Mr. Bill was a large rotund man with a red face and somewhat bloodshot eyes. I had never seen him without an unlit cigar in his mouth, which he chewed constantly. Briefly I looked away, but I could feel his eyes burning deeply into me. There was a tense silence; he chomped on his cigar, switching from one side of his mouth to the other.

"Boy," he began and continued letting me know how he felt in no uncertain terms laced with his own colorful profanity. He ended, "And if you don't like the way I run things around here, you can find another job somewhere else."

He turned and waddled off, and I had no chance to reply. Neither did I want one!

I knew segregation was present in the southern United States, but I did not know it was also prevalent in other parts of the world. Years later when we were living in Hong Kong awaiting visas to go to Vietnam, a huge problem developed. In Aberdeen Bay, there were literally hundreds of houseboats occupied by Chinese called "boat people." These families lived on boats, carried on businesses on boats, had their own boat schools, and went ashore only when they had to. The government of Hong Kong decided the schools for boat children were inferior. They decided to close down all of the schools for the boat people and have them attend schools with the Chinese children living on the land. Immediately, there was an outcry among the Chinese "land people." They did not want their children going to school with those inferior Chinese boat people. On the other side, the Chinese boat people did not want their children going to school and being corrupted by those Chinese land people. The police had to escort the boat children to schools on the shore.

Perhaps everyone in the world seems to want someone they can look down on so they can make themselves feel more significant and powerful!

My sensitivity to the African American culture was the beginning of my interest in other cultures in the world. When I was twelve years old, I heard about an international pen pal agency for young people. I immediately applied and was given the address of a young girl who lived in the Hawaiian Islands on the big island of Hawaii.

She was a second-generation Japanese raised in a Japanese/Hawaiian home. In letters to me, she occasionally transliterated Japanese characters into the Roman alphabet and then translated them into English. This introduced me to another language. She described in detail the food she ate, the games she played, the work in the pineapple fields, and her relationship with her Japanese/Hawaiian mother and father. I could hardly wait for each letter to come, longing someday to visit that strange place. I fell madly in love with her, but at that young age, I didn't dare let her know it! I continued the correspondence for two years. Unknown to either of us, this young pen pal was opening my eyes to Asia, the part of the world that one day would become my home for most of my life!

Liberty was certainly not a tourist destination. Nor was it a place requiring foreigners who speak another language to come and work. Every chance I got, I continued to pursue my knowledge of other cultures, world religions, and languages, and I developed a long-term interest in geography. I studied Latin when it was offered one year and took all the French taught at our school.

All of this produced in me a desire to experience the world. It was probably because of this that, just after my sixteenth birthday, I decided to hitch a ride to Florida and get a job for the summer. The night before I left, my father came into my bedroom, sat on the end of the bed, and shared with me that, as a young man of twenty-four years, he had gone to Florida and worked in a meat market for more than two years. He really loved living there. He said, "We don't have much money to help you, but here is twenty dollars you can use." I knew he had very little money and this was a big sacrifice for him. It was a way for him to express love and confidence in me on the eve of my trip.

Neither my mother nor my father questioned the wisdom of a sixteen-year-old boy thumbing to Florida for the summer knowing no one, with no job in hand and no place to live. This represented the way my parents related to their boys. They were never overprotective. They trusted us until we gave them reason not to trust us. At every turn, they encouraged high aims and maximum independence. I always knew I could never rely on them for financial support, but I could always rely on them for moral and emotional support. They were there at any point to give advice and counsel whenever my brothers and I needed them. Seldom did they ever question our decisions or try to dissuade us from attempting our various pursuits.

My father always said, "I would rather you attempt, fail, and learn from it than for me to tell you what and how to do it and you learn little!"

The next morning, I packed a lunch and went to Highway 421, leading south. I thumbed every car for hours. Finally, a truck stopped and asked where I was going. I said, "I am going to Florida."

He said "Son, tomorrow I am driving to Florida. If you wait a day, I'll take you."

The next morning, I began my trip. He offered me a job for the summer, which I accepted. In Florida, I was provided a cot in a small shed sheltered by an old tin roof, which at the very least kept my bed from getting wet when it rained. This would be my home for the summer.

One morning shortly after we arrived, a worker asked me to go with him to collect rent from some tenants. On a dirt road, apparently rarely used, we were approaching the house when we came upon a wooden bridge across a small river.

We stopped. He looked at me and back to the bridge and then back at me. He said, "This bridge ain't very good!"

"No, it looks like it is not used very much. Looks like it'll fall down any minute."

He got out of the truck, looked closely, got back in the truck and said, "One thing you need to know about me. I always do what I want to do, and I don't worry about what might happen. Life's too short to worry."

With that, he started the engine; pushed his long hair out of his eyes; grinned a wild grin; and shouted, "Yee haw," at the top of his lungs. And away we went. Arriving at the bridge, we began creeping slowly across. At one point, a plank broke and fell into the river. He said with a laugh, "One down and a bridge to go!"

We crossed the bridge. I heaved a sigh of relief and was conscious of a pain in my right hand where I had held tightly onto the door.

A lady came out on the porch and shouted, "Which way did y'all come in here?"

He yelled, "We came across the bridge."

She yelled back, "Ain't nobody used that bridge in three years. It's fallin' down."

We went back another way.

On another occasion, he called me in from the field to go with him to another house to collect the rent. As soon as I climbed into the truck, I could smell the strong aroma of whiskey. Looking a little closer, I could see he was very drunk. We arrived at the house and turned into a dirt driveway. He leaned toward me and passed out. I had no idea what to do. A big truck and a drunk driver passed out, at a home where I knew no one, too young to drive, and no idea how to shift gears in a truck! I went to knock on the door.

Halfway there, a huge snake was crawling toward me in the weeds. I yelled for someone, but there was no answer. Almost in a panic, I ran back to the truck, pushed the driver over on the other side of the seat, and sat behind the wheel. I started the engine and engaged the gear. The truck went forward, not backward. I put it in another gear and again went forward. Many times, I put it in various gears, only to move forward until I was a few feet from the end of the driveway and the closed door of a garage. Finally, I pulled the gear down as far as it would go and, thankfully, began to back out. I drove all the way back to the farm using almost every gear the truck had. It was almost dark when we arrived home. I jumped out of the truck; went into my shed; lay down on the cot, my heart beating wildly; and didn't move for hours.

I have no idea how I found the farm that afternoon. Perhaps the Lord was protecting this sixteen-year-old boy who was certainly over his head in that environment!

Sometime during the night, I woke up. My first thought was, "How did I do what I did to get home?" I asked myself over and over. It really was impossible for me to drive that truck and then find my way back to the farm. I felt a lot of pride welling up in me. I had not allowed that experience to paralyze me. I remember saying to myself, "Sam, you see, don't ever say you can't do something. There will always be a way out, and never forget it. Today you proved you can always do something and survive! You've just learned to never give up!"

The truck driver must have spent the night lying in the truck because the next morning my job was to wash out all of the vomit and clean the cab of the truck. That was pretty much the last straw! Two days later, with a million mosquito bites and a low-grade fever, I informed the foreman I should return to North Carolina. He was very understanding and kind. He told me a truck was leaving right away for North Carolina. He would see to it I was on board.

It would be impossible to enumerate all the things I learned, especially about myself, during that brief trip. Perhaps overcoming fear, handling feelings of helplessness, overcoming adversity, and learning to act independently while at the same time learning to depend on others were valuable lessons. They impelled and enabled me to keep moving forward in years to come.

***

"Dad, I am going to join the Naval Reserves!" I had practiced all day deciding how to break this news to my father. I knew the minimum age to join the Naval Reserves was seventeen years old with a parent's signature. I was just over sixteen. I was faced with two problems: First, how could I change my age? Second, I would have to have my father's signature, and he knew my age. How could I get him to sign?

World War II had been over only three years and was still fresh in everyone's mind. Because I'd played "Taps" for so many military funerals, I had come to know a number of young World War II veterans. One of them from my hometown was active in the Naval Reserves in Greensboro, North Carolina. Knowing these men and the military funerals had a lingering effect on me. Memorizing the Preamble to the Declaration of Independence, learning each article of the Bill of Rights, and understanding the history of our great country, all in high school civics, influenced me to want to serve my country.

Before going to my father, I decided to go to Asheboro, the

county seat, and get a copy of my birth certificate. I worked for hours to change the 1932 birth date to 1931. With all preparations made, I then went to my father to request he sign for me to join at seventeen years of age. I showed him my birth certificate. He asked me why I wanted to join at such a young age. I shared with him my love for my country and how I was inspired to join. He didn't say anything but took the paper and signed it.

Every week I caught a ride to and from Greensboro to attend reserve meetings. In the summer of 1949, I was obligated to take a six-week training cruise. I boarded a destroyer, the USS *Hugh Purvis* (DD-709), for the trip to San Juan, Puerto Rico, and Guantanamo Bay, Cuba. We left from New Orleans in early afternoon down the Mississippi River out into the Caribbean Sea. My first night out, I was assigned to stand watch on the starboard bow of the ship. The farther we went into the Caribbean, the rougher the sea became. The bow was the absolute worst place for a novice seaman to stand watch, especially in rough seas. Soon I was nauseated beyond description, lasting the entire two-hour watch. In all my years at sea, I was never seasick again.

We arrived in Guantanamo Bay, Cuba, early in the morning. With the ship secured for port, some of the crew was allowed to go ashore. Several crew members invited me to go along to Havana for the day.

We took a navy bus to Havana and began visiting several tourist sites. Late afternoon, we all went into a bar. Everyone ordered drinks. It was my first time in a bar, and the others pressured me to order a drink.

"Guys, I have just turned seventeen, and I am not allowed to drink alcohol."

They broke into laughter and began persuading me.

"Boy, the law doesn't apply to sailors in Puerto Rico," they said.

"It's not just that," I continued. "You see, my father is an alcoholic. For two years, I have had to drive him home at night often because all day long he has sipped his alcohol and by closing time he is just too drunk to drive. So many Saturday nights I have had to help him into the house. My mother and I get him to bed. I have been so sad and embarrassed to see him that way and resolved I will never drink alcohol."

For a few moments, all was quiet. Then, "We understand. Let us order you a nonalcoholic drink." One of the men ordered a Tom Collins.

Trusting they had my best interests at heart, I found the drink refreshing on such a hot afternoon. I ordered another. Little did I know this drink was made from vodka, which does not have the taste of alcohol but is highly intoxicating, After the second drink, I was not feeling well and excused myself to go outside for fresh air. When I left the bar stool and stepped on the floor, it was like the floor was leaning at a forty-five-degree angle. I fell several times trying to get out of the door, much to the laughter of my fellow seamen. I lay in the gutter and threw up countless times. One of the men carried me back to the ship. After that, unintended by my "friends," I learned a valuable lesson that has followed me all of my life. I've never touched even the smallest drop of alcohol again!

Even at this early age, God was preparing me to be involved in a world of different cultures, though I had no way of knowing what this would mean in the future. The potter knows what the vessel will be used for. In much of secular life, we can practice and perform until we can do whatever it is we need to do. However, in the spiritual life, we must first become who we need to be so then we can do what we need to do. Being precedes doing.

So it is with our childhood when we begin having those experiences that mold our life and our future. God was preparing me through so many experiences for the task He wanted me to do in the world. I was not an object of fate. God never forced me beyond my will into some kind of mold, and I had choices. There were many opportunities to choose other directions. But all these experiences had a way of nudging me in the direction I needed to go. The Potter was molding the vessel!

CHAPTER 4

FORMED BY ONE WORLD, LIVING IN ANOTHER

It was just after daybreak when my father dropped me off on the side of Highway 49, where I planned to begin my trip hitchhiking to New York City. I would take highway 49 to US 70 leading me to US Highway 1 north. I was fortunate to get rides fairly quickly and arrived at US Highway 1 about midmorning.

Hardly had I lifted my thumb high in the air when a rather large truck screeched its brakes and pulled off the highway. I ran to catch up to see if the driver was offering a ride.

He stuck his head out of the cab and motioned me toward him. He spat a huge splash of chewing tobacco out the window, looked down at me from his cab, and yelled, "Boy, where you headin'?"

I looked up into a very weather-beaten face, deep wrinkles plowing across his face. His uncombed hair was hanging low on his forehead almost to his eyes. At first, I just wanted to run away. As I looked into his eyes, there was a certain softness that entranced me. I sensed this would be okay.

I yelled back, "I am going to New York City."

"Git in, young feller, you're in luck. I'm haulin' fish from Ft. Lauderdale, Florida, to Fulton's Fish Market in Brooklyn, New York. Hurry up. We got a long day ahead of us."

Just the day before, I had walked on stage and had been awarded a high school diploma along with twenty-six other seniors in the class of 1950. A college education seemed so distant and almost impossible for me to ever attain. But one thing seemed absolutely certain; if I stayed in Liberty, I would never accomplish it.

My uncle, Charlie Langley, lived in Weehawken, New Jersey, just across the Hudson River from New York City on the Palisades looking down on the Hudson River. He managed the distribution warehouses in Jersey City for R. J. Reynolds Tobacco Company. Knowing my desire to go to college, he graciously agreed to let me stay with him until I could find a job and enroll in a university night school in Manhattan. I would need to find my own place as soon as possible.

We arrived in the central area of Manhattan in late afternoon. The driver asked me where I wanted to get out. I was suddenly almost sick to my stomach. Tall buildings and masses of people were everywhere. I had no idea where to go. I said, "I'll get out at the next large intersection." He stopped, but I could not bring myself to get out. I suggested another intersection and then another. Finally, with a stern voice without looking at me, he said, "Here is where you get out."

I left the truck in the midst of tall buildings, swirling crowds of people, and traffic such as I had never seen. It was nothing like Liberty, North Carolina. Now I had to find my way across the Hudson River and on to Weehawken along the Palisades where my uncle lived.

Uncle Charlie and Aunt Ershall never had any children. When I arrived at their home, they accepted me like I was their own. Early the next morning, I was in Manhattan searching help wanted ads in newspapers. I asked everyone I met where I could find a job. At noon, I found a place called an Automat, where you put a coin in a machine and received a sandwich. The place was full of young adults. It seemed they were all looking for a job. I heard one of them say, "Marine Midland Bank and Trust Company is hiring right now. Let's go down and apply."

When I heard that, I gulped down my sandwich and raced to Marine Midland Bank and Trust Company, located on Broadway in the financial district of Manhattan. After inquiry, I took the elevator to one of the high floors where the company's personnel office was located.

Exiting the elevator, I immediately was standing in front of a wall of frosted glass with double doors labeled "Personnel Office." I was not sure whether to knock or to simply push the doors open and walk in. I felt my face flushing, my palms wet with sweat, and I was trembling just a bit. I gently pushed one of the doors open and was confronted by an elegant lady sitting behind a large desk. She looked up, rather surprised and said, "Sir, do you have an appointment?"

"No, ma'am. I just arrived in New York yesterday afternoon. I didn't know I needed an appointment. I am so sorry. I heard some young people say you are hiring, and I need a job. I hope I am at the right place."

She looked at me curiously. "Where in the world are you from?"

"Ma'am, I am from Liberty, North Carolina, and this is my first experience up north."

Laughing almost uncontrollably, she said, "Well, I knew you're not from around here. You are the first Southerner I have ever met in person, and you really talk differently!"

"Yes, ma'am. I know I do, but I can change."

With that, she laughed again. She said, "I have never had anyone call me ma'am.' I have heard Southerners are very polite, but I did not expect this!"

Her eyes wandered from the top of my head to my feet. Fixing her stare directly into my eyes, she said, "Who taught you to dress?"

"Ma'am, being from the South, I wondered this morning how to dress when I am applying for a job in a big city like this. I hope you don't mind my wearing a suit and tie. Actually, I bought this suit before I left home thinking I would need it in New York."

With that she laughed again. "You'd be surprised. I have young people from all over New York come here for an appointment wearing the worst clothes possible. I just tell them to go home, get another appointment, and come back looking decent. After all, this is a financial institution!"

She looked at me again with a different expression. Her stare was long and uncomfortable. I felt like running away, but there was a slight softness in her expression.

After a long silence she said, "There is just no way I can give you a job without an application completely filled out and an appointment. You have no application filled out. You have come in here with no appointment. I should send you home, but I can't do that. Here is an application. Go in that room. There's a typewriter there. Fill it out right now and bring it to me quickly. I have other appointments coming up."

I had never used an electric typewriter, but within moments the application was typed and in her hands. It took just a few minutes to fill out my résumé. There was little to put on it. After all, working in tobacco fields, delivering the morning paper, and working in a grocery store part-time would not excite an employer in downtown Manhattan in a leading financial institution!

She said, "I have never had anyone type so fast with no errors. Take this paragraph and go back in that room and type it for me."

Within a minute, it was in her hands.

She took a hard look at it and said, "No errors and so fast. I can't believe this. You wait right here."

She picked up the phone and made a call, and within a few minutes a young man appeared in the doorway. "You called?" he said.

"I have someone I want you to meet. He is exactly what you are looking for."

He took me into a small room, sat down, and began to ask questions. He too laughed when I began speaking. I shared with him that. more than anything in the world, I wanted a college education. I explained that coming to New York to get a job would enable me to go to night school. I said finally, "This is the only way I can get a college education."

After a rather long interview with seemingly interminable questions, he finally said, "Since you are in the Naval Reserves, just like I am, you will probably not be drafted and have to go in the army. For that reason, I can give you this job. You can start to work tomorrow."

My aunt and uncle shared a duplex with an Italian couple who also had no children. The Italian couple were first-generation children of immigrants so they were very Italian in every way and still lived in the midst of their broader Italian family, who were almost too numerous to count. I actually became a member of their extended family. Frequently I was a part of large dinners, weddings, celebrations, and other family occasions where all the relatives would gather. These occasions were filled with joy, excitement, singing, flares of tempers, debates, honest sharing, and a lot of love. Much of the activity was in Italian. They were loud, and everyone was expected to be involved.

I was fascinated by the Italian language. Being an introvert made it difficult to adjust to these cultural experiences, yet I found myself eager to be there. They would not allow introverted behavior! My Southern accent and manner of speaking was hilarious to them, yet I felt accepted. This was another of those introductions to another language, people, and culture and an opportunity to learn to become an "insider" in a strange culture.

Everywhere I went in New York, I was an oddity. My Southern accent got the job. I got free movie tickets when I tried to pay. I was often given a dessert. People took me for a meal just so they could hear me talk.

There were so many mixed emotions. I often felt like a freak exhibit in a circus. I was always the center of attention in any crowd. Even at my work, people would come from various departments of the bank just to engage me in conversation and get to know this strange young Southern boy in their midst. This was difficult for an introverted country boy. I often longed to go back to my comfort zone in Liberty, where everyone knew me, and I was not odd.

From my early days, I was fascinated by other cultures. Now, I was the culture others were fascinated by. I began to understand what it is to be looked on as an "outsider." This was a key experience preparing me for the future.

One Saturday morning, I was walking on 5th Ave and the Avenue of the Americas looking in shop windows and experiencing the huge city. A young man slightly older than me, a perfect stranger, greeted me with a smile and engaged me in conversation.

"Where are you from?" he asked.

"I am from North Carolina and just arrived in New York City," I responded.

After a brief conversation, he asked, "Have you ever been in Radio City Music Hall, a very famous building near here?"

"No," I said. "I have seen very little in New York."

"I can show you around New York, if you like. Would you like to see Radio City Music Hall now? I can take you behind the scenes, and you can see programs being filmed."

"Yes!" I responded with enthusiasm.

He showed the doorman an identity card. We entered the building and went from studio to studio, watching radio and television being created. At noon, he invited me to lunch and afterward to visit his apartment. I was thinking perhaps he could be a friend, and I accepted his invitation.

Entering a small crowded café/bar, I noticed it was crowded with young men. Everyone turned to look at me. Some began to whistle and wink. Suddenly, I felt very uncomfortable. Several came and stood near me. One sat unusually close and placed his leg next to mine. I had never experienced anything like this. It began to dawn on me these guys were homosexuals. It was the first time I had ever met or been around a gay person. As we waited for our food, my new friend sensed my nervousness and said, "Don't pay any attention to these people in here. They are being very impolite." He put his hand on mine and said, "You're safe with me. I'll take care of you." He winked, tried to catch my eyes with his, and continued to hold my hand. "Don't be afraid. We'll get out of here after we eat. I can't wait to show you my apartment very near here. I want you to spend the night with me."

I grew up around Southern rednecks, where a man holding hands with a man just didn't happen! I tried to be calm, but inside I was very uncomfortable. I asked him to excuse me for a moment so I could find a pay phone to call my uncle and let him know I would not be coming home tonight. I went outside and quickly disappeared into the crowd.

I went to Central Park and sat on a park bench for a long time, reflecting on what had just happened. This experience awakened me to my innocence. I realized how extremely naive and vulnerable I was. In this large city, it was like I was in a rapidly flowing river, twisting and turning, carried by the current in directions beyond my control. Somehow in this alien environment, I was going to have to find the still waters and the deep channels, which I could control so that I could navigate in the direction I needed to go. I reminded myself that I had just turned eighteen-years old. I was coming from the sheltered, safe environment of a one-culture town and had been suddenly thrust into a multicultural world I knew nothing about. I was going to have to learn to live in this new world.

CHAPTER 5

JOINING THE NAVY, SEEKING THE UNKNOWN

Standing at the lectern, shifting from one foot to the other, breaking into a cold sweat, I looked out on an entire class of New Yorkers laughing uncontrollably, looking at me! I faintly heard the professor saying, "Quiet! Quiet, class! This is highly impolite!

"Okay, Mr. James, begin your speech again."

The room suddenly seemed deathly quiet. As bravely as I could, I took a deep breath and broke the silence: "I want to tell y'all how to raise tobacco."

The class again broke into peals of laughter.

One by one, each of the students from every borough of New York City and towns in New Jersey had presented his or her speech. I was the last to speak. I could not understand why everyone was laughing at me! I had enrolled in a communications class to begin night school at Pace College (now Pace University) in the business district of Manhattan. This seemed like a fairly easy course for me. The first assignment was a five-minute talk on how to do something.

The professor calmed the class and turned to me. "Mr. James, please sit down and listen." From the podium to my seat seemed like a thousand miles.

"In the first place, you don't have to say 'y'all.' The word 'you' includes everyone. Also, you don't raise tobacco. You grow tobacco." He repeated to be sure I understood, "You raise children. You grow tobacco!"

At that point, I was feeling frustrated, helpless, embarrassed, and angry. I spoke back, "Where I come from, you raise tobacco."

With an overly condescending attitude, he said very slowly, "But you are not there anymore. You are not going to be able to speak your colloquial dialect and expect to be taken seriously. You will have to learn to say things where you are living, not where you formerly lived. I will challenge you in this class to listen to your fellow students and learn how to express yourself in an understandable way—in this context."

Though this was a painful moment, this lesson defined much of my cross-cultural communication through the years.

On June 25, 1950, seventy-five thousand troops from North Korea crossed the 38th parallel, invading South Korea. By July, the United States fully committed to defending South Korea and began sending troops into the war. At the age of eighteen, I was a prime target for the draft into the army. I was already in the Naval Reserves, so there was little question I would be called upon to go to war.

My experience participating in the military funerals nurtured my patriotism and my respect for those who gave their lives for our freedom. My status in the Naval Reserves caused me to want to accept my responsibilities. I felt it was not right for me, a young man, to let others give their lives for their country at this crucial time while I stayed at home pursuing my own desires. On the other hand, I had this tremendous longing to get my college education. What was I to do?

I went home for Christmas, still not sure which direction I should take. My mind said to stay in college. My heart said to fulfill my responsibilities to my country and go to war. I made my decision to leave my Naval Reserve status and join the United States Navy. I returned to New York, finished my semester of college, and gave notice of my departure from my job at Marine Midland. And on March 8, 1951, I was sworn into the US Navy. I did not tell them I was already in the Naval Reserves for fear they might see I had not told the truth about my birthdate. Two years into my four-year assignment, I received a notice from the Navy Department. The navy had discovered I had two years of service in the Naval Reserves. They were increasing my longevity pay. Nothing was said about my birth certificate. Thus, when I was discharged, I had six years of naval service.

After boot camp in San Diego, I was sent to Alameda Naval Air Station and boarded the USS *Sitkoh Bay* (CVE-86), which would be my home for the next three years. *The* USS *Sitkoh Bay* was an aircraft carrier with a distinguished career during World War II in the South Pacific.

When I boarded the ship, I was what was called a "deck-ape." I was a seaman apprentice assigned to keep the ship's deck clean and handle any jobs related to our ship's seaworthiness. A few days into my first trip at sea, I watched men on the bridge of the ship signaling other ships by light using Morse code or by semaphore (the use of flags to send and receive messages). When getting my Eagle Scout award, I had learned both Morse code and semaphore, so this was of great interest. I watched them use a sextant to locate the position of the sun and stars in order to plot the ship's course. The bridge was the nerve center of the ship. I was fascinated by this and determined I would pursue a rating on the bridge. I immediately applied for transfer from the deck to become a quartermaster on the ship's bridge. It was almost impossible for a seaman apprentice on his first trip at sea to get into the quartermaster division. My prior experience as an Eagle Scout made it possible.

Almost immediately, I was transferred. The quartermaster's job was to become expert at handling the ship's wheel, communicate either by flashing light using Morse code or by semaphore, and work with the navigator to plot the ship's course. In addition, one of us was always stationed on the small boats, including the captain's gig any time the captain was going ashore. As quartermasters, we always kept someone on duty on the bridge to keep a sharp lookout for other ships at sea. When anchored in port, we maintained a watch to make sure the anchor was holding steady in place. During wartime, such as the Korean War, this job required personnel who could excel at their responsibilities, especially when operating in convoy.

In December 1952, the USS *Sitkoh Bay* was involved in a collision with a merchant freighter hauling coal from the United States to Japan. The ship was so badly damaged we had to turn around and go to the naval shipyard in Long Beach, California, for repairs.

At that point, I knew very little about what believing in Jesus really meant, even though I was a member of a church. I felt joining the church was what was required of me. For so long, I was troubled that something was still missing from my life. The collision at sea left me feeling vulnerable. I was a good church member. I tried my best to do good things for people. I didn't participate in bad activities. What was bothering me? I guessed my intense feelings of loneliness and restlessness were because I didn't care to participate in many of the activities my fellow seamen were engaged in. This isolated me to a degree from those around me. Yet, I knew this was not the whole story. What was it that troubled me so?

I remembered that, during my childhood, our radio at home was often tuned to a program called "The Old-Fashioned Revival Hour." Dr. Charles Fuller was the longtime preacher. It was broadcast from the Long Beach Auditorium every Sunday afternoon. I decided, since it was Sunday and I was in Long Beach, I would go and experience the service in person.

I shared with three of my friends what I was going to do. They all said, "We'll go with you."

We were seated in the balcony. The music was superb. The pianist, Rudy Atwood, could play the piano like no one I had ever heard. Dr. Fuller preached a powerful sermon. I was deeply moved. As Dr. Fuller drew toward the end of the sermon, he began to invite people to come forward to accept Jesus as Lord and Savior. He turned his attention to the balcony.

"I see a number of sailors in the balcony. Won't you come today and accept Jesus?" It must have been a hundred yards from my seat to the pulpit, but I was sure that I could see him looking straight at me, no one else!

I was not sure why I would go forward, and I did not want my friends to have to wait for me. I simply stood there, gripping the seat in front of me.

I heard Dr. Fuller say, "With every head bowed and eyes closed, no one looking around, if you just want prayer, raise your hand, and we will pray for you."

The collision at sea was just three days earlier. I was still feeling the impact of that experience. The fact that I had spent the whole night in that small boat had intensified the experience. I needed prayer. I raised my hand.

"Who raised their hand?" I heard the voice of an elderly gentleman standing at our row looking at the four of us. "Which one of you raised your hand? Come with me, and I will help you."

I had not bargained for someone to approach us like that. I just wanted prayer! He went to each one of us, "I know one of you raised your hand."

We all just stared ahead. No one, including me, acknowledged him. Over and over, he urged.

The service mercifully ended, and immediately my three friends turned to me. "What did you raise your hand for? You got us all in trouble!" For days afterward, they teased me and never let me forget that experience.

A month later, my ship was docked at Alameda Naval Air Station. I heard about a famous evangelist who would be preaching at the Oakland municipal auditorium. Feeling restless about my life and lonelier than ever, I decided to go to this meeting. The night in the small boat after our collision at sea was still fresh on my mind and powerful in my heart. This time, I did not tell anyone and went alone. The sermon moved me emotionally. I wanted so badly for something to happen in my life to bring peace of mind and heart.

When the invitation was given for people to come forward

to accept Jesus, I stepped out and went forward. When I stepped into that aisle, I was not intending to accept Jesus. I was already a member of the church, so I felt I did not need to accept Jesus. What impelled me to step out was I was desperately seeking whatever was missing in my life that perpetuated my intense longing for something I could not define.

An elderly man met me and ushered me into a counseling room.

"Why did you come forward tonight, young man?" he asked.

"I am not sure," I replied. "I feel very lonely and unsettled in my life. I don't seem to fit in anywhere."

"What makes you feel that way?" he asked.

"I don't know. I feel like something is missing in my life, and I don't know what it is. I don't understand why I feel like this because I live a clean life. I don't drink alcohol. I don't smoke. I am careful not to use curse words. I try to live a clean life. Compared to others on my ship, I have very good behavior. Maybe this makes me feel lonely and cut off from my shipmates."

"Have you ever been baptized into the church?" he asked.

"Yes. I was baptized in a Baptist church when I was fourteen years old. I attend the chapel services on my ship every Sunday, but I feel something is missing from my life," I responded. "I just don't know what it is."

"Then you evidently know Jesus and what He can do for you. We just need to pray."

He prayed for me and moved on to the next person. I returned to my ship carrying the same feelings, which now were intensified. My problems were still unresolved.

I continued to attend the chapel services. I even sang in a quartet led by the chaplain's assistant. In spite of all my efforts, it seemed whatever I longed for was just out of my reach. I did not know what it was. I was truly a seeker but had no idea what I was seeking!

CHAPTER 6 _____

I FOUND IT!

Saturday afternoon, we were docked at Alameda Naval Air Station, where my ship was being loaded and prepared for sea. A friend and I were leaving to go ashore when an older gentleman who was working as a carpenter on the ship came rushing up behind us and yelled, "Wait up!"

Somewhat breathless, he continued, "Would you like to go to a party tonight?"

"What kind of party?"

"It's a party with a lot of young adults like you. They really enjoy having sailors come and spend Saturday evening with them. In fact, it is designed for people just like you. You'll love it."

We checked with each other and decided to go. We had seen him on the ship but had no idea who he was. He introduced himself as Thomas. He was dressed in well-worn work clothes. He looked in great shape and his graying crew cut suggested former military of some kind. He led us to an old, battered car. He said, "I always try to pick the sailors carefully and choose those who I think would profit from the party. I really enjoy inviting sailors going ashore to come to this party."

We stopped in front of a church. I read the sign: "Melrose Baptist Church." It was located on 47th and Bond Street in East Oakland. He took us across the street into a building with a name over the door, "The Say-So House," which sounded very strange to us.

Upon entering, we met dozens of teenagers and young adults. The old carpenter took us over to an elderly gentleman and introduced us to him.

This man said, "Welcome. My name is Watson. Sailors call me Pop Watson. My wife and I have worked with our young people with a special love for sailors since early in the Second World War. We enjoy having sailors visit with us, and we'd be glad if you could spend the night at our home." He shook our hands with a grip that almost hurt. His hands were strong and gnarled, suggesting years of hard work. He smiled slightly, but there was a happy twinkle in his eyes. We were noncommittal about going home with him.

The young adults were working in the kitchen baking cookies and making all kinds of refreshments. We realized this was some kind of church function. Everyone was friendly and spent time talking and visiting with us. Gradually, the crowd grew, with more sailors and young people flooding in until the room was full. We played games. We sang choruses. I had never seen so many beautiful girls in one place. I was so overwhelmed, not just by their outer beauty but by their inner beauty as well. I could hardly speak!

One by one, the young people shared how they had found Jesus as their Savior or what Jesus had come to mean in their life. These young people had an indescribable joy. One of the young men gave a brief message from the Bible and challenged everyone regarding the Christian life. In the message, he made a statement that penetrated deep into my consciousness. He said, "It doesn't matter how good you think you are or even if you are a member of a church. You will never feel complete until you accept Jesus into your life and begin to follow Him." My long-term feelings of loneliness and "something missing" flooded my mind. He seemed to be speaking directly to me! Could it be that this was what I was missing?

I learned the building was called the "Say So House," taken from the Psalm: "Let the redeemed of the Lord say so, whom he hath redeemed from the hand of the enemy" Psalm 107:2 (KJV).

I'd spent my early years in a Lutheran church and my teen years in a Baptist church, but I had never experienced anything like this. I realized they were not talking at all about the church but emphasizing Jesus. Yet, they were faithful members and very active in their church. All of this, their vocabulary and testimonies, was so strange to my friend and me, but we were also captivated by it.

When the party was over, Pop Watson came and asked if we'd like to go home with him. Six sailors piled into his car. As soon as I saw Mom Watson, I felt at home. She was short, a bit overweight, and had a beautiful smile. She was like a grandmother who could calm any storm of life.

We slept on the couch, in chairs, on the floor, wherever there was a spare place. The next morning, Mom Watson cooked waffles and served them with fresh strawberries and whipped cream. Pop Watson led us in prayer and prayed for each one of us by name. He especially prayed for my friend and me and our safety, as we would sail the next morning to return to Korea. I'd never felt so cared for. He then very tactfully invited us to attend church that morning with him and Mom Watson. This man and woman were so humble and sincere that being in their presence felt like nothing I had ever experienced before. They did not "overtly witness" to us. There was no pressure. There was no preaching. There was just something about their caring, their genuineness that made us want to be with them. We all agreed to go to church.

The choir was filled with young adults. I had met most of them the night before. Everyone in the church was singing joyfully and seemed to know all of the songs, many of which I had never heard. The service made me feel alive and joyful. Throughout the service, I felt that, in some way, I had come home. I had an indescribable peace that I was in the right place.

Pop Watson took us back to our ship. As we exited his car, he turned to face us. "Fellows, the next time your ship docks at Alameda Naval Air Station, would you like to come back to church?" We both responded with a resounding yes and thank you!

That night, lying on my bunk, I was filled with longing for an opportunity to go back to that place. Testimonies of so many young people reverberated in my mind. The devotional at the party had especially touched me. My whole life was in transition in a way I could not understand, but I was moving toward whatever I was yearning for.

The next day, we sailed for Yokosuka, Japan, where we would take on additional planes and cargo and proceed to Pusan, Korea, through the Inland Sea of Japan. It was going to be a challenge to navigate an aircraft carrier through the very congested and narrow Inland Sea.

Upon arrival, I was asked to go to Tokyo to obtain some up-to-date charts of the Inland Sea. In early afternoon, I boarded a very crowded train to make the trip around Tokyo Bay to Tokyo.

The only empty seat on the train was beside me. People were reluctant to sit with a young American sailor. After the train began moving, a beautiful young Japanese girl asked permission to sit in that seat. Almost breathless, I managed to stutter, "Yes, yes, please do."

She spoke English quite well. She was a student at the University of Yokohama and on her way back to school. She wanted to practice her English, which I was overjoyed to do! We talked of many things, especially her life as a university student. Then she looked at me very seriously, held out her hands, and said, "My professor told me to believe in Jesus. I want to believe. How do you believe?" This question shook me.

I was a member of a church. I had been baptized. I had sat in many church services. I had attended summer vacation Bible schools and Sunday schools as a child. Just days before, I'd had the stirring experience at the "Say-So House." Surely, I could tell her something. It pierced my heart when I realized I had never consciously expressed a belief in Jesus. It wasn't that I didn't believe or did not want to believe.

During my early years in the Lutheran Church, I had learned all about the church and what the church means. I'd learned the rituals of the church. I'd learned the names of all of the special days and the various colors used on the altar on various Sundays. I'd memorized responses repeated by the congregation. I'd learned about the life and teachings of Jesus and all the stories about Jesus as a human being interacting with His disciples. Basically, I had learned nice stories about the historical Jesus.

After I was baptized in the Baptist church, I had learned a lot in Sunday school about the Bible and the importance of faithfulness to the church and participation. To me, Christianity was the church. I didn't really know what else there was to do except to try to be good, moral, and faithful.

I also knew that, for much of my life, I had been struggling with finding meaning in life and my lifestyle. I was hungry for something that was missing, but I didn't know what! Since our collision at sea, my restlessness and questioning had intensified.

I told her a few things about Jesus. I told some of the stories about how Jesus healed people and how He taught them. As I shared with her, the stories seemed lifeless, no joy or excitement. I was sharing a history lesson about Jesus more than anything else. We arrived at the Yokohama Station. She politely bowed and left the train. Through the window, I watched until she disappeared into the crowd. She never learned about believing in Jesus from me.

The train slowly began moving toward Tokyo. As they gathered speed, each turn of the wheels seemed to be saying "Howdoyoubelieve? Howdoyoubelieve? Howdoyoubelieve?" This echoed in my mind all the way to Tokyo. I went to the hydrographic office and got the charts. Then I walked the streets of Tokyo until long after dark. Where do I go for answers? What do I have to do? I was troubled to the very depth of my soul.

It was late when I arrived at my ship. Due to the war, no lights were allowed anywhere. I made my way to my locker and retrieved a small flashlight. I went to the ship's ward room and found a New Testament. I made my way to an empty ammunition room under the flight deck. There was no electricity in that room, so I closed the hatch; sat down on the deck; and shining my flashlight on the Gospel of Matthew, I read all of it. I read all of the Gospel of Mark. I read all of Luke. I had an insatiable hunger to learn everything I could possibly learn about Jesus. It was as if I was seeing all of this for the very first time.

When I read the account in the Gospel of Luke about the betrayal of Jesus, His death on the cross, His burial, and His resurrection, I stopped reading. I was overflowing with emotion. Suddenly, I knew why Jesus died on the cross. I knew why God raised Him from the dead. He was taking on Himself my sin and dying on the cross in my place. On the cross, my old life died, and I was being raised with him to a new life. God raised Him from the dead to prove His sacrifice on the cross was accepted for my sin and not for my sin only but for the sin of the whole world. All I needed to do was trust Him that this news was truth.

At that moment, I realized I was being given a new life. This was what it meant to believe! I could not keep the tears from flowing. My whole life had been lived in a dense fog, and suddenly the sun had broken through and was shining directly on me. I could start life all over again. Everything I'd heard over the years, the services I'd attended, the songs I'd sung, and the stories I'd heard suddenly became meaningful. The piece of the puzzle I had looked for all my life and could not find fell into place. The loneliness, the troubled heart, the restless soul all were being healed. I entered a place of total trust in the Lord for my new life.

I continued reading into the early morning hours until I finished the Gospel of John and then began to read the Acts of the Apostles. It was as though my hunger to know more could not be satisfied. I could not stop reading. The silence was broken by the boatswain mate piping reveille. It was time for the ship's crew to wake up. I had been up all night.

It was my responsibility to muster the operations division on the flight deck, share information, and assign responsibilities for the day. Some would stay on the ship; some would go ashore. Before I finished, I shared with them what had just happened to me as a result of reading the Bible.

In sharing this with these men, I was a bit naive. Hardly anyone in the operations division was a Christian as far as I knew. Most of them probably grew up in a church but were no longer following Jesus, if they ever did. At first there was stunned silence. In the days following, there was a lot of joking about me "getting religion." I endured much harsh criticism and some kidding and joking about my "new life." Later, unknown to me, the men were taking bets. They were betting ten dollars that I would last a week, twenty dollars I would last two weeks, and forty dollars I would last a month and then return to my old life.

When I finished the morning muster, I stood alone on the flight deck looking out over the city of Yokosuka. This huge city, still bearing the marks of war and extreme poverty, stretched out before me. I wanted to give my life to helping this city know Jesus. I wondered if the Japanese people would ever have a chance to hear about Jesus. I wondered if there was anyone there who knew Jesus. In all of my wandering around the city, I had never noticed a church of any kind.

At that time, I knew nothing about the concept of missions or being a missionary. My question now was, "Where should I invest my life?" Would I go back to Liberty, North Carolina, my hometown, and share with my own people? Then I thought about all the churches in and around Liberty. There were six churches of various denominations inside the city limits for about fourteen hundred people, at least three African American churches, and many more churches in the surrounding countryside. If anyone there was not a believer in Jesus, it would not be because they were not privileged to hear. It would be because they had every opportunity afforded to humankind to hear the gospel and still rejected Him. No, I would not go where the gospel was already known. Instead, I determined to set myself on a path that would take me to the far corners of the earth where people had never had an opportunity to hear. One thing was for sure: I would share this good news about Jesus somewhere.

I realized all these years I had focused on the church. I came to understand that morning that the church was not an end in itself. It could not give me peace for my restless heart. The church was the channel that brought people to know Jesus. The church should be made up of people who have their faith in Jesus and have this new life. Faith in Jesus saves us, not faith in the church. For some reason, I had seen the church as an end in itself. What I needed was to accept Jesus's death and His resurrection personally for me and let Him fill my life with meaning. Receiving this new life gave the church meaning. Receiving Jesus gave me the motivation, the power, to live for Him.

Then the church becomes the community of followers of Jesus and has great meaning. Otherwise, without Jesus, the church is simply another socially conscious organization among many showing various concerns for people.

Standing on the flight deck, I vowed to the Lord that my calling in life from that point forward was to lead people to know Him. Whatever church came from this witness would be a church that had as its mission bringing people to know Jesus as Savior and Lord and leading them to live out that life enriched by Him.

Sometime later, lying on my bunk at night, I thought of my childhood. I thought of my loneliness as a child even when I had no reason to feel lonely. For the first time in a long time, I remembered that brief moment when I was fifteen years old—December 27, 1947, when I wrote in my diary, "I got a Bible today. I am deeply troubled. I think something wants me to be a preacher." Why did I turn away so rapidly from that thinking? Perhaps I really did not know then what I would preach or why!

I soon discovered many on board were setting me up for temptation. They were looking for whatever they could find to show I was not really a Christian. In that environment, one either has to be a genuine Christian or not one at all. There is no middle ground.

On one occasion, just after docking in Yokosuka, mail call was almost immediate. I kept listening for my name. I did not receive one letter after all those weeks at sea. I was extremely depressed by this. The men kept urging me to go with them to The Golden Pheasant, a popular bar/night club in Yokosuka. Feeling sorry for myself and feeling no one loved me or cared, I decided to go with them.

As we were about to leave the ship I heard one say to another, "I knew we'd get him!"

I immediately turned around and went back to my sleeping quarters. I lay on my bunk and wallowed in my self-pity.

Within ten minutes, there was another mail call. I received ten letters! I learned something from that experience: I was going to have to be careful to not follow my feelings but just follow Jesus!

I soon discovered my constant chatter about Jesus was beginning to turn people away. It wasn't that they did not respect me or did not believe me. They were annoyed by my constant talking about Jesus every time I talked with them. They also did not want me to keep talking about their need to forsake their present lifestyle. They were not ready for that.

I decided to change my approach. First, I would be the best at my job that anyone could ever be. I did not want there to be any criticism about me not doing my job or not doing it right. "Now that I am a Christian," I thought, "I will show what Christ intends for me to be and to do in every area of life." Second, I decided to let my Christian life speak for itself. I needed to restore the friendship I had with most of my shipmates and become someone they enjoyed being around. I needed to earn the right to talk with them about Jesus without forcing myself on them.

Before long, one at a time, men began to come to talk with me about their problems. They often shared with me how they had gone to church before coming into the navy and how they had fallen away. It was interesting how sailors returning to the ship intoxicated would come to my bunk; sit down; and, under the influence of alcohol, weep and share with me their troubles and their shame at the way they were acting. They often shared with tears about a loving wife and children who begged them to stop drinking. They wanted me to pray for them.

I often wanted to refer them to the chaplain or the chaplain's assistant. The problem was the chaplain's assistant was a member of the Christian Science religion and often poked fun at evangelical Christianity. The chaplain was more a naval officer than a pastor or minister of the gospel. There was just nowhere for these men to turn for spiritual help.

Slowly, a small group began to form. We read and discussed the Bible. Often the debate about the meaning of a passage would become almost violent. That usually happened because none of us had much training in interpreting the Bible. We had no authority figure to resolve an issue with a reasonable interpretation. Usually it fell to me to provide a final say, even though I myself had never been in a serious Bible study. Nevertheless, we enjoyed the discussions, and the group grew. Evidently, the Holy Spirit led us as we struggled together to discover the truth in the scripture!

For the first time since joining the navy, I could hardly wait to be discharged. I wanted to begin my education and preparation to serve the Lord. The Potter had spent years preparing the clay. He had taken a long time, but now the clay—me!—was in His hands, a potential vessel ready and yielding to His plan.

PART II
FORMING THE VESSEL

CHAPTER 7

SHAPING THE VESSEL

ANCHORAGE ALASKA, SUNDAY MORNING, MAY 1953

The USS *Sitkoh Bay* was the first aircraft carrier ever to navigate Cook's Inlet into the Bay of Anchorage. We navigated the channel through ice floes, arriving in the dead of night, carefully timed to catch high tide in the shallow bay.

Early in the morning, a note posted on the bulletin board shared the name and addresses of several churches in Anchorage with offers of a ride to any of them. Noticing the First Baptist Church of Anchorage, I immediately made the contact. A young couple met me at the gangway. I felt badly because they had prepared for many sailors to attend that morning, and I was the only one who attended. My royal welcome by the congregation was exciting. The same couple took me to lunch and then to their home for the afternoon.

As we sat in their living room, they began to share with me about life in Anchorage. Being just slightly younger than this couple, I was somewhat disturbed when our conversation turned to problems they were having in their marriage. Within minutes, the wife was sharing through tears. The husband, evidently embarrassed, was looking off in the distance as she talked. Being so young, unmarried, and a new believer, I was not sure what to do with all of this except to listen and understand what they were saying. I tried to draw him into the conversation but with little success. The wife began to have trouble speaking through the tears flowing more profusely with each moment.

Finally, she took a deep breath, swallowed hard and turned to her husband. "I'm so sorry. I shouldn't have bared my soul like this. I love you, honey, but it has been so hard. Please forgive me for talking so openly. Is there anything you want to say?"

His response was a shrug of his shoulders and a stare out of the window that lasted what seemed an eternity.

Then he turned to me with a distressed look on his face. "Sir, I want to apologize for putting you in this awkward situation. You are a guest in our home, and I am so sorry you had to hear all of this. These things have been pent up inside of us for a long time. Neither of us has felt like confronting the other. When we have confronted issues, we began arguing. I can't stand that."

She responded, "Maybe this is a good time to talk about some of these things while we have someone here to help us."

With that, they both began to share in a loving kind of way many things that bothered them. They poured out months of pent up unhappiness, misunderstandings, and struggles. They did it calmly but expressed their feelings fully. It was evident they had a great love for each other. I sat silently through it all.

Finally, they looked at each other for a long time in silence. Tears began to flow down their cheeks. Through his tears, he spoke with tenderness. "I am so sorry for the way I have acted. I love you so much and never intended to act the way I have. We must learn how to talk with each other. I just don't know how to talk without hurting you. Please forgive me."

He arose from his chair, knelt beside her, hugged her close, and they both wept.

I waited a while and then arose from my chair, knelt beside them and hugged them both close. I could not help but cry with them. There was an uncomfortable silence for a long time.

Suddenly she began to laugh, slipped out of her chair onto the floor, and all three of us were piled up on the floor laughing.

"I can't believe what just happened!" she said. "You don't know how long I have wanted to cry but couldn't. Here you are, a total stranger. All we wanted to do was to take you to church and to lunch. You didn't ask anything, and for whatever reason, I just opened up months of wounds and suffering. I didn't know how good it feels just to cry! If this gets my husband to hold me close like that, I'm going to cry a lot more often!"

The tension broken, we all three broke into almost uncontrollable laughter.

They suggested we return to my ship.

Just as I was getting out of the car, the young wife put her hand on mine and, with a pleading look in her eyes, said, "May I share something with you? Please get your education and come back to Anchorage to minister to all of us here. Our church is small, and everyone knows everyone else. We just can't share our problems. We have no one to talk to. Unless someone like you gets your training and comes here, we will continue to struggle and only hope for the best. Please come back."

I left that young couple, my heart broken. "If I just had a few days," I thought to myself, "I think I could help them." I went aboard ship and stood alone on the bridge looking over Cook's Inlet. I could not stop the tears from flowing. I prayed, "Lord, someday I am going to help people like that, somewhere in this world."

Little did I know, later in life counseling would become a very important part of my life.

One evening, Lieutenant Commander Rapp, the ship's navigator and commander of the operations division, was lingering in the chart room where we did the navigation calculations daily to plot the course of the ship. By this time, I had taken a great interest in navigation and spent hours in the chart room practicing plotting the ship's course on my own. In those years, we still used a sextant to visually locate the position of the stars and took sun lines to determine the precise location of the ship at all times.

On this occasion, we had completed our calculations. Lieutenant Commander Rapp began to talk with me about the Naval Air Station in Pensacola, Florida, where he trained as a naval aviator.

After going into much detail about his training and the joy he found in flying, he asked me, "Would you give me permission to recommend you for flight training to become a navy pilot? I have looked at your records and determined I could easily get you admitted into the training program. The navy will pay for your college education, after which you would go to Pensacola for flight training. In fact, you could do both at the same time if you want to."

I was immediately intrigued. I thought, "I could be a Christian, and the navy would be my place of service for the Lord as a layman." This was another of those forks in the road of life. My choice would determine my future direction for years to come.

"Can I think about this for a few days?" I needed to know if taking this opportunity was in line with the promises I had made to God and consistent with His calling.

"I expected you would need time," he said. "It's a big decision. I would like to know before we reach port. That's all."

My overwhelming desire to go to college could be settled with this decision. My schooling would be totally paid for, and I could begin immediately.

That night, I prayed earnestly about what God would have me do. At this point, my great desire was to give my life to the Lord for His service. I was no longer trying to find a missing piece in my life. I was no longer troubled about a restlessness, looking for an answer to a question I did not know. I now stood between two directions in my spiritual life. I would have to decide.

"Surely, I could be a pilot and also serve the Lord, just like I am currently doing on this ship," I thought. However, the more I prayed and thought about it, the more convinced I became that I was already on the right course for what God would have me do.

That night, I could not go to sleep. I kept thinking about the direction of my life. At sea, I learned to navigate the vast Pacific

Ocean. Every morning just before daybreak, when only the brightest stars were visible, and late in the evening just after the setting of the sun, I would go up on the ship's bridge and, with my sextant, take bearings on three predetermined stars, noting the exact latitude and longitude of those stars in the sky and the precise time. I would then plot their location on the chart. The very second these three stars intersected pinpointed our exact location. I thought about navigating life. What were the "stars" by which I could determine the course of my life?

First was the Bible. Then there was prayer. And finally, life experiences offered guide posts for life. These all spoke to direction. Usually, life's tough experiences teach us the most about who we are and who we need to become. As I lay there struggling with the decision about naval flight school, experiences as far back as early childhood flooded my mind. "God has been preparing me all this time for what He wants me to do," I realized. Learning to love people of other races and cultures, entering a declamation contest, practicing living under difficult conditions as a young man, realizing the presence of God in a little boat tossed around in the middle of the Pacific Ocean, exposure to youth groups and the church—all were a process of discovering my gifts and calling. Meeting Pop Watson and the Say-So House brought me face-to-face with Jesus. That meeting with the young Japanese girl on the train, which resulted in my coming to know and trust Jesus, was not just a "chance experience." I had to believe God brought her into my life at just the right moment. I pictured myself again, standing on the flight deck of my aircraft carrier, burdened for a Japanese city that needed to know Jesus. I simply could not abandon the clear call God had given me.

I decided to decline the offer.

The evening before we entered San Francisco Bay, Lieutenant Commander Rapp entered the chart room. "Well, what are you thinking?" he asked.

"Sir, I have considered every angle I can think of. I have relived every experience and tried to be objective in making a decision. I realize how significant this invitation is and what an honor to be offered this opportunity. I want to thank you for that. As you know, some months ago, I became a Christian in Yokosuka, Japan. God has called me to serve Him. I am aware that everything in life has prepared me to serve God. He has given me a clear call. I must follow Him in this call."

Commander Rapp responded, "I think I knew all along what your response would be. I have watched you, and I have no doubt about your sincerity. I just want to wish you well in your choice of vocation."

He stared deeply into my eyes, smiled, shook my hand, and left. He received orders for another assignment, and I never saw him again.

On July 27, 1953, the Korean War ended. Within two months, word came that our ship was to be decommissioned. Everyone would be transferred to other assignments. I had only a year and a few months left on my enlistment. I began to pray I would get an assignment on shore and have an opportunity before leaving the navy to at least begin my college education.

Just before Thanksgiving, I received my orders to report on January 10, 1954, to the Adak Naval Base in the Aleutian Islands for duty.

Adak is a small island near the end of the Aleutian Island chain leading out from Alaska. It is like a barren rock located in the Pacific Ocean with the ocean on the south and the Bering Sea on the north. I knew this would provide no opportunity for me to go to college. I could not see how serving on that island would result in growth in my knowledge of the Bible and the Christian life.

"Why am I being sent to a place like that? I will have no opportunity to be in a Christian environment or attend a university," I complained to the Lord. I made a firm commitment that, other than my work, I would read nothing but the Bible while on Adak. I would read no books, magazines, or entertainment materials. I wanted to take this opportunity away from the world to learn all the Bible had to say.

I was able to take leave from the navy prior to going to Adak. I had long been concerned for my father and his health. He was under tremendous stress financially and worried about his declining health. After I accepted the Lord, I occasionally encouraged him to come to know the Lord and join my mother in church. While I was at home over Christmas, my folks saw my faithfulness in attending church, my prayer life, and my commitment to the Lord. After I left to go to Adak, my father began attending church and joined the Lutheran Church where my mother attended. This was joyful news for me. Though he never gave up his smoking habit, he quit drinking alcohol. However, much damage had already been done to his health, which continued to deteriorate.

In early January, I arrived on Adak. It was the dead of winter, with howling winds called "williwaws" frequently sweeping the island. There was more snow on the sides of buildings than on the ground, which was a solid sheet of ice. Many buildings were underground and could be reached by underground passageways. "Zip your parka up before you step foot outside," my commanding officer reminded me in our first meeting. "The wind will treat it as a sail and carry you right into the ocean, where you will last less than one minute in the freezing temperatures." The island was almost devoid of vegetation. Halfway up Mount Moffett was a stand of about fifteen trees many years old, only about three feet tall. An old sign said, "Adak National Forest." In the spring, one small white flower began to bloom here and there around the island. I must have taken a hundred pictures of that one flower since it was such a rare object.

I was cleared by the Office of Naval Intelligence to handle top secret material, especially regarding shipping both in the North Pacific and the Bering Sea all the way to Vladivostok, a major Russian naval base in Russian Siberia north of the Chinese border. At times, I went by tugboat out to the end of the Aleutians to Attu

Island to pick up materials that were too sensitive to be transmitted by radio. I brought them back to Adak for analysis and forwarding to Washington. I dreaded those trips because of the rough seas, freezing air, and sparse quarters.

One of the first persons I went to meet on Adak was the navy chaplain. I immediately felt a warm, pastoral spirit. I was impressed and felt this would be my first time in the navy with a real chaplain. Worship services were fairly well attended. I joined the chapel choir immediately. I heard about a small group of about ten men who met together one night a week to study the Bible. They called themselves the Adak Christian Fellowship. After a few weeks, I was asked to lead the group in Bible study. I had no idea what I was doing. Three weeks later, a chief petty officer named Gene Farrell came on the island. He attended our Bible study.

Afterward he met with me and said, "Do you really want to learn that Bible?"

"More than I can say."

"Would you like to meet with me one night a week and study together?"

"Yes, more than anything in the world!"

Gene had somehow escaped without injury when Japan attacked his battleship and others in Pearl Harbor on December 7, 1941. Years later, he met Dawson Trotman, who had founded an organization called "The Navigators." The "Navs," as they were called, were the primary follow-up organization for the Billy Graham Crusades. Billy had just begun conducting crusades with literally thousands of people in attendance. Large numbers were accepting Jesus. Billy Graham asked the Navs to disciple new believers. They produced numerous follow-up materials for discipleship.

Gene Farrell had been active with the Navs for several years. "You must begin memorizing scripture," he commanded me. "By memorizing scripture, you will always have your Bible with you. By putting the Bible in your mind and heart, it will constantly remind you of what the Lord would have you do."

The Navs taught what was called the "topical memory system" for memorizing scripture. Small cards contained Bible verses divided into categories for easy memorization. I immediately began memorizing scripture. Each week, we would discuss the verses I had memorized.

"Let's go together out into the barracks and find people we can share with about Jesus," he said. As we went, he talked about Jesus and shared scripture verses while I listened and prayed. Then one night, he led a young man to the point where he was ready to accept Jesus. Gene looked at his watch and asked to be excused because he had an appointment. He asked me to take over the conversation. I was nervous about this, given that I had not done this since studying with Gene. The young man accepted Jesus, and we prayed together. It was the first time I had used the Bible verses I had memorized to actually lead someone to Christ.

When I left the barracks, I discovered Gene outside waiting for me.

I asked him, "Why did you leave me like that? You scared me half to death!"

Gene responded, "I had to do something to get you started. Now you can go on without me."

From that point on, I had no trouble sharing with people about Jesus and followed Gene's example discipling those who believed. As Timothy had the apostle Paul to mentor him, I had Gene Farrell. The foundation he helped me lay as a new servant of the Lord kept me grounded in the scriptures throughout a very challenging college and seminary career.

A cook, a large heavyset Pentecostal Christian from Oklahoma City, came on the island and became a good friend. He was very concerned I had never spoken in unknown tongues as recorded in the New Testament book of Acts and in Paul's letter to the Corinthians.

"Sam, don't you know that speaking in tongues is the gift of the Holy Spirit of God? Speaking in tongues is proof you have been filled and baptized with the Holy Spirit. God gives you the gift of speaking in unknown tongues as a testimony to the fact you are now baptized with the Holy Spirit of God. You need to ask God to give you the gift of tongues!"

He was much older in the Christian faith than me, so I followed his instructions. Every night, he and I met in an old, abandoned Quonset hut for prayer. Yielding to his teaching, I knelt and prayed night after night, even begged God to allow me to receive the gift of "unknown tongues" and, with that gift, receive the baptism of the Holy Spirit. I became confused and discouraged with my faith. He tried to teach me how to use my tongue and form the sounds, but it just didn't seem right to me. This was artificial and in no way a supernatural gift from God.

One Sunday night, at my lowest point, I was listening on my shortwave radio to the Old-Fashioned Revival Hour. Dr. Charles Fuller was preaching on the "Gifts of the Spirit." One of the points he made was that anything we have to beg for ceases to be a gift. He went on to say the various spiritual gifts are given at the pleasure of God Himself through the presence and power of the Holy Spirit. If we are open and ready to receive whatever gift God has for us, then He will give the gift that enables us to meet whatever need He wants us to meet. Then it will be truly a gift from God. When we must plead for something, it ceases to be a gift. This is especially true of the gifts of the Spirit. This message was tailored for me.

I determined to keep myself open and willing to exercise whatever gift God wanted to give me. God gave me other gifts but not the gift of unknown tongues. There is absolutely no doubt I have been filled and continue to be filled with the Spirit of God. This has been evident every time I face a challenge. I experience His fullness, especially when I meet tasks beyond my ability, and there have been plenty of those!

Years later, when I began serving God as a missionary overseas, language came somewhat easily for me. I could communicate the good news of Jesus in the language people could understand.

This was more like the experience of Pentecost in Acts 2 when people heard the gospel, each in his or her own language. To me, speaking in tongues that people understand is the greatest gift I could receive.

Years later, as I reflect on that experience on Adak, I am convinced my miraculous opportunity to take Latin as an eighth grader in school and my desire to study all of the French available was an indication of a supernatural gift God was developing in me. He gave me a gift of loving to communicate the gospel in other tongues and a love for learning language. Learning these languages in middle and high school prepared me to become fluent in the other languages I needed to communicate the good news about Jesus. Paul never ruled out speaking in unknown tongues. He said, "But, in the church I would rather speak five intelligible words to instruct others than ten thousand words in a tongue" I Corinthians 14:19 (NIV).

Our Adak Christian Fellowship began to grow. As we grew, attendance at the chapel on Sunday mornings increased. People who had never attended worship services began attending. Naval and Air Force personnel began arriving on the island ready to serve the Lord. It was as though God was sending choice servants to serve on Adak. The chaplain preached with new power. Many came to know Jesus. My last week on Adak was emotionally overwhelming—I was able to see over one hundred men in our Adak Christian Fellowship attend that special service. What I thought would be a year of no opportunities for spiritual growth became a year of practical and rapid spiritual growth.

On February 1, 1955, I departed Adak, and on February 17, I received my honorable discharge at the Naval Air Station in Seattle, Washington. What at first seemed to be a most undesirable assignment on a small, isolated island in the North Pacific Ocean had become the most powerful agent of growth and spiritual development in my life. For me, it was the same as Moses's forty years in the wilderness, Jesus's forty days in the wilderness, or the apostle Paul's two years of mentorship with Barnabus. That period of time became the best preparation I could have to become a servant of the Lord. I was truly in a process of being molded into that vessel equipped to do whatever God called me to do in the world.

CHAPTER 8
THE VESSEL NEARING COMPLETION

Immediately after my discharge from the navy, I went to the San Francisco area to visit my mentors, Mom and Pop Watson. I arrived late Friday afternoon and heard that the Melrose Baptist Church in Oakland, now my home church when in the States, was beginning its annual World Missions Conference that night. This church lived and breathed world missions in everything they did. I could hardly wait for the service to begin. It would be my first experience meeting international missionaries. They were there from almost every major part of the world.

A missionary from Africa preached a powerful missions message on Saturday night. He invited anyone feeling a call to be a missionary to come forward as we sang an invitation hymn. I was the first to step forward. I told him, "I want to drive a stake down firmly tonight, committing myself to follow God's call to go wherever He leads, especially to those who have no access to the gospel of our Lord, and I want to do this for the rest of my life."

Mom and Pop Watson welcomed me to spend a few days with them. While there, I prayed for the Lord to lead me to a good used car I could drive home and depend on for my years in the university. After visiting a number of used car lots, I walked onto a lot in Hayward, California. I immediately saw a two-tone blue Plymouth with ridiculously low mileage. I knew this would be my car.

"Who owned this car previously?" I asked the salesman.

"Well, I could tell you it was owned by an elderly, unmarried schoolteacher who only drove it to school and back each day, but I doubt you would believe me."

He gave me the name and telephone number of the woman who had owned the car. I called her, and he was right. She was an unmarried schoolteacher who seldom drove her car. I returned to the dealership to bargain for a lower price.

When I walked in, the salesman said to me, "I don't know why I am doing this, but something tells me you really need this car. For some reason I don't understand, I feel like I just have to practically give it to you." He made me a very low offer.

I bought the car on the spot. I could have told him the real reason he felt compelled to sell it to me was because the Lord had told him to do it! I drove the car across America, home to North Carolina. It never needed repairs during my entire university career.

On my way home to North Carolina, I was driving through Oklahoma. It was late Wednesday afternoon, and I had an urge to find a church where I could attend a prayer meeting. I prayed the Lord would lead me to the right place. Hardly had I finished praying when, just ahead, I saw a small, white church with cars parked around it. I knew it must be a prayer meeting. The service was just starting. It was a Pentecostal church of some kind, and the service was like nothing I had ever experienced. Singing, praying, praising, unknown tongues, prophecy, casting out demons, and healing were taking place pretty much all at the same time. Several fell to the floor as though unconscious. Others shook violently. Sometimes the pastor would pray for a healing to occur, and that person would fall to the floor as in a trance and then rise healed.

My eyes must have been as big as saucers! I was totally astounded at all of the confusion and activity in a worship service. As a new believer, my only exposure in a church in America to date was Melrose Baptist in Oakland. My first reaction was, "I'm in the wrong place. Let me out of here as fast as I can get out!" Then, I became utterly fascinated by what was happening.

An old man with silver hair and a white beard rose to pray. The church immediately grew quiet. He lifted his voice at first softly and then powerfully to the Lord. I was deeply moved. He ended his prayer with a statement I have never forgotten. He prayed, "Oh God, I know you can fill a bent vessel. I know you can fill a damaged vessel. I know you can fill an ugly vessel. But, oh God, I know you will never fill a dirty vessel. Cleanse us, dear God, that we may be filled with your Holy Spirit so we can live like you want us to live." If I came into that church for no other reason, it was worth it to hear this prayer, which has influenced my life throughout my years.

After arriving home and consulting the pastor of the First Baptist Church, Liberty, I applied to Wake Forest University (then Wake Forest College) located at that time in Wake Forest, North Carolina. I was accepted for the fall semester. I had been away from home for five years, and it seemed right to spend time near my parents. A part of my reasoning for choosing Wake Forest was that it was a highly academic Christian college. Because it was a small school with high academic qualifications, it was very difficult to be accepted. I wanted a school that would challenge me academically and prepare me for service overseas.

I had debated at length between two different directions. I could go immediately to the mission field under the auspices of the Navigators who discipled me and grounded me in the Bible as the Word of God. I could raise support and return overseas quickly with no more formal education. Or I could go with the Foreign Mission Board (in 1997 changed to International Mission Board, abbreviated IMB), which also had a good reputation but required very high academic and practical preparation before going overseas to serve. Having been overseas extensively in the navy, I was convinced I needed all the preparation I could get to be an effective missionary. This meant a minimum of seven years of college and seminary, including two years of practical experience before I could go. This seemed like an eternity to wait. I could not get away from the conviction that I needed to prepare and mature mentally, academically, and spiritually so I could be ready for whatever God would call me to do on the mission field.

This was another of those forks in the road. I appreciated the Navigators and all they stood for. The Holy Spirit knew what was going to be required of me as a missionary. God, the Potter, was shaping a vessel exactly like He needed for His task. I chose to go to Wake Forest for my undergraduate education!

At the urging of Dr. Carl English, pastor of Liberty's First Baptist Church, in 1955, I wrote a letter to the Foreign Mission Board to let them know of my interest in foreign missions. I told them of my desire to go as a missionary to Asia with a special interest in Vietnam. My service in the navy had stimulated my interest in Vietnam. The percentage of evangelical Christians in Vietnam was extremely small, which further impressed me.

Dr. Winston Crawley, at that time secretary for the Orient, responded with gratitude for my interest in missions. He wrote that the Foreign Mission Board had no missionaries in Vietnam and no plans to send anyone there. I would need to choose another field. He suggested I finish my education and then make application to the board.

I knew I needed to become more familiar with the people who would be supporting me as a missionary, so I chose to spend my summer on the staff at Ridgecrest Assembly near Black Mountain, North Carolina. It would be a great learning experience.

During that summer at Ridgecrest, an experience powerfully influenced the course of my life. During a week called Sunday School Week, the major focus was training to teach the Bible and the ministry of Sunday schools. Dr. Ralph Herring, pastor of First Baptist Church, Winston Salem, North Carolina, was the principal Bible teacher for the week. He was born and raised by missionary parents in North China. Many of his illustrations were based on his experiences growing up in North China. He was a Greek scholar and almost all of his Bible teaching used word studies from the Greek language of the New Testament.

I was fascinated and inspired by his explanation of Greek words, which so clearly and simply enlightened especially the Pauline epistles. As a result of my discipleship training by the Navigators, I was thoroughly committed that the Bible is the authoritative Word of God. I needed to be thoroughly grounded and trained in the scriptures.

By the end of the week, I made my decision to major in Greek at Wake Forest University. I did not know then that Dr. A. T. Robertson, one of the foremost scholars of the Greek language, was a graduate of Wake Forest and had left a legacy of Greek and Latin scholarship in the Classical Languages Department.

Introductory Classical Greek was a two-semester, five-hour-per-week course. It took major commitment of time every day to prepare for the course. I received an A+ each semester. To speed up my education, I decided to attend summer school each year; that way, I could graduate in three years. In summer school, I registered for a Greek course translating Xenophon's *Anabasis*. It would meet every day during summer school. I arrived in class early. Dr. C. B. Earp, dean of the Classical Languages Department, entered the room and closed the door.

I looked around and saw I was the only student in the room. I rather hesitantly asked, "Dr. Earp, am I in the wrong room? I don't see any other students in here."

Dr. Earp responded, "Mr. James, you are the only student to sign up for this course."

I realized that this would mean I would have to translate every day with no break in my assignments. I slowly rose from my seat, closed my book, and said rather fearfully, "Dr. Earp, I don't want you to spend your summer teaching just one student. Excuse me, I will leave now."

Dr. Earp frowned, glared at me, and said with great authority, "Mr. James, you sit down and open your book to the introductory page. You will learn Greek in this class. You will have three tests and a final exam. Now, let's get acquainted with the author, Mr.

Xenophon! I sheepishly sat down, avoiding his intense stare, and opened my book.

I made an A+ and learned more Greek than I could have ever anticipated. From that point, I studied every Greek course available ending my final year with New Testament Greek translating all of First John. I was also obligated to study two semesters of Latin.

***

I was seated with a team of Wake Forest students in the office of the pastor of a large conservative church in Wilson, North Carolina. In just a few moments, our team would enter the auditorium to lead in music and worship. During those years, Wake Forest sent out a number of teams to churches to conduct weekend meetings for youth and participate in the Sunday morning service. I was a freshman, and this was my first experience with a team.

The pastor entered his office, looked each one of us over, and asked, "How many of you are using the Revised Standard Version of the Bible?" which had recently been published.

Everyone raised his or her hand but me.

"What are you using, young man?" he asked.

I swallowed real hard and said, "I always use my old trusted Thompson Chain Reference Bible. It is only printed in the King James Version."

He said, "Then you are the preacher this morning. I do not allow the Revised Standard Version in my services."

With that said, he walked out.

I felt the eyes of the whole team on me. "What are you going to do?" they said almost with one voice. I could tell they were very worried and sympathetic.

"I have ten minutes to prepare a sermon. Please leave me by myself so I can prepare."

Later, the team described me as white as a sheet and shaking all over. I prepared a very simple sermon using one of the scripture memory categories I had memorized with the Navigators. I walked out into the pulpit and faced around five hundred people. Never had I felt so young, inexperienced, and incapable of doing a job!

The team led a wonderful worship service, and the Lord was in that place in power. I stood to preach. As I preached, I began to recall all of the scripture I had memorized. I felt an unusual presence of the Lord. Time came for the invitation to accept Christ or rededicate one's life to the Lord. People, both young and old, from all over the room began to come forward. Many knelt at the altar. Some talked with the pastor. Some were weeping. I was overwhelmed with the way God moved in the hearts of the people.

From that time on, any time we received an invitation from a conservative church, I was assigned by the team to preach. As I became more fluent in the Greek language, I gravitated to the American Standard Version and other newer versions of the Bible that had a clearer translation of Greek words into modern English. When a very conservative church demanded the King James Version of the Bible, I could use that version and draw illustrations from the original Greek to explain meanings. Greek allowed for great versatility!

These trips to various churches to preach were excellent training for my future ministry. If I wanted to minister in churches, I was going to have to be very sensitive to what each church expected of a team and be prepared to adjust accordingly. Also, I knew knowing the original Greek language would be invaluable for teaching the scriptures in other languages.

When Wake Forest moved its campus from the little town of Wake Forest in eastern North Carolina to a new campus in Winston Salem, North Carolina, I moved with it. I watched as the college took on an increasingly Ivy League approach to education. I watched as the distance between the school and its traditional foundation as a church-supported school became greater and greater. The number of students studying for the ministry drastically declined during the first two years on the new campus. I watched as Wake Forest made the change from an intimate, personal-oriented college to a highly academic, more formal university. It continued to pride itself on being a small school, emphasizing humanity's search for truth.

I will always be grateful for the challenging education I received at Wake Forest University. The best thing that happened to me was everything I had come to believe was intellectually challenged in the emphasis on academia. I became a much stronger apologist for the Christian faith as a result of this. This education thoroughly prepared me as a missionary to face the religions and worldviews of the world outside the Christian religion and culture. My six years in the navy had matured me. My discipline in scripture memorization and detailed study of the Bible on Adak were invaluable. A foundation was laid, which helped me sort through and make choices.

Sometimes in college the use of the Bible was quite humorous. In my regimented life in the navy, any day could be an inspection day. Everything had to be kept neatly organized. Living space was expected to be spotless. My first roommate was a young man right out of high school. Every time I returned to our room, his side of the room was a mess. His bed was seldom if ever made. When he undressed, his clothes fell to the floor wherever he was standing and stayed there for days. I was going out of my mind with frustration over the mess in our room.

I complained about it to a mutual friend, a German student. recently arrived from Germany. He was typically German in his obsession with order and detail. One day he looked around the room and asked my roommate, "Do you believe the Bible?"

My roommate answered, "Of course."

"Then," he said, "you want to live like Jesus?"

My roommate answered, "Of course."

My friend said, "Have you not read in John's account of the resurrection when Peter entered the tomb where Jesus was buried, he found Jesus's linen separated out and neatly folded? Why is your room so messy?"

From that point on, our room was at least a little neater!

CHAPTER 9

MADE COMPLETE WITH A PARTNER FOR LIFE

I answered the phone and heard the voice of a woman I did not recognize. She asked, "Is this Sammy?"

I knew immediately it must be somebody from my childhood.

When I responded, "Yes," she said, "Can you come to my house for dinner this coming Friday or Saturday night?"

"Who is this?"

"This is your aunt Mamie. Don't you know me?"

"Oh, I'm so sorry. Yes, I know you, but I haven't seen you for at least five years."

"Well, are you able to come or not?"

"Aunt Mamie, I remember you live in Durham, so I can stop by on my way home on Friday night."

"Good. Be at my house by six o'clock."

With that, she hung up. This was a voice from my past. I had no idea why she was inviting me to her home. I gave little thought to it until I arrived at her house. She was waiting outside. She immediately said, "We need to go and pick up somebody."

Nothing more was said, and I didn't dare ask questions. We drove a short distance around the corner, where a young lady was waiting. Completely dumbfounded, I asked myself, "What in the world is going on here?" We rode in silence back around the corner to my aunt's house.

As we entered the house, my aunt introduced the young lady.

"Sammy, this is Rachel Kerr, a nursing student at Duke University and a member of my church. She sings in the choir."

Unknown to me, she had invited Rachel to dinner telling her, "I want you to meet my nephew, who has been in the navy and does not know any girls." Later, Rachel said she hardly knew my aunt but felt she needed to be polite and accept the invitation.

Only two places were set at the table. Quickly, food was served, and my aunt disappeared into the kitchen, coming out only occasionally to see if we needed anything.

Dinner over, she invited us into her living room. "Y'all sit on the couch, and I'll be back in a few minutes."

A few minutes later, she came back with dessert and left it on the coffee table. Rachel and I found ourselves in deep conversation.

It was surprising how easily we talked. I discovered that Rachel was called to missions when she was fourteen years old. She had wanted to be a missionary nurse from the time she was a small child. She was interested in serving in Japan. She was completely committed to the Lord. I shared with her about my own salvation experience in Japan, my call to missions, and my interest in serving in Asia.

My aunt returned again with popcorn and drinks and left without saying anything. Soon Rachel and I were conversing deeply about the Lord and our experiences in our Christian lives.

When the evening was over, she invited me to attend her church on Sunday evening. I told her that, if I finished my Greek assignment in time, I would stop by on my way back to Wake Forest. That weekend, I could not get Rachel out of my mind.

When I'd arrived home after my years in the navy, I had pledged to the Lord I would not date anyone who was not committed to going to the mission field. I did not want to get involved in anything that might sidetrack me or possibly hinder me in the future from my missionary call. Now, I had met someone who was not only committed to the same goals in life but completely compatible spiritually. In those few moments, we discovered we shared the same doctrine, the same value system, and the same call to the mission field overseas. It was almost frightening to realize I just might have met my life's mate.

The weekend dragged by. I could hardly wait to go to church on Sunday evening. As I arrived at the church, the pastor met me on the front steps of Holloway Street Church. He introduced himself as Jack Wilder and asked about my experience with the Lord. He then invited me to go with him for a time of prayer with the choir and then to give my testimony in the evening service. After the service, I took Rachel back to Duke to the nursing dormitory. We sat in the parking lot at the nursing dorm and talked until midnight, the hour of curfew for nursing students. Before I left that night, we prayed together for the Lord to continue to guide us on the path He had called each of us to walk.

While driving back to Wake Forest that night, I could not stop praying. My thoughts were sharply focused. I recognized I was falling in love with this girl. But what was I falling in love with? Was I falling in love because she was heading for the mission field? Was I falling in love because we had the same spiritual commitment and core values in life? Was it that she was very attractive and intelligent? She was all of those things, but were they really enough to say we belonged together for the rest of our lives? What if, for some reason, we could not go to the mission field? Would our love be strong enough to sustain us through all the trials of life?

I prayed, "Lord, if this is the one you want me to join my life with for eternity, please show me unmistakably your perfect will! Help me to know what genuine love really is!"

Two weeks later, I invited Rachel to go to a ministerial banquet held each fall for the ministerial students at Wake Forest. When I took her back to the Duke campus, we sat and talked again until curfew time. On that third night, almost with one breath, we shared our deepest feelings that God just might have brought us in His perfect will to serve the Lord together. In my own heart and mind, I knew without a doubt I loved Rachel simply because of the beautiful person God formed her to be. Whatever circumstances we found ourselves in in the future, I wanted us to be together. From that moment, there was never a doubt we would become one. If, for some reason, we could not take the gospel to those who had never heard, we would serve Him together wherever God placed us.

In January 1957, I was at home following the Christmas holidays. I was between my sophomore and junior year at Wake Forest. I had gone to summer school and intended to go one more summer so I could finish college in three years. Mr. Boyd Poe, a deacon from Mt. Pleasant Baptist Church, a small rural church just south of Liberty, my hometown, came to visit me. I had known him since he'd returned to Liberty from the navy after World War II.

After a few pleasantries, he began speaking. "Sammy, our pastor of twenty-five years has just retired. I am the lone member of the pulpit committee of Mt. Pleasant Baptist Church. I am representing our small congregation. We would like to invite you to become our pastor." He continued almost without stopping. "Our church has Sunday school every Sunday morning, but we only have preaching once a month. We have Training Union every Sunday evening and prayer meeting every Wednesday night. If you accept our invitation to come as pastor, we want you to be our full-time pastor with worship every Sunday morning."

"Boyd, I appreciate this invitation very much. I do have some reservations though. I am only twenty-four years old, with no pastoral experience. I have only been a believer for about four years. In addition, I am a full-time university student."

"Preacher Sammy, we have discussed that, and we still want you to come. Also, our church has gone down in attendance, and because we have so few people, we can't guarantee you a salary. We will try to give you as much of the offering each Sunday as we can."

Continuing my reservations, I said, "As you know, I am a single man and have been advised against pastoring until I get married. There are just too many complications that arise. Besides, so many are trying to introduce me to their daughters and granddaughters and friends, and it has become annoying!"

"We understand and have discussed this. We heard you are getting married in August. Is this right?"

"Yes," I replied. "We are getting married in August."

"Then that is no problem at all! Honestly, if you can't come, the continued existence of our church is questionable. It will be hard to find a pastor with the small amount of money we can pay. I know we are small and weak, but we will try our best to do right by you, financially."

"Boyd, I will accept your invitation. I promise I will do my best to become a good pastor. I will depend on you and the church to help me to become the pastor you are hoping for."

I knew I would need to have at least two years of pastoral experience before I qualified to go to the mission field. Also, it would be good experience for me to learn how to grow a church and to be involved in preaching and discipling believers.

So, at the age of twenty-four, single, a sophomore in college, and a Christian for a little over four years, I became the pastor of Mt. Pleasant Baptist Church at the end of January 1957. I followed a pastor who had preached for sixty-five years and had served this church for twenty-five years. He was well known and had the respect and love of people throughout the county. Following him was intimidating to say the least!

There was some dissension among two of the families in the church. For six weeks, I preached, and nothing was happening. I felt strongly that the dissension in the church was holding back any progress. I also wondered if I was just too young, untrained, and inexperienced to pastor a church. I felt like I was just practicing preaching.

Thoroughly discouraged, one Saturday night, I went to the church to pray. I parked under the maple tree and felt my way through the darkness into the church. I turned on a small light in the pulpit area and prostrated myself on the floor behind the pulpit.

I poured out my heart to the Lord. I asked forgiveness for anything in my life that might be hindering the flow of God's power to the people. I confessed every possible sin in my life. I asked for a fresh cleansing so that nothing would hinder the fullness of the Holy Spirit in me.

Sometime in the wee hours of the morning, I felt my tongue swelling to the point I could hardly speak. I was frightened by this. I thought about going to a doctor, but I knew I was going through a deep spiritual experience. In just a few hours, I would be in the pulpit expected to preach. How could I preach with this handicap? How would I be able to explain it to the congregation? I went home to get a couple hours of rest before the service, but rest wouldn't come. I arranged to arrive at the church just before the worship service, so I would not have to speak to anyone. Anxiety overwhelmed me. With my tongue essentially paralyzed, I had no idea how I would be able to preach even if I had a sermon.

Just before I entered the pulpit, I bowed my head and prayed. "Lord, I am completely dependent on You. I can't speak. I don't have a sermon. Whatever you would have the people experience this morning is in Your hands. Lord, please don't let me get in the way. I am totally surrendered to You." I felt my whole body begin to relax.

As I joined in singing a hymn before preaching, I felt my tongue soften.

In the pulpit, I began to share about last night's time in prayer. I shared how I had felt since becoming their pastor. "I have tried to do everything in my own power. Up to now, I have felt like a complete failure as your pastor. Last night, lying prostrate on this altar where I am standing now, I totally surrendered myself to the Lord. I confessed every sin and every weakness. I confessed my lack of ability for this task. I asked for forgiveness. I asked the Lord to make me a channel through which He could work unhindered by my ego, my weaknesses, my lack of faith and trust, and my sinfulness.

"The sermon I prepared is now no longer appropriate. This

morning we are going to have to let the Lord speak to us in whatever way He will. Please respond to whatever He is saying to you."

With that, I simply bowed my head and waited.

I felt the powerful presence of the Lord among the people. Everyone was silent. There was a quiet, reverent atmosphere. The silence was broken when the leader of one of the dissenting families stood and asked forgiveness for his actions over the past several years. Then the leader of the second family stood and asked forgiveness for his behavior. Soon a number of people began to hug one another and weep. It was a service like none I had ever experienced. It was as though, in my own weakness as pastor, the Holy Spirit took over the service in my place and brought about His perfect will. That was a historic turning point for the church. Everything changed. Perhaps most of all, I was changed.

From that point on, the church began to experience phenomenal growth. This was one of those life-shaping experiences of yielding in complete trust to the Lord and then radically obeying what He evidently wanted me to do.

The long-anticipated time finally arrived when Rachel and I would be joined together with the Lord for the rest of our lives. After my first two final exams on August 8, 1957, I drove to Durham for our wedding rehearsal. After that rehearsal, Rachel and I talked for hours. We reviewed our almost two years of dating.

Rachel said, "Almost exactly two years ago, just two months before we met, I was kneeling alone in prayer at the altar where we will be married tomorrow night. It was a week of special prayer for our church's revival services. The sun was just beginning to rise. I felt the warmth as it began to shine through the stained glass window. The rays were coloring the image in the glass so brilliantly and shining on the altar where I was kneeling. I was deeply moved. I began to pray. 'Lord, you know I am going to the mission field. I have dated boys, but none of them have shared my call to missions. I have wondered about going alone as a single nurse, and many things have made me uncomfortable about that. This morning,

Lord, I want you to know now I am completely willing and ready to go alone. But, Lord if you send me somebody, and we can go together, that will be okay too.'"

Rachel continued, "At that moment, I felt perfectly at peace, willing, and ready to go alone to the field. There were no doubts. There was no fear. That special time in prayer was my time of complete surrender to God's will for my life. Three months later, we met."

I told her, "When I arrived at the university, I determined I would not date anyone who was not called to the mission field, lest I get drawn away from my call and commitment to the field. I knew my weakness after years in the navy, at sea most of the time. Especially on Adak, I longed to have someone to share my life with, but there was no one. I knew there would be numerous people in college, and my hunger for companionship would grow. In my third month at Wake Forest, I met you. I knew that first night that God was bringing into my life someone very special."

As I drove back to my dorm to prepare for my final two exams the next day, my mind was flooded with so many emotions. I was anticipating that great day tomorrow when Rachel and I at last would stand before the Lord and vow our eternal love for each other. I thought how much I loved Rachel. I thought of the almost two years of sharing together, our closeness, our intimacy. I was filled with a deep appreciation that both of us had been committed from the beginning of our relationship to keep ourselves pure before the Lord. Sexual intimacy was too precious to share before we entered into the sacredness of marriage. Though at times it was difficult, we realized that, when a relationship becomes physical, it is so powerful that it has a way of inhibiting communication. We knew that what happens too often is the longing for physical intimacy is stronger than the longing to share deeply who we are, how we feel, what bothers us, and what gives us joy and peace. As valuable and precious as it is, sexual intimacy does not keep two people in love through the trials and tribulations of life. Instead, it is knowing one another deeply and loving with that deepest of loves that keeps a marriage strong. It is being able to communicate what is inside that draws two people together in genuine love and sustains that love through the years. I was filled with gratitude for all God did in us through those months of getting to know one another so that our love could be genuine. August 9, 1957, we pledged to each other and before the Lord our vows of marriage.

In many ways, the Lord, the Potter, molded each of us into two unique vessels, each designed to work together to accomplish His divine purposes.

Mt. Pleasant Baptist

CHAPTER 10

DECISIONS AND JOYS OF MINISTRY

Dr. C. B. Earp, chairman of the Classical Languages Department, sent an urgent message for me to come to his office. It was graduation day. In just a couple of hours, I would receive my degree from Wake Forest University. I was nervous beyond description. Had something happened to keep me from graduating? What could he want?

Dr. Earp was waiting for me. He invited me to sit down. He pulled a letter from his desk drawer and handed it to me. It was a letter from Columbia University in New York City announcing they were prepared to give me a full academic fellowship to pursue PhD studies in Classical Greek.

Dr. Earp looked deep into my eyes. "I have just one question to ask you. Are you positively sure that you are going into the ministry?"

I have to admit I was completely astonished at this offer, and for a moment, I was speechless. Immediately I was tempted to accept the offer. Quickly, I realized I was facing another of those forks in the road of life. My choice of direction would determine my commitment, perhaps for the rest of my life. Many thoughts flooded my mind. Was I really called by God to be a missionary? Could I pursue this new direction and also fulfill that calling? Perhaps they would need Greek professors overseas. This was one of those times when all my past experiences informed my decision.

"Yes, I am called to the ministry to serve the Lord somewhere overseas. I have never been surer of anything."

Dr. Earp replied, "Then, I will not pursue this matter further. I do not want to tempt you away from the ministry."

I would have to admit this choice of direction was worth considering. The study of Classical and New Testament Greek was extremely important to me. I had invested the largest portion of my studies in that field. On the other hand, I also remembered standing on the flight deck of my aircraft carrier, the USS *Sitkoh Bay*, just a few years before, looking over the city of Yokosuka, Japan, and seeing the multitudes of people with no knowledge of Jesus. It had been only six hours since I, myself, had believed in Jesus. I was overwhelmed with the need and desire to share this good news. I committed my life to the Lord that day—to be His servant wherever He called. That call had never changed. There was also the time when I'd had to decide whether to go to Pensacola for Navy Flight School. In spite of the great temptation, my call to serve the Lord somewhere in the world had remained steadfast.

My decision to reject this offer was final. I chose the fork in the road that past experience and present commitment best informed. I communicated this decision to Dr. Earp, and the issue was closed.

At first, Wednesday prayer meetings at Mt. Pleasant Church had only a handful of our faithful members present. As the Lord began to work in the hearts of the people, Wednesday night prayer meetings began to be the highlight of the week. Attendance steadily grew. I asked the church if we could begin Sunday evening services each Sunday after our Training Union meeting. They agreed. Within three years, the church was crowded, and there was no more room.

There were days when I would drive through the countryside on the myriad of dirt roads that wound through fields of crops and huge tracts of wooded lands. I knew this area of Randolph County was an area rich in making moonshine whiskey. So many of the homes in the area were occupied by bootleggers. I began to wonder if anyone ever visited these homes, tucked back in the woods and fields, to tell them about Jesus.

The truth is I knew many of them. As a young boy working for my father in the grocery store, I had loaded their cars every Saturday night with sugar and fruit jars for making whiskey.

A young woman who recently began attending our church said her grandparents lived not far from the church. One day, I decided to ask a trusted lady in the church who knew the area intimately to go with me to find them. I soon spotted the house partially hidden in a grove of trees well off the road. She said, "You know, it is strange. I have lived here all my life, and I never noticed this place."

We drove up a long, dirt driveway through the woods into a yard full of chickens, several goats, and barking dogs. In the middle of the yard was a large black pot sitting on a fire waiting for a load of clothes to be splashed in and washed. An elderly man with a full beard and a cane sat in a chair in the yard next to an old well. He didn't move but just sat there staring at us.

An elderly lady came out on the porch and before I could say a word she yelled, "What do you want?"

My gut feeling was this was probably one of the families of bootleggers who ran stills in the woods surrounding their houses. These people were highly suspicious of strangers. I shouted back, "We are from the Mt. Pleasant Church. I am the pastor, and this lady is one of our church members. We would like to visit you for a few minutes."

The woman seemed to relax when she met the lady with me and invited us to come into the house. We stepped up on the wooden porch and followed her in. The front door was standing wide open even though there was a chill in the air. A large stone fireplace took almost a whole wall in the living room, kitchen, and eating area, all one big room. A large, heavy black pot was hanging in the fireplace near the fire. An old couch sat almost in the middle of the floor facing the fireplace. She invited us to sit down. Two chickens were roosting on the back of the couch. She shooed them out the front door, took a rag, and wiped off the seat. It was then I noticed a large hog, alive, stretched out across the hearth in front of the fireplace. She tapped him with a broom, and he ran squealing out of the house.

After a few pleasantries, I asked her, "Ma'am, do you attend church anywhere?"

"No, we ain't never been to no church."

"We'd like to invite you to come to our church. It isn't far from here, and everyone in the church would be so glad if you could come."

"My granddaughter told me she started agoing to a church som'ers around here."

"Yes, we know your granddaughter. She has started coming to church, and she is about the nicest young lady I have ever met. We would be so happy if you would come with her sometime."

"We ain't really been nowheres in a long time, since the children moved out. My granddaughter might be willin' to bring me down to the church sometime."

"I think your granddaughter would love to bring you. She is so friendly and polite. Everybody just loves her."

"I don't know how she got that way growin' up in mess like we'uns is. Her daddy and uncles all worked down yonder in the woods fer years. My husband and her daddy did a year and a day in the pen fer bootleggin', so she didn't have much of a upbringin'. The sheriff put us out of business, and we ain't done much or gone nowheres since."

With that said she got two bowls, wiped them out with her apron, and ladled out a large spoon of pinto beans cooking in the black pot hanging in the fireplace. I thought of chickens roosting on the living room couch, a hog sleeping on the fireplace hearth where she cooked their food, and litter and junk lying around everywhere. Eating food prepared there just didn't seem very appetizing.

I asked permission to pray before we ate. The beans were absolutely delicious. The lady from our church visiting with me was more reluctant to eat than me, but she ate her bowl and later told me they were the best she had ever eaten!

We thanked our host for welcoming us and feeding us. We expressed our great pleasure that she might come to church on Sunday and worship with us. With that, we excused ourselves and returned to the car.

The old man with the cane had not moved in all that time. I spoke to him, but he did not speak to us. He kept his eyes intently on us until our car was out of sight. It was an eerie feeling.

My church member said as we drove away, "I grew up here from the time I was a little girl. I knew a lot of families just like this one. They lived just like this. The daddy and the boys were bootleggers who drove nice cars but lived very private lives. I had no idea there were people within a few miles of our church still living like this in the 1950s. It makes me want to find every house, visit, and bring some joy into their lives by introducing them to Jesus."

Sunday morning, just as I invited the congregation to stand and open our service with a hymn, I saw a beautiful young woman enter the church, her arm guiding an older lady down the aisle to a seat, both with a huge smile. The elderly lady looked up at me and grinned. Her hair was freshly washed and cut. She had on a new dress, held a new purse, and the deep wrinkles in her face took nothing away from her elderly beauty. When I finished my sermon and gave the invitation for people to trust Jesus as Lord and Savior, she and her granddaughter stepped out into the aisle and walked forward with strong, deliberate steps. They both pulled my head down to their level and said, "We want to follow Jesus." Oh, what a day that was!

Experiences like this were some of the greatest preparation I would get for serving the Lord overseas. The Potter was now beginning to fill the vessel for His use. Little by little, these experiences were continuing to shape my life. How many times, years later while serving in various countries overseas, was I faced with eating in places where living conditions according to my standards were not good, where people were suspicious and on guard, and where relationships had to be established? But it is all worthwhile when people come to know Jesus!

PART III
FILLING THE VESSEL

CHAPTER 11

CONVICTION + CONFRONTATION = PREPARATION FOR THE FIELD

One Sunday afternoon, Rachel and I sat down with Mrs. Ora Langley in her living room. We prayed together. Then I said, "Mrs. Ora, something is greatly troubling me."

She responded with a sly grin. "I thought you might come to talk with me."

She knew when I needed help, clarification, enlightenment, or just good advice, I always came to her. She was deeply spiritual, a woman of prayer. Her years as a follower of Jesus gave her a lot of experience. As a young pastor, God blessed me with a variety of good, mature people in that small, rural church to whom I could go for advice. From Mrs. Ora, I could always get the temperature of the congregation and the community around us.

"Mrs. Ora, I am sure you have noticed our prayer meeting attendance has suddenly gone down significantly. This morning only about half the people were there for Sunday worship. Something is wrong. I need to know what it is. Please help me."

She was quick to respond. "Last Sunday night, you went to preach at Edwards Grove Baptist Church (an African American church). Now some of the men in the community are saying you are going to try to integrate our church with black people. They are determined their families are not going to come to Mt. Pleasant Church anymore."

I was shocked.

The pastor of Edwards Grove Church had invited me to speak to a Sunday night meeting. I took a quartet from our church to sing. It was my first time to preach in an African American church, and it was a wonderful service. When I gave an invitation for people to accept Jesus, decisions were made. One young man responded to a call to become a pastor. I was thrilled at the opportunity to preach in the church that had influenced me so much when I was ten years old. It was there I'd sat in a side ditch on many Sunday afternoons to hear the joyful singing of the congregation and choir. Now I had an opportunity to share God's Word with them. The thought of integrating the two churches had never entered my mind. Nor had it entered theirs.

Suddenly and without warning, I was plunged into a dangerous controversy. My mind went back three weeks before when a neighboring pastor had made a simple statement about segregation from his pulpit. That Sunday night, someone using a shotgun had blasted the front window of the parsonage. The year was 1959.

To put this in perspective, we have to look at the atmosphere of the South in the 1950s and early 1960s. In 1954, the Supreme Court ruled all laws establishing segregated schools were unconstitutional. On December 1, 1955, Rosa Parks refused to give up her seat in the white section of a city bus in Montgomery, Alabama. She was arrested, and this began a period of great unrest throughout the South. On September 4, 1957, in Little Rock, Arkansas, the National Guard was called out to protect a group of nine students who were enrolled and attempted to attend classes in the segregated Little Rock High School.

In 1958, Martin Luther King, Jr. was the new leader of the Southern Leadership Conference and led in twenty meetings to achieve voter registration for African Americans. Numerous demonstrations began to be held throughout the Southern states.

On April 15, 1963, four little African American girls died in the racially inspired bombing at 16th Street Baptist Church in Birmingham, Alabama.

That same year, June 12, 1963, Medgar Evers was assassinated by a member of the White Citizens Council and died in the hospital in Jackson, Mississippi.

At 4:30 p.m., February 1, 1960, four black students from A&T University in Greensboro, North Carolina, entered a Woolworth Store. Greensboro was just twenty-two miles north of my hometown, Liberty. The students purchased a few things and then went to the segregated lunch counter. They ordered food but were refused. They sat at the counter until closing time. The next day, students from the all-female Bennett's College joined the sit-in with A&T students. Woolworth Company's national store management was called, and they supported the local Woolworth's store management refusing to seat African Americans. By the fourth day, more than four hundred people had joined the movement.

This sit-in spread to other colleges throughout North Carolina and then out into the entire South. Fights began to break out in various locations as people flocked to Woolworth stores and then to Kress stores and other locations to either defend the blacks or show hostility toward them. This pioneer movement began just twenty miles north of Liberty.

Liberty had always maintained a staid, quiet but racially divided culture. However, key experiences had transformed my own attitude toward race. Now as a young pastor, I was facing a new reality in a directly personal way.

I not only needed to deal with this personally as a pastor, but Rachel and I were also facing our first big crisis as a young married couple. What we were going to do was not just my decision but our decision. Not the least concern was that we were barely making it financially. If we left our pastorate, we would face a disastrous situation financially. We immersed ourselves in prayer.

"Lord, you know our heart. The African American people are just as much your children as we are. You love them just like you love us. We all worship you, Father, Lord, and Savior of us all. There is no way we can allow hatred or division to have the victory here.

Lord, guide us through this difficult decision. Give us strength to make the right decision."

As we prayed, we both realized we would have to take a stand. We both had the same theology and biblical understanding. We could not, under any circumstances, abandon our convictions regardless of the outcome.

Knowing that, in that rural community, news traveled very quickly, I shared with several key people that, on Sunday morning, I would have an important announcement to make. I hoped all the community would come to church and hear it.

Sunday morning was a morning of intense prayer. I knew what I must say to the people. The church was full. There was a hush over the congregation. I could see the serious looks on every face. I trembled a bit because I couldn't tell if these were angry expressions or expressions of concern. A moment of fear welled up my heart. For just a moment, I asked myself, *Sam, do you really want to do this?*

Soon after the service began, I entered the pulpit. I did not try to preach a sermon. I simply shared from our hearts as Rachel and I understood it. "I have been your pastor for more than two years. I was your pastor when I was a young, single man. You walked with me through our courtship and our marriage. You have patiently allowed me to grow from an inexperienced, young pastor and have forgiven so many mistakes I have made. You have helped Rachel through her first pregnancy and the birth of our first child. Now, we have come to a crisis point.

"You know we are going to the mission field. Every Sunday, I have preached how God loves all mankind no matter where in the world they live, what color skin they have, what economic strata they belong to, or what social standing they have. Above all, God loves every single one of us, whoever we are, even though we are all sinners. He gave His unique Son to die for us on the cross that we might receive forgiveness, a new life, and hope for eternity. He is the heavenly Father of us all and everyone, I repeat, *everyone* who believes in Him is a child of God—we are brothers and sisters in Christ, with the same heavenly Father, no matter what the circumstance or who we are.

"For me to preach one gospel in America and then go to the mission field to preach to other people a different gospel would be the height of hypocrisy. For me on this day to make a decision contrary to what the Bible teaches and what I know to be true would be hypocrisy of the worst kind.

"Here is what we are going to do. Rachel, Deborah, and I are going go home now. I am asking you, the church, to take a vote. If you want us to stay, then you are accepting the teaching of the Bible about God's love for all people, and we are going to accept and treat all people with dignity and respect, regardless of the color of their skin. If you do not want us to stay under those conditions, then vote no, and Rachel and I will resign. I will turn this service over to the chairman of the deacons, Mr. Boyd Poe, and he will lead you in this vote."

With that, Rachel, Deborah, and I left the church and went home to await the outcome.

I remember so clearly the perfect peace we had in our hearts as we waited. All the anxiety about the future was gone. That peace came from two things: First, we had complete trust in God's will and knew we were in the center of His will. Second, I knew the people of Mt. Pleasant Baptist Church. I knew the community. They were all good people. They were people of honesty and integrity. They were, above all, Christian people grounded solidly in God's Word. They loved the Lord and wanted to do His will. I had complete confidence in that.

About a half hour after we arrived home, Mr. Boyd Poe came to the door. He had a beautiful smile on his face. He sat down and, in his quiet, wise way, shared the outcome of the vote. He informed us the congregation wanted to take a secret ballot. This was such a controversial and dangerous subject that some people were afraid others would see how they voted. The counting of the secret ballots was done and 100 percent of the votes were a resounding yes. Then he said, "Preacher, we want you to stay with us."

Some would say pastoring a small church in rural America has little to do with preparation to serve overseas. I beg to differ. This was where I learned to love people for who they are, to negotiate and compromise, to overcome prejudices, and to see God work His work of grace in the everyday lives of people. I learned to appreciate the preciousness of family and the honor of doing a hard day's work.

The intimate involvement of a pastor in the lives of ordinary people taught me the value of integrity and honesty. These are the people who taught me the beauty of a simple faith and trust in God. I learned from them how to receive love and expressions of respect. This was great training for the task of carrying the gospel into the dark places of the world where people are in so much need of learning how to relate to one another and to know the value and joy of following Jesus.

That little, white clapboard church house, with a cemetery on one side and a tobacco field on the other, with a bell in the tower that resounded across the fields and woods, will always be my point of reference, no matter where I go in the world. The people of that church took in a very young, inexperienced pastor and, with their love and patient support, gradually helped mold me into the servant of the Lord I have been for more than sixty years of ministry.

In the seminary, I was studying such high subjects as premillennialism, postmillennialism, and amillennialism; higher textual criticism with multiple sources of the Bible; the problem of evil; the problem of biblical authorship; postmodern theology; and on and on. What kept my head out of the clouds and my feet planted solidly on earth was those old farmers who had been Christians for many years, those young men who knew what it was like to live in a tough world of farming, small businessmen in a competitive world, factory workers, laborers, and skilled craftsmen; women who gave their lives day by day ensuring their family's emotional, spiritual, and physical health; women who worked at a job all day and came home to cook meals and do all the necessary things for the family; and men and women who knew what it was to worry about finances and securing their future—people who knew what it was to be tired and struggling day by day. What they longed to hear on Sunday was the wonderful, simple story of Jesus and His love—the story of forgiveness, redemption, and salvation—and that there is a beautiful hope waiting for us when we finish this tough journey on earth. All of the lessons I learned from that small church cannot even begin to be enumerated.

I remember writing a paper in the seminary on my pastorate. In that paper, written in the early days of my ministry, I complained that all the church wanted to hear were old Stamps-Baxter songs with the shape notes and every song a message about heaven. My ethics professor, Dr. Olan Binkley, wrote in red on the top of the page, "Remember, these are country people who toil on their farms and who are subject to fickle expressions of nature, which often puts them on the razor's edge of survival. They know suffering and toil. It is only natural they look with great hope and anticipation for that day when God wipes away all tears from their eyes, and they find themselves in the glorious presence of Jesus. Don't take that away from them!"

Easter came a few months after this crisis of racial division. The rumor was that black folks were going to go to white churches on Easter Sunday and demand to be seated. On Easter Sunday morning before the service, I called our deacons together and asked them, "What are we going to do when they arrive at our church?"

"Pastor, we have already talked about that and prepared a place in the center section of our auditorium. We will welcome them and seat them just like we do everyone else."

In spite of a beautiful and worshipful Easter service, I was very disappointed when the service ended. Not one African American attended our church.

After lunch, I went straight to the Edwards Grove Baptist Church. "Pastor, I was disappointed this morning. Not one African American came to visit our church.!"

He responded, "We knew your church would seat us. We didn't have go to your church."

CHAPTER 12

DELAYED FOR A PURPOSE

In early 1959, the board of trustees of the Foreign Mission Board voted to open work in Vietnam. We got in touch with Dr. Winston Crawley, secretary for the Orient, to remind him of our interest in Vietnam. We were immediately named candidates, with appointment scheduled for April 1961.

As we neared graduation from the seminary, a detailed plan was worked out. We would go through an eight-day orientation in January 1961, our baby was due in early February, we would be appointed in April, and we would proceed to the field immediately after graduation from the seminary in May. We were excited, but God had other plans.

In January, we were oriented as scheduled in a nonstop orientation for eight days. I have always been amazed at Rachel's stamina and patience. At eight months pregnant, she sat ten to twelve hours a day in classes; slept on bunk beds; and flew to and from Gulf Shores, Mississippi. As I watched her go through this time so uncomfortable yet maintaining her beautiful Christian spirit, I realized again how special was her call and commitment to missions. I was once again filled with a deep love and admiration for this special person God had given me so we could spend our lives together in His service on the mission field.

Our second child, Stephen, was born on February 3. The obstetrician was an unusually tall and well-built man. It was striking to see this large man holding our tiny little baby in his huge hands. His gentle spirit was comforting.

"Sam and Rachel, your baby is healthy. There is one small problem. He is having difficulty taking his milk, because he has a very small opening in his palate area. At some point, he will need an operation to close that hole, and he will be as healthy as any other baby."

"Doctor, when can we have this operation performed?"

"Well, you have two options. You could possibly just leave him as he is. He will learn to take his milk, and he will survive. The problem is he might develop a speech impediment for the rest of his life. This is not certain but highly probable. The other option is to wait about a year and have the operation. He will be perfect then, and there should be no more concerns."

"Doctor, there is no question. We want this corrected."

We immediately notified the Foreign Mission Board of the problem. "Their response was, "Bring him to our headquarters in Richmond, Virginia. Our doctor will check him over, and we will make a decision about the timing of your appointment."

My first words to the doctor were, "I hope this will not put in jeopardy our appointment to the mission field!"

The doctor checked Stephen over carefully and agreed to let us know their decision within a few days.

Two days going on an eternity passed. Just as we sat down to eat lunch, the telephone rang.

"Sam and Rachel, we have made a decision about your appointment. There is no question we will appoint you. However, we feel it best you have the operation on your baby, and then you can go to the mission field with your minds at ease with no more concerns about this healthy little boy." The voice on the phone was kind and filled with compassion.

"We agree with you, but it is going to be very difficult for us. Thank you for being so kind and considerate of us."

We understood with our minds the wisdom of this decision,

but our hearts were broken. We had spent six years in the university and seminary preparing to go. We were filled with excitement at finally being on the brink of going to the mission field. Why was this happening to us? Surely God must have a plan not yet revealed to us!

I asked for a meeting with the deacons. "Brothers, you have heard our going out in the field is being delayed. I know it is urgent to begin the new church building. I cannot conscientiously lead in this building process and leave in the middle of it. Rachel and I are going to have to resign so you can call a new pastor and begin building."

The chairman of deacons responded, "We have already talked about this, and we are willing for you to stay as long as you need to. We will delay our building as long as necessary."

"Men, I really appreciate this, but we cannot hold up the progress of our church. It is growing rapidly, and you need to begin searching for a pastor as quickly as possible. You must maintain this growth. Rachel and I don't know what our next step is going to be, but we are certain God has a plan for us."

We had made our decision, but that did not prevent us from worry and concern about how we would live with no income. What could we do? No one would want a pastor just for one year. The Lord would have to intervene in some miraculous way. But how?

As we were in concerted prayer regarding our next steps, a man identifying himself as Ray Rogers from Durham, North Carolina, contacted us.

"Pastor James," he said, "we are five laymen from Grace Baptist Church here in Durham. We would like to meet with you about an important matter. Can you come to Durham for a meeting?"

For some reason, I could not ask him about the important matter. We were desperate for something to happen and felt like going through any possible open door.

Rachel and I sat in the living room of one of the men. They, with their wives, sat around us.

"Sam and Rachel, our church, Grace Baptist, has decided to plant a new church in north Durham. We five have volunteered, and the church has commissioned us to plant this new church. We have already acquired a piece of property but have built nothing. We have no idea how to start. We have never been a part of a new church start. We heard about your delay going to the mission field, and we believe God has led us to you to join us in this new challenge."

"Listen, I have never started a church either," I told them. "This would be a new experience for me. I have helped a small church to grow, but it was a rural church. Also, I have not pastored in a large city before."

"Sam, to us that it good news. We don't want to start a traditional church. We want to start a New Testament church. We are not looking to model after so many old churches with all of their tradition. You are young. You have not had time to be cemented into old ways of doing things. You are still open to trying new things and keeping everything biblical. That is what we want!"

"Thank you for that. I would delight in our looking at the New Testament and building the foundation of a new church on that."

Ray Rogers responded, "Please understand we don't have much money to pay a salary. We five families will give as sacrificially as we can, and just as soon as the church begins to grow, we will increase the salary. The North Carolina Convention is willing to provide a salary supplement, since we are planting a new church, but we declined that. We are determined we will be self-supporting from the beginning. Would you be willing to move to Durham and spend the year planting this new church?"

Rachel and I were impressed with the dedication, the spirituality, and the commitment of these five men. Before we left that day, we accepted this invitation. Salary or benefits never entered our mind. We met again, knelt together, and had the sweetest prayer time of our lives with these five spiritually committed men and women.

It was miraculous that, just at the right moment, God opened this door for us. He knew I was going to the field to be a church planter. I needed some experience planting a church before going. In His time, He brought this opportunity to us. Our emotions went from disappointment and frustration to excitement and renewed commitment. I could hardly wait to get started! The Potter was again forming and reforming the clay to make the vessel He could use in His great plan!

It was late February when we moved to Durham. Dr. Henry Anderson, pastor of Grace Church, had conducted services on three Sunday afternoons in Holt Elementary School. Dr. Anderson was advanced in age, with silver hair, his taller-than-six-foot body erect and steady. His voice was clear and strong. His preaching was thoroughly biblical and always applicable to real life. He was known all over the city as a great preacher and compassionate pastor. I was twenty-nine years old and felt very much like a novice preacher. I wondered how these wonderful, seasoned veteran laymen, accustomed to being led by this great spiritual giant, would accept my comparatively inexperienced ministry. Added to that stress was the fact I had pastored a rural congregation with a very different culture and mind-set from this urban community. Also, a number of pastors in the area objected to a new church start in that area of Durham and were very verbal about their objections.

I began, as a first step, to lead our laymen to think about our vision for the future. We discussed important questions: "What and who is the church?" "What kind of church do we want to plant?" "What are the essential activities we should begin?" "What are our priorities in these first weeks?" I recognized immediately I was now working with some of the finest, most dedicated laymen I had ever met. Together we spent hours in prayer, discussing our vision for the future. We arrived at key elements we wanted to give highest priority in shaping the new church.

We stated five foundational pillars for our church: (1) It would be a church thoroughly committed to Jesus Christ and to the Bible as our authoritative source for living, worshiping, witnessing, teaching, stewardship, and missions. (2) We would be committed to minister to every person whatever their color, social and economic strata, and past history. (3) We would focus our efforts on "lost people," rather than enlisting members of other churches. (4) We would focus on discipling and training every person who came into the church. (5) Our church would have at its very core a commitment to carry the good news of Jesus to all the peoples of the world. We began to develop strategies to carry out all of these things as priorities.

These five laymen joined together with me to go out in teams of two at least one night a week and do everything possible to visit every home in our area with no distinction made to race, national origin, or economic strata. In choosing homes to visit, we determined as much as possible to refrain from visiting people already active in other churches. While we would listen to the past history of individuals and pray for those individuals, our focus would be on their future as children of God in Christ Jesus. We decided from the very beginning that, no matter what the church's income, we would always give as a minimum a tithe to the work of carrying the gospel to the world.

We absolutely refrained from "recruiting" people from other churches lest we lose our commitment to founding a new church free from old problems and long-held traditions of other churches.

We led the members of our new church to commit together to make these principles our core strategy by which our plans and personal involvement would be measured.

We immediately began Sunday morning and Sunday evening worship services. From that point until I preached my last sermon, not one Sunday service passed that someone didn't accept Jesus as Savior or, after careful screening, move his or her membership to our new church.

In early August, 1961, Rachel and I discovered we were expecting our third child. It was a total surprise and created much anxiety. We were looking forward to finally being appointed missionaries in

March. Our second child needed an operation to correct the small defect he had been born with. This experience made us wonder whether our next child would have a similar problem that might further delay us. We would be making the long journey to Vietnam aboard a ship with a three-year-old, an eighteen-month-old, and a newborn. How would we survive mentally and physically? How would the Foreign Mission Board look upon this new development? Once again, as so many times in the past, we had to submit to God's perfect will. We knew we could not "blame" this on God. We also knew He knows best and had always given us everything we needed to get through situations. We knew He would not fail us now! It was a matter of putting our complete trust in God.

Our son Stephen underwent surgery in February 1962. The operation was perfect with no complications. We notified the Foreign Mission Board. They responded with an invitation to arrive in Richmond, Virginia, on Sunday afternoon, March 4. We would be appointed Thursday evening, March 8, and free to return home on Saturday, March 10. After that, all we needed to do was wait for our baby to be born, and then we would be free to leave. Finally, after so many years of waiting, we would be on our way to the field.

Plans were made to organize the new church on Sunday morning, March 4, 1962. The name would be the Homestead Heights Baptist Church. The new church would conduct its organization service and have a noon fellowship meal together. Immediately after the meal, the new Homestead Heights Baptist Church would send their pastor and his wife, Samuel and Rachel James, to Richmond for our appointment as missionaries. This would be our last Sunday as pastor of the new church.

My final sermon text was:

> Enlarge the place of your tent,
> Stretch your tent curtains wide,
> do not hold back;
> lengthen your cords,

strengthen your stakes,
For you will spread out to the right and to the left;
your descendants will dispossess nations,
and settle in their desolate cities." (Isaiah 54:2–3)

At the organization service, 50 percent of the charter members were new believers. Almost immediately, plans began to be made to sell the previously purchased property and purchase a large tract of land next to Holt School to build a new church building.

How could we possibly ever dream what would happen to Homestead Heights Baptist Church in the years to come. After forty years of growth and loss, good and bad experiences with leadership, Homestead Heights Baptist Church still struggled with about three hundred people in attendance. In 1999, a young man, J. D. Greear, who had served as a journeyman missionary, was called as student pastor. On January 1, 2002, he became the lead pastor of the church.

Dr. J. D. Greear led the church into an exciting new future. In 2002, the name of the church was changed to The Summit Church, and it moved to a new location. Now with over eight thousand people in regular attendance, The Summit has been named year after year as one of the twenty-five fastest-growing churches in America. It has sent out more than 550 people to carry the gospel to the world, both at home and abroad. It has started 227 churches and has a vision of starting one thousand new churches around the world in this generation.

As I think back on the very beginning of Homestead Heights Baptist Church more than fifty years ago, I recall the vision stating clearly that missions to the ends of the earth would be the highest priority of the church. Involvement in missions, sending and supporting missionaries throughout the world was planted within its DNA. The Summit Church has epitomized in every way the original vision of the old Homestead Heights Church.

The apostle Paul's words, "I planted the seed, Apollos watered it, but God made it grow," I Corinthians 3:6 (NIV), are illustrated beautifully in the founding of the old Homestead Heights Baptist Church and now the new Summit Church.

The only thing remaining was the birth of Philip James on May 3, 1962. We were relieved and elated to see Philip healthy and ready for overseas service! After a long wait and then a delay, the birth of a church, and the birth of our third child, we were on our way to Vietnam.

CHAPTER 13

THE VOYAGE BEGINS

I heard a voice shouting loudly over the din of hundreds of voices as the band on the dock played Auld Lang Syne. "Jes' git 'em on board," he shouted. "Git 'em on board." I can still hear the echo of the urgent shout of the officer of the deck.

Our family flew from Durham, North Carolina, to San Francisco, California, to board our ship to Hong Kong on our way to Vietnam. We stayed a couple of days in Oakland, California, with Mom and Pop Watson, my first mentors in the faith during my navy days.

We followed directions meticulously. The night before sailing, we took our luggage to the docks to be stored on the ship. We were to board the ship no later than 2:00 p.m. the next day. Pop Watson was taking us to the dock. On the way, we stopped at a store and bought a number of things we thought the children would need for the trip. As we crossed the Oakland Bay Bridge, we found ourselves in a huge traffic jam. For a long time, we inched across the bridge. By the time we were on the road to the ship, the 2:00 p.m. deadline had passed. We were nervous wrecks!

We arrived at the huge, beautiful SS *President Wilson* just minutes before the last line would be thrown from the dock and the ship would be under way. As we rushed toward the gangway, the band was playing its last song. Hundreds of people lined the decks waving goodbye to the huge crowd on the dock. Rachel started up the gangway carrying eight-week-old Philip in one arm, leading three-year-old Deborah with the other, and balancing an oversized diaper bag across her shoulder. I followed with eighteen-month-old Stephen in one arm and a large pasteboard box of things under the other arm. Just as I reached the halfway point up the gangway, the bottom fell out of the pasteboard box.

Horrified, I watched boxes, cans, diapers, and everything imaginable bump and roll down the gangway. I then looked up and saw every one of the several hundred passengers lining the decks looking down at us in the middle of the gangway. About that same time, the music of the band began to lose its beat. The musicians had lost their place in the music. I was debating with myself whether to put Stephen down and run quickly down the gangway to catch the rolling items or to continue up the gangway and hope for the best.

Then I heard an officer at the top of the gangway yell, "Jess git 'em on board. Jess git 'em on board." A deckhand was retrieving all of our things and putting them in a nice box with a handle designed especially for bringing things on board neatly. Perhaps the greatest relief was when we disappeared into the ship, away from the eyes of what seemed to be the whole world!

We were shown to our stateroom a couple of decks below the waterline. The room was small, with a bed for Rachel and me, a pull-down bed for Deborah, a portable crib for Stephen, and a bassinet for Philip. This was to be our home for the next three weeks at sea. The ship stopped in Honolulu for a day and during the night sailed for Hong Kong.

As we slowly made our way west, we had to turn our clock back one hour almost every day. For our three-year-old, time was no problem. Our eight-week-old, Philip, could care less what time it was. Our eighteen-month-old, Stephen, could not change his body clock. At 3:00 a.m., he was awake and ready for the day. Morning after morning, Stephen and I were alone on the deck taking our walk. He enjoying the fresh air and open space on deck, pointing out and trying to inspect everything of interest to him. I, in turn, stumbled around, trying to get my eyes open enough to keep him from falling over the side.

It was a great relief to arrive in Hong Kong and meet a veteran missionary couple on the dock, who identified themselves as Carter and Agnes Morgan. They both exuded confidence and joy. Everything about them seemed to say, "Everything is okay now. Relax!"

Agnes was in charge of hospitality for new arrivals. They took us to a Chinese hotel in downtown Kowloon. It was one of the old hotels built originally as a lavish hotel for British colonialists, but time had taken its toll. Now it was used mostly as a low-budget hotel. She confessed they had never used this hotel but wanted to try it out for future guests.

We were delighted to find a large hotel room with the old colonial British-style high ceilings and plenty of space for our children. After three weeks in a small stateroom on the SS *President Wilson*, we could hardly believe all this room was available to us.

Agnes left us alone to recover from our long voyage and the time change. The carpet was plush, and our children enjoyed tumbling on a carpeted floor after three weeks on a steel deck. When we put them to bed, we were stunned to see their clothes, legs, feet, arms, and hands black with some kind of soot, most likely from the coal-fired factories in the area. We bathed them and put them to bed. Due to the time change, we were all up very early in the morning. We made our way down to a beautiful, cavernous dining room, where every little sound echoed all over the room.

We were the first to arrive for breakfast. A waitress came to our table to take our order. To the great annoyance of our children, she could not keep her hands off their white skin and blond, curly hair. The tables were covered with white, linen tablecloths and set with beautiful plates and silver utensils. We were impressed!

As we sat there alone, waiting for our breakfast, I noticed black marks, which looked like cat paws, on the white linen tablecloth. We decided to move to another table. That one also had cat paws.

We looked across the room, and a large cat was sitting on a table licking the catsup from the top of a catsup bottle. When he finished that one, he leaped to the next table and repeated his morning meal of catsup. Our first impulse was to get up and walk out. Then we thought about the impression that would make on the hotel staff. We also realized this was the mission field, and we were going to have to get accustomed to dealing with things like this. We determined we would eat but leave the catsup off of our food.

By noon, we had bathed the children twice to try to keep them as clean as possible from all the soot in the room.

At noon, Agnes walked into the room. She exuded a "mothering" spirit that was welcome to us. It had been a difficult twenty-four hours adjusting to the hotel.

"Well, how are you doing? Is everything okay? How is the hotel?" She waited patiently for a reply.

At first, we were unwilling to share about the soot in the carpet, the cat on the dining room tables, bathing the children constantly, and blackened clothes piling up for laundering.

Agnes was persistent. She noted our reluctance to share. "I don't think you are telling me everything. Please, tell me what is going on!"

"Agnes, we don't want you to think we have just arrived and are already complaining about things. Yes, there are some problems, but we will find a way to deal with them. We know we are in a different culture and an environment foreign to us. We do not expect everything to be perfect."

"Sam and Rachel, you have just arrived. This is the most important time to be honest. Getting a good start on arrival is important for your long-term future on the field. I am waiting to hear everything!" With that she sat down with a determined look, eyes blazing, and folded her arms, a small frown creasing her forehead.

We had no choice. We had to share with her. "Last night, before putting the children to sleep, we noticed their clothes were black with some kind of soot. When we bathed them before putting them to bed, we noticed the tub was grimy so we washed it out as best we could. We bathed them, changed their clothes, and put them in bed. While doing this, we noticed a slight film of soot on the bedcover. This morning, a cat was licking the top of all the catsup bottles in the dining room. The children awakened early and have been playing on the floor. We have bathed and changed their clothes twice. We just can't keep them off of the floor. We are running out of clean clothes. Rachel and I don't dare walk around barefoot! I noticed there are some factories around here with black smoke coming from the chimneys. This could be the source of what we are experiencing."

Agnes looked horrified. "As I told you yesterday, we have never used this hotel before and thought this was a good time to try it out. Please forgive me! Pack up your things right now. We are leaving this hotel!" Her command for obedience could not be ignored!

Reluctantly, Rachel and I packed everything up and took our things to the lobby. Agnes had already checked us out. Within minutes, we were on our way to a small, three- story Chinese hotel. It was on Waterloo Road very near the Baptist mission office, the seminary, Baptist College, Baptist hospital, and several missionary residences. This hotel looked and smelled clean and spotless. The room was small but adequate. To us, this was heaven!

The hotel was small and very Chinese. Few westerners stayed there. We settled into a room with just enough sleeping space for all of our family, including a small closet just large enough to put a bassinet for our now twelve-week-old son, Philip. The restaurant was unusually large and served only Chinese food. Often, we were the only ones eating in the restaurant and usually the only foreigners there. Every sound seemed to echo especially loud in that huge dining room. Every meal, we tried our best to make our children behave and whisper our conversations, but eighteen-month-old and ten-week-old children don't understand that. It was one of those small stresses that gather strength with each passing day. We anxiously waited for the moment we could leave for Saigon.

At that time, Hong Kong was considered the most densely populated city per square mile on earth. It was a colony of the United Kingdom and an economic powerhouse in Asia. Dr. Carter Morgan introduced me to Hong Kong. He took me to visit a complex of refugee housing built by the British government. I saw ten apartment buildings in a row. Each building was ten stories tall. Each building housed ten thousand people. Carter shared a vision with me: "One day we will have a rooftop school on each building for all the small children in that building, especially preschoolers. We will plant a church in each building to minister to the people in those buildings."

I thought, "My hometown, in North Carolina, has six churches for the population of fourteen hundred people. The pastor I followed at the rural church near Liberty had pastored that small church for twenty-five years. If each building has ten thousand people, would I be willing to spend twenty-five years of my life ministering to the people in one of those buildings?"

"Carter, how many people in those buildings know Jesus as their Lord and Savior?"

"No one has researched that yet. Our Chinese convention estimates not more than one-tenth of one percent are Christian, if that many."

Suddenly I felt the enormity of the task. My mind ran wild! No way would I want to invest my whole life in just one of those buildings! I might do it in a city of ten thousand people. Then I thought, "What's the difference between investing one's life in a town of ten thousand people and investing a lifetime in a building of ten thousand people?"

For days afterward, I reflected on this experience and tried to justify my unease. Questions flooded my mind. "Is this a spatial problem unique to Hong Kong?" "Is there some difference between investing oneself in a vertical society versus a horizontal society?" "Is it a feeling of so many people limited by space rather than a similar number of people in open space?"

It was one thing to be in America and contemplate the millions and millions of people in the world without a saving knowledge of Jesus but another thing to stand looking at a hundred thousand people in ten buildings in a row in one small space. Slowly I began to realize the real challenge would be leading the first ones to the Lord, investing time and energy in those few as they became disciples. Then it would be a matter of seeing them go out to their own people and watching the gospel begin to spread like a wildfire to thousands of people through them in their own space. It became no longer a question of space or density but a challenge of leading to know Jesus those individual people who would become salt and light among their own people. No, God did not call me to win the millions to the Lord. He called me to be a living witness to those I came into contact with, and through discipling them, I would get to watch millions come to know Jesus through them.

Our visas for Vietnam were supposed to be ready when we arrived. They were not. We checked with the Vietnamese embassy. They had never heard of us.

Herman and Dottie Hayes were our first missionaries to arrive in Saigon, in November 1959. Herman was now business manager and had guaranteed our visas. He went to the appropriate Vietnamese ministry and inquired about our status. No one seemed to know anything about our visa application. Later, he discovered that an employee at the Ministry of Foreign Affairs had questioned whether the government wanted Protestant missionaries coming to Vietnam. Rather than forward the matter to his superior, he had put the visa application in a drawer and left it there untouched.

To put this in historical context, we need to understand the situation of Vietnam in 1962. In 1954, in the Geneva Conference, the Geneva Accords divided Vietnam into two countries, Communist north and democratic south, after the victory of the Vietnamese forces led primarily by the northern Communist revolutionaries over the colonial French government in May 1954. When we arrived in Hong Kong in 1962, the government in South Vietnam was under the control of President Ngo Dinh Diem, whose family members, along with Diem himself, were strong Catholics. Diem's father had studied for the priesthood but left the seminary to become a leader in the government of Emperor Bao Dai. His older brother also studied for the priesthood. As a young child, Ngo Dinh Diem entered the Catholic monastery, where his older brother was studying. He did not stay long because he was unable to accept the life of the monastery. His younger brother, Ngo Dinh Thuc, would later be named archbishop of Hue, Vietnam, and then archbishop of Indochina. Ngo Dinh Diem from birth was intimately connected to the Catholic Church.

Diem was an ardent nationalist. Because the Communist regime in the north put a price on his head, he fled to America in the early 1950s. He lived at Mary Knoll Seminary in New Jersey and later moved to the Mary Knoll headquarters in New York. While there he lobbied the US government to help Vietnam defeat the Communists.

In July 1954, the Geneva Accords were signed by nine countries—Cambodia, the Peoples Republic of China, France, Laos, the United Kingdom, the Viet Minh (in other words, North Vietnamese), the United States, the Soviet Union, and the State of Vietnam (in other words, the South Vietnamese). It divided Indochina into three countries—Laos, Cambodia and Vietnam. It further divided Vietnam into two countries. The north was declared Communist, and the South was declared a Republic. As an addition to the accords, the Geneva Convention directed that an election be held within two years (before July 1956) throughout the two countries of Vietnam to decide whether to unify or keep the nation divided. The US government and the South Vietnamese never agreed to this addition in the accords.

In 1954, Diem was invited by Emperor Bao Dai to return from the United States to Vietnam to become prime minister even though the relationship between the two was not good. Diem accepted and returned to Vietnam in 1954. In 1955, the name of the State of Vietnam was changed to the "Republic of Vietnam" (Việtnam Cộng Hòa). A break in the relationship between Emperor Bao Dai and Diem was inevitable. On October 26, 1956, following a special election, which he himself called, Diem proclaimed himself president. Many people felt the election was rigged. A number of sources say about four hundred thousand people registered to vote but Diem was elected by six hundred thousand votes.

Almost all of his support was concentrated in the Roman Catholic Church. Many leaders in the American government were cool toward his presidency from the beginning. Many saw him as a man of integrity and demonstrated courage but also a rabid, uncompromising nationalist who lacked the administrative skills to bridge all of the swirling political and religious currents flowing through the country. On his arrival in Vietnam from the United States, several newspapers quoted him as saying that, as president, he would unite the country and make it a Roman Catholic nation. This infuriated the Buddhist people who make up 90 percent of the Vietnamese population.

Almost all of the educational institutions in South Vietnam were founded and run by the Catholic Church. Preference for admission was given to Roman Catholic students or students coming from Roman Catholic families. This insured that almost all of the educated people in the south were Roman Catholics or sympathetic toward that religion. In numerous ways, Buddhists were discriminated against. Buddhist organizations, including Buddhist monasteries and temples, were not allowed to own property legally. It was also difficult under this government for Protestant Christian organizations to achieve legal status. It took nine years for our Vietnam Baptist Mission to be recognized as a legal entity in Vietnam. This explains the very slow process of granting visas to new evangelical missionaries coming into Vietnam.

Herman Hayes wrote to us, telling us it could be a long wait in Hong Kong before our visa request could be processed, if it was approved at all.

In late July, a call came from the Vietnamese embassy in Hong Kong. "We have received a cable from the Foreign Ministry in Saigon. If you want, I will read it to you."

"Please do. We have been very anxious to hear."

"This is to inform you your visa request for entry into Vietnam is hereby rejected." It was very short and clear. No reason was given.

We sat on the edge of our bed for a long time. We did not feel like talking. Weighing heavily on our heart was the fact we had spent years preparing to invest our lives in Vietnam. It would be difficult to describe the pain of that moment.

We sent a cable to the mission business manager in Saigon. He sent an immediate reply. "Under current conditions, it is unlikely the Vietnamese government will reconsider and approve another application. The only hope would be if the American embassy intervened in some way. You need to decide whether to seek to serve somewhere else or continue to pursue a visa for Vietnam. Two others of our personnel had to wait over a year for a response."

Rachel and I had spent much time praying and together felt God's leading to Vietnam. We knew no Vietnamese language. We knew nothing of the culture. We had no Vietnamese friends. However, we knew God wanted us to plant our lives in Vietnam. On the large, blue application form the Foreign Mission Board had required us to fill out in those days, now fifty-five years ago, we had signed a statement at the very end of the form that stated, "As far as we know, this will be our service for the remainder of our life." We had gladly signed it.

Now the doors were closed. Had there been a mistake? Did God really want us to serve somewhere else?

As we prayed for His guidance, not once did we doubt our place of service would still be among the Vietnamese people. With dogged determination, we would not accept no for an answer. We reapplied for a visa. Anticipating a long wait, we began to see what God would have us do among the people of Hong Kong while we waited.

The Kowloon Baptist Church (English language) met in the auditorium of Pui Ching Middle School. In early August, they invited me to become the interim pastor while they awaited the arrival of Rev. Hamp Ware, a retired veteran missionary to China. When he arrived, I was called to pastor the Hong Kong International Baptist Church as interim pastor.

Mrs. Ward, a faithful Eurasian Christian who had fled from China to Hong Kong to continue her work for the Baptist Mission, asked if I would begin teaching her English Bible class, which met in her home each week. Most of the attendees were university students from Hong Kong Baptist University.

Following that, Pui Ching Middle School asked if Rachel and I could teach English classes in the middle school. Then, the Hong Kong Baptist Seminary asked if I would teach Greek in the seminary. We found a Chinese "Amah" who would watch our children during the day, and we accepted all these invitations. Rather than wasting valuable months waiting for visas, we were serving full-time with Chinese people. We learned much about serving the Lord in another culture. We learned how to adjust to living in one room of a Chinese hotel, eating Chinese food every meal, and living with a minimum of physical belongings. We learned that, even though we did not know the Chinese language, we could communicate with our hands, our eyes, and especially with our hearts. Reluctantly, we unpacked our suitcases into the small dresser drawers provided in the room.

Much of our belongings had to stay in suitcases for lack of room. Rachel was startled that first night when she opened a drawer to get something out, and a small lizard jumped from the drawer to the wall and ran up on the ceiling, where he sat looking down at her. Thoroughly unnerved, she could just see that little lizard crawling up our baby's nose! She called immediately for someone to come and spray or get rid of the lizard in whatever way that could be done. The hotel room boy came immediately and, seeing her fear, broke into a loud laugh. He took her outside and showed her the light bulb just outside of our room. There were dozens of lizards hanging around the light. In his best broken English, he helped her to know these lizards don't have any teeth. They eat mosquitoes, which is a good thing. We should protect them and be glad they are there. From that time on, the little creatures became our friends, and we delighted in watching them crawl up the walls and even across the ceiling without falling.

One night, two young university students accepted Jesus following the Bible study in Mrs. Ward's home. These were the first two people to accept Jesus through our ministry in the mission field. It seemed to be an affirmation of our presence in Hong Kong.

As interim pastor of the Kowloon International Church, on my first evening, I looked out over the congregation. Numerous missionary families from many different mission agencies and denominational groups attended the Sunday evening service. Most of these missionaries had spent years in China. They were forced out in the early 1950s when the Communists took over. They moved their ministries into Hong Kong, always hoping for the day when they could return to China.

I remember looking out over the congregation and thinking, "Lord, what do I have to say to this congregation of some of your greatest and most faithful servants?" I was a young, thirty-year-old pastor who had spent all of three weeks in the mission field. I felt so young, so immature, so vulnerable, so inexperienced. I asked, "Lord, what am I doing standing here in this holy place?"

I had come to know the names of these spiritual giants through years of reading various publications, books, and mission studies. As I looked at the faces, I saw Dr. James Belote, a seminary professor from the seminary in Guangzhou, China, and now president of the Hong Kong Seminary; Dr. Jaxie Short, longtime teacher at the Chinese Pui To Middle School in Guangzhou and now teaching in Hong Kong; Dr. Sam Rankin, a medical doctor and contemporary friend of Dr. Bill Wallace, who was martyred in a Communist prison in China; Dr. Carter Morgan, born in North China of missionary parents and now a seminary professor in Hong Kong; Millie Lovegren, a longtime student worker in China; and many others.

I confessed all of this to the congregation and asked for their prayers that God would use me in spite of my weaknesses. In truth, I had never spoken to a more attentive, patient, interested congregation in all my life. The Holy Spirit was powerfully present in that congregation of God's servants.

Following the service, Dr. Jimmy Belote pulled me aside. He said, "Sam, remember all of us have worked hard all week ministering in the Chinese language. All day Sunday we have been in Chinese churches sharing from the Word of God. Now, on Sunday evening we can all come here to vespers with our families and worship together in our own mother tongue. Our children can hear a message they understand. They can sing hymns they understand and enjoy. Many of us have been praying our children, who have so few opportunities to hear the gospel in English, will hear, understand, and accept Jesus.

Dr. Jaxie Short, a single female missionary, who in 1952 was one of the last missionaries to leave China, pulled me aside and said, "Sam, did you see all these missionary children in the service tonight? You and Rachel are not much older than most of these high school missionary children. They will listen to you because you are closer to their age and teenage culture than any of us old folks. We haven't had anyone young like you to work with them. I watched them tonight. I have never seen them so attentive and focused on a preacher before."

I learned veteran missionaries are some of the most affirming and encouraging people I would ever meet. As I heard these comments from a host of people, I knew then I must not waste my energy on self-doubt. I just needed to renew my trust in the presence of the Lord in my life and ministry. There lay my strength!

Day by day, we waited for an answer to our visa request. The little hotel room seemed to get smaller every day. Our children became more restless and frustrated, which made Rachel and me more restless and frustrated. We would take the children out on the sidewalk, sometimes going to a nearby park to play. Chinese people, especially older women, many of whom had fled China and had little prior contact with foreigners, were fascinated by our three children's blond, curly hair and very fair skin. They loved to pinch their cheeks and feel their hair. Soon, every time I said to the children, "Let's walk down to the park," they would say, "No!" "Why not?" "They pinch our cheeks and feel our hair. We are not going anymore!"

August went into September and September to October. The first of October, Rachel reminded us that, on October 17, she would have a birthday. Her name would be on the prayer calendar for the first time. People all over the world would be praying for us. We determined we would not worry any more but pray expectantly for God to grant us those visas. As we went to bed on October 16, Rachel said, "Don't worry. Tomorrow is my birthday. This is the first time our names will appear on the missionary prayer calendar. We will get our visas!"

In early afternoon, October 17, a call came from the Vietnamese embassy. "We have a notice for you from the Foreign Ministry in Vietnam. Would you like to hear what it says?"

Yes, please read it," we replied.

"Your visas have been approved. You may proceed to Vietnam."

Never did a message sound so good! We both wept for joy. For us, it was confirmation that it is important for our people to pray faithfully on missionaries' birthdays. There is no way they can know what a missionary is going through on that day, but God knows very well. The prayers of His people are always in His heart.

We began to make preparation for departure. As we look back on this time in Hong Kong, everything that happened was formative for our future service. It was a time of cultural adaptation, experiencing intimacy with both missionary personnel and Chinese people. We learned to adjust to less than desirable circumstances. We gained new confidence that whatever the Lord calls us to do, He always gives us everything we need to accomplish it!

CHAPTER 14

BEGINNING A LIFETIME COMMITMENT

November 3, 1962, had to be the most exciting day of our lives up to that point. After so many years of preparation, practice, and hard work, we finally arrived in Saigon, Vietnam. Missionaries met us at the airport and took us to a small apartment to rest up for a couple of days. From there, we would go to Dalat in the central highlands for language study. We were scheduled to study language there for a minimum of two years.

Our crates of household goods were already at the port in Saigon. Herman Hayes and I drove to the home of the truck driver who would haul our crates up in the mountains to Dalat. Arriving at the truck driver's home, I saw an old truck with the hood up. I noticed there was no engine. An emaciated old man, covered in black grease and oil, squatted in the backyard with an engine block and dozens of parts scattered over the yard. Herman greeted him, "Chao Ong." He mumbled a reply but never looked up from his work. Herman asked, "When will you be ready to take our crates to Dalat?"

"Tomorrow afternoon."

"Are you going to drive this truck?"

"Yes."

We were shocked.

"Are you sure you'll be ready?"

"Yes."

"We will come back tomorrow morning, and if you are ready to leave, I'll pay you the money."

"Okay."

Those were almost the only words he spoke—yes and okay.

The next morning, the truck was sitting in the same place, but the hood was closed. The driver came out to greet us, rag in hand cleaning the grease off of his hands. "Is the truck ready to go?" Herman asked.

He responded, "Yes."

I went out to look. A gas tank was sitting on top of the cab. A small plastic hose ran from the gas tank across the windshield and entered the engine compartment through a hole in the hood. From there it went directly into the carburetor. My first thought was everything we owned, everything we planned to use for the foreseeable future would be in crates on that truck. He was going to climb the mountains on a steep, winding road to the city of Dalat. The things in that truck were just irreplaceable in the current situation in Vietnam.

Just as I was thinking those thoughts, I remembered the day we stood in the chapel of the Foreign Mission Board to be appointed missionaries. Dr. Baker James Cauthen, executive secretary of the board, said to us, "There are war clouds on the horizon in Vietnam. Take whatever you want to the mission field, but always remember, take it in your hands because, if these things ever get into your heart, you are through as a missionary." He was talking about the potential loss of everything in time of war or disaster. Dr. Cauthen had experienced this loss three times in the Communist takeover of China. I, on the other hand, was looking at an ancient truck in terrible repair, hauling everything we owned into the mountains.

I wanted to say to Herman Hayes, "Wait, surely there is another company we can use to take my things to Dalat?" A second thought kept me silent. As a new missionary, I didn't want to come across in the beginning of my career as a demanding person who wanted everything perfect. I ought to be able to accept and be grateful for whatever came and learn to adjust!

We flew to Dalat in an old twin engine plane belonging to Air

Vietnam. As we climbed in, I saw an identification plaque on a wall at the entrance. It read, "Made by Douglas Aircraft Company, 1944." This meant it was probably originally built as a World War II military plane (C-47) and most likely converted at some point to a civilian aircraft (DC-3). I wondered if anything in the country was not ancient or at least just slightly used! Later I learned this was probably the most reliable, sturdy aircraft ever built. The Republic of Vietnam had been wise getting their national airline started with these great planes, regardless of their age. At that point in history, Vietnam had very few airports. The DC-3 was one of the few passenger aircraft that could land on most of the landing strips in Vietnam.

We were met at the small Lien Khuong Airport by Bob and Ida Davis and their four little girls and Sam and Marian Longbottom with their three boys and a girl. Both of these families had served as missionaries in Hawaii for several years and transferred to Vietnam. The Longbottoms arrived in Saigon in August 1961, and the Davis family in September 1961. They became the fourth and fifth Baptist missionary families to be assigned to Vietnam. We were the sixth family to arrive. Both families moved rather quickly to Dalat to begin their language study.

They took us by car from the airport up the mountain to the former French resort city of Dalat, the "garden capitol of Vietnam."

Dalat was surrounded on all sides by beautiful vegetable and flower gardens, and beyond the farmlands lay the thick jungle countryside, green and smelling of fresh pine trees. Dalat is a little over five thousand feet in elevation. Living there was like living in perpetual springtime, the air pure and clean.

We spent our first night in our new city with the Davis family. Tired from all the activities of the past few days, we went to bed early. About 11:00, I was awakened by a loud thud and a man's voice, "Got him!"

Somewhat alarmed, I ran to the door into the hall just in time to see Bob Davis come out of his bedroom dressed in pajamas, dangling a rather large rat by the tail and a big grin on his face.

"These houses in Dalat have a lot of rats and mice running around all over the place. I usually go to bed early and read. Often, a rat or a large mouse will come out in my bedroom, sit, and watch me read. I keep a slingshot (a forked stick with a piece of rubber tied to each fork) by my bed with a large metal tap. When a rat sits down to watch me, I quietly put the tap in the slingshot, pull it back, aim, and shoot the tap toward the rat, hoping to hit him. Tonight, I killed my first rat!"

The next morning, we went to see our house. It was an old, partially wooden, partially rock house built many years ago by the French during colonial times. It sat on a small knoll surrounded by pine trees.

The mission realized that studying Vietnamese in the large city of Saigon would be very difficult, so they decided to put language students in Dalat to study. Dalat was a small city with very few people speaking English. Missionaries studying there would have plenty of time to study and would have to learn Vietnamese to survive.

Lewis and Toni Myers, the third Baptist missionary family to arrive in Vietnam, had moved to Dalat a few months after their arrival in Saigon. They'd rented this house for a very cheap price. It had been empty for many years and was in poor condition. During their five-month residency studying Vietnamese, they had managed to make some repairs to the house so that it was in fairly livable shape when we moved in.

After we began to understand Vietnamese, we learned from the neighbors why the house rented so cheap and sat empty so long. A man had killed himself in the upstairs of the home some twenty years ago. That meant a curse was placed on this property, and his spirit would remain there forever as a malevolent spirit. Everyone watched our family closely those first months because they knew something bad was going to happen to one or more of us in that house. No one would visit us, lest something happen while they were there.

After a number of months, people relaxed, thinking perhaps the curse and spirit would not do any harm. We had plenty of company after that.

At first, I was very uncomfortable living in a house where someone had killed himself. But I soon learned living in this house taught us a lot about culture and the spirit world. We became a living witness to the community about the sovereign power of Almighty God over all spirits!

We had to go to Saigon for a meeting. An elderly man who lived on the street in Dalat became a friend. He was alone with no place to live, so we let him fix up an old storage house on the back of our property in exchange for maintaining our yard and generally watching over our house. When we returned from the trip, he was slow answering the door. I banged on the front door for him to let us in. Slowly the door opened slightly; the old man peered out suspiciously and then partially opened it. There was a frightened look on his face. In one hand, he held a hammer and the other a saw. It was rather comical to see this.

I asked him in Vietnamese, "What are you doing with the hammer and saw?"

He said, "Many times during the day and especially at night, I hear the sound of chains rattling in the attic. I know it's the spirit of the man who killed himself. I am carrying this hammer and saw for protection!"

To him, like so many in that culture, this spirit was very real. Many people live in great fear of the spirits and conduct all kinds of rituals to guard against them. A verse in the book of Psalms became a favorite: "The Lord is my light and my salvation, whom shall I fear? The Lord is the stronghold of my life—of whom shall I be afraid?" Psalm 27:1 (KJV). Whatever we would go through in that house, I wanted to be able to say, "The Lord is greater than any spirit!"

Vietnam is a country of two seasons, rainy and dry. In Dalat, the monsoon rains began in early April and continued into early

November. Sometimes torrential rains continued unabated for seventy-two hours without stopping. At five thousand feet in the mountains, during October and November, the wind and rain penetrated everything with a sharp chill. We were grateful for a large fireplace. With two boys in diapers, during the rainy season, the living area was completely covered with cloth diapers drying as close to the fireplace as possible.

From the time we arrived in Vietnam, we were determined to have a language teacher who knew no English. That way, we would have to learn Vietnamese by being immersed totally in the language. A teacher fluent in English would inevitably explain things in English or carry on conversation in English. Language students are tempted to ask questions in English or make comments in English, which keeps them from learning to think and converse in Vietnamese.

We found a former Vietnamese pastor to teach us. He did not know even one word in English. The first few weeks were frustrating and slow, but we made progress. Our progress was like that of a little baby, who hears and mimics sounds, thereby learning to speak. We had language books, which the Christian and Missionary Alliance missionaries had used for years. These proved to be extremely valuable resources. Before long, we were asking questions and understanding answers in Vietnamese. We reached that critical point where we could use language to learn language.

Periodically, a Vietnamese language teacher came from Saigon to assess our progress. One middle-aged teacher spent the night with us in our guest bedroom. In the morning, he came out of the bedroom with his nightgown on, a toboggan on his head, and an overcoat draped over his shoulders.

He said, "I have not slept a wink. All night, mice ran up and down inside of the walls of the bedroom. I just knew they would come out in the room and get in my bed.

"I used up all of my matches trying to light a piece of incense to keep the mosquitoes away, but every time I struck a match, the cold wind came through the cracks in the wall of the house and blew it out. How can you live in a house like this?" he asked. "I couldn't do it!"

By then, we were accustomed to the house, mice and all, and had adjusted to the wind so we were not bothered. It was a reminder to us that adjustment to hard conditions is not impossible if the call to serve stays strong.

Our small mission adopted a policy that missionaries in language study could not participate in ministries during their first year of language study. They reasoned it would be easy to get so involved in ministry that language students would lose the priority of language study. However, it was our conviction that we would only remember what we used. Rachel and I developed the kind of ministries that required us to keep speaking Vietnamese and learning new vocabulary.

To regularly use what we learned, we adopted a schedule. For every hour we spent in class, we spent an hour outside of our home using what we'd learned.

Even before arriving in Vietnam, we decided both of us would learn language equally. To give Rachel time to study, we hired a helper, a young Vietnamese girl, to help with marketing, cooking, and watching our children. In those days, freezers were nonexistent. Refrigerators were small. Everything had to be purchased fresh in the market, prepared carefully for health reasons, and cooked. Also, there were a lot of vegetables and fruits we had never encountered. We needed to learn to eat these. It was difficult for someone new in Vietnam, without language, to accomplish all this and also study Vietnamese. In addition to a helper, we worked out a family schedule each day. Part of the day, I would study and Rachel would take care of the children and house. Then she would study, and I would take care of the children and the house.

At first, her language ability far surpassed mine because she had to learn to converse with our helper to teach her how to do the work in our house and take care of our children. Rachel would go to the market with her to learn to buy food. I would spend the afternoons after class down in the valley behind our house talking with the farmers. Sometimes I would squat with them in the field, and we would talk while they worked. If the family was in their yard, I would stop and visit for a while. We learned educated language with our teacher and practical language with the ordinary people in the community. Our language abilities began to grow by leaps and bounds.

I decided to begin an English Bible class in our home once a week. I shared this with Vietnamese friends, and in no time, the class filled with eight people. Some of them were significant people in the community. The sister of the mayor of Dalat began studying in the class. The daughter of a prominent professor at the university began studying. A shopkeeper and a medical doctor joined the class.

We invited all of them to dinner in our home. We made the mistake of serving Vietnamese food. It was a mistake because I did not know yet how to be a Vietnamese host. As the dinner began, I led in a prayer of thanks. I then began to pass the plates and bowls of food around, inviting them to put the food on their plate. It was evident after a while as the food was passed they were either not taking any food or taking very little.

I decided to set the example for them. As the plate reached me, I took out a lot of food. I invited them to eat, but they still did not eat. I ate voraciously, thinking that seeing me eat, they would relax and feel free to eat. I knew something was not right. The atmosphere was tense. There was no conversation. Finally, I stopped and confessed to them, "Please help me. I have not learned yet how to be a Vietnamese host. Would you please teach me how a good Vietnamese host would act at a meal like this?"

The oldest guest spoke up immediately with a big smile on his face. He said, "In the first place, a Vietnamese host eats before the guests arrive or after the guests leave. He eats very little while the meal is being served. The reason is he is putting food on each person's plate. He serves everyone and makes sure everyone has some of everything on the table. During the meal, he watches his guests so, when the guest eats all of something, he immediately puts more on the guest's plate. We feel it is highly improper for a person to fill his own plate with food as though he or she is hungry. Also, we do not eat all of a dish if we do not want any more because the host will think we are still hungry and want more, which would be very impolite."

I realized immediately I had done it all wrong! I began to apologize profusely for my ignorance.

The old man stood and gently said, "Let me show you how we do it." He proceeded to demonstrate how a good Vietnamese host serves his guests. He picked up some chopsticks and began to put food on everyone's plate, including mine. Everyone began to laugh excitedly and talk together in Vietnamese. They were enjoying seeing me learn something new. From that point on, the table began to be a joyful place, as everyone relaxed and ate. Also, as a result, from that point on they delighted in teaching me the Vietnamese way in everything.

I learned that night that people who laugh at our mistakes are really laughing with us in a good way. I also learned it is a great joy for people to be able to teach a foreigner something new about their culture. It gives them a sense of importance to be able to teach a foreigner.

I learned that making mistakes has great potential for significant learning and can result in real bonding with others. So often we foreigners think of ourselves as the teacher. Too often, we are teaching people how to live and behave like us. This makes us feel significant. However, when we become learners and begin to learn from our friends, they begin to feel significant and enjoy helping us become people of their culture. This way we both learn how to live the Christian life in a culture that has little to no knowledge of Christian values and life. The result is a genuine Christian bonding. If we learn from others, then they are willing to learn from us!

One night, a class member looked very serious and said,

"According to Vietnamese law, no more than three people can gather for a meeting in a private residence without permission from the government. This means our class is actually illegal!" He continued, "The Catholic government is not against Christianity, though they don't like Evangelicals. However, they are desperately afraid of being undermined by people such as the Communists who want to take over the government. The government trusts no one, so they are intent on stopping any meetings that include several people, lest it is an enemy cell."

As a result, my Bible class was illegal. I could be suspected of undermining the government and arrested. This plunged me into a dilemma. Should I ask permission and risk being told no? Should I go ahead and teach and hope no one in the government would notice and take action? It seemed the best thing to do, since I was new in Vietnam, would be to see how the authorities responded to my openness and honesty.

Though somewhat fearful of what might happen, I made an appointment with the mayor's office. When I arrived, I was shown directly into the presence of the mayor of the city. He was taller and more muscular than most Vietnamese and formed a rather intimidating presence. After we sat down, his serious expression changed to a pleasant smile. My anxiety about the visit lessened somewhat.

"What can I do to help you, Pastor?"

"Your Honor, Mr. Mayor, I have an English class that meets in my home once a week. My students are learning English, and in return, they teach me Vietnamese culture. I just found out my class is illegal. We have eight people meeting every week. All of them have a rather prominent place in society and are good students. I understand if we have three or more people meeting in my home without permission, we are illegal. Is this true?"

"Yes, it is true. I know about your English class because my sister studies in that class."

"Wonderful! I did not know that. I am honored!"

"I want to share something with you very important. You are correct. Your class at present is illegal. If you ask me for permission to conduct the class, I will have to say no! Then you must stop! However, if you do not ask for my permission, then I will not have to say no. Is my meaning clear?"

"Yes, sir! I understand very well. Thank you for seeing me today. I am relieved about the class now. I hope to visit you again in the future and would welcome you to my class or to visit us at my home!"

With that, he took me to the door, shook my hand, and said, "Goodbye!"

As a result of that class, many things happened to facilitate our language and our relationships. People invited us to their home to eat. We had to speak Vietnamese with families of our students, since most families usually knew little or no English. From time to time, the mayor of the city invited us to key receptions at the mayor's home, where we met and spoke in Vietnamese with numbers of significant leaders in the city. We were invited to the graduation of the Vietnamese Military Academy (the West Point of Vietnam) to sit with the highest dignitaries and watch the graduation service. We watched as the president of Vietnam gave his address to the academy. As a result, our Vietnamese language and relationships in the city grew by leaps and bounds.

Beginning in early 1963, the open confrontations between Buddhists and the Catholic Diem regime grew in intensity. The population of Vietnam was 90 percent Buddhist and only 9 percent Catholic. A Buddhist monk protested the government by burning himself to death in front of the Catholic Cathedral in Saigon. This was like pouring coals on an already glowing fire across the entire country!

As Buddhists in the city of Hue prepared to celebrate the birthday of Gautama Buddha in May 1963, the government issued a decree forbidding the flying of the Buddhist flag anywhere in Vietnam. The city of Hue was the ancient imperial capitol of

Vietnam and also the residence of the archbishop of Indochina, Ngu Dinh Thuc, the president's youngest brother. As morning dawned over Hue on Buddha's birthday, the entire city was a sea of Buddhist flags flying over almost every building and house in and around the city.

The Vietnamese army moved in with force to remove the flags. A huge confrontation occurred. Many people died in those clashes. Much of this confrontation was led by President Ngo Dinh Diem's brother, Ngo Dinh Nhu, who was the head of the dreaded Public Security Police and a very ardent Catholic. He was intensely disliked by the Buddhist population.

Already many in the American government and Vietnamese military had become convinced the country would never accept the Diem brothers as leaders of the country. These and many other clashes convinced the American government regime change must take place.

On November 2, 1963, the Vietnamese Army moved against President Diem and his brother. They fled from the palace by an underground secret passageway disguised as Catholic priests and were secretly transported to a Catholic church in Cholon, the Chinese section of the city. There they were found and arrested by the Vietnamese Army. They were being transported to an army base just outside of Saigon. On the road to the army base, they were killed. The army said they were killed while attempting to escape.

Rachel and I were listening to a Vietnamese radio station when we learned of the death of the president and his brother. We heard about huge masses of people gathering in various cities to celebrate the death of these two leaders. Curious, I went to the downtown plaza in the center of Dalat in front of Dalat's only theater to see what was happening. Twisting and turning, I made my way through hundreds of people to get as near to the podium as I could. The arrival of the commandant of the Vietnamese Military Academy was imminent.

As I found a place in front of the crowd, I saw someone on

the steps of the theater immediately behind the speaker's podium motioning me to come to him. I immediately recognized this was the famous national photographer of Vietnam. I had met him earlier at a reception at the mayor's home. He called to me, "Ong James, come up here with me. You will be able to get good pictures!"

The commandant of the military academy arrived in his jeep surrounded by a heavily armed contingent of troops. He went straight to the podium and raised his arms in victory. The applause and shouts of the crowd were deafening. Briefly he stated the struggles of the past few months and the divisions that developed among the population. He then announced to the crowd, "I am pleased to announce President Ngo Dinh Diem is dead."

A cry of excitement and applause arose from the people.

Then the commandant held his arms up for quiet and shouted, "I am pleased to announce Mr. Ngo Dinh Nhu is dead."

With that, the celebration was wild. There were shouts of joy, people were crying, people danced in the street, and the celebration was twice as noisy as it had been with the announcement of Diem's death. The greatest joy among the people was the death of Ngo Dinh Nhu, the director of the Public Security Police.

Later many people were saying, had it not been for Diem's brother, President Diem might have continued as president. Of course, unless the government changed its attitude toward the Buddhist people, Vietnam would continue to be a divided populace with no central rallying point. This division of the country without acceptable leadership in place would prove to be the Achilles' heel of the South Vietnamese government.

These events revealed the serious problems Vietnam faced in its struggle with the Communist north. The north was unified behind a popular hero beloved and accepted by the northern people. Ho Chi Minh, or Uncle Ho as he was affectionately called, was almost revered by the people in the north. He was a hero of the revolution against the French. His commanding general, General Vo Nguyen Giap, was a battle-tested hero who led Vietnam to victory over the

French colonial power. Now these two heroes were leading the north to unite all of Vietnam under Communist rule.

Unlike the north, South Vietnam had no one who embodied their hopes and aspirations in the struggle for a free, democratic country. South Vietnam was an agrarian society. For the people of South Vietnam, their first loyalty was to their immediate family. After that, if they trusted anyone, it was their own extended family. If they broadened their trust at all beyond their extended family, they trusted people from their own village and possibly their own province. Beyond that, there was little trust in anything or anyone from other regions of the country and especially a central government. In the agrarian society of the south, the concept of freedom meant being left alone to pursue one's family's life and welfare. It had little meaning beyond that.

After Diem's death, a succession of coups d'état was led by one military officer after another.

Perhaps the greatest comparison between the two enemies was that the north was committed to something, which most of the people saw as positive, a clear nationalist philosophy or ideology embedded in Communism, which would last beyond the war and unite the country. This philosophy was embodied in a simple man, living in poverty with his people, Ho Chi Minh, who was loved and respected by the people of the north.

The south attempted to inspire and challenge the people with something essentially negative—a hatred for and the defeat of Communism. In itself, this was a noble goal for those who knew and understood the brutality and absolute control over the population inherent in Communist Marxism. To the majority of the agrarian population, such a goal had little meaning. There was nothing and no one who captured the people's imagination. There was no commanding figure, loved and respected, to provide vision and inspire commitment. If the south won, then what? The concepts of freedom and democracy meant little to them. What would happen after a victory over Communism was an unspoken and perhaps unconscious question. An answer to this was never communicated clearly to give the people something to live and die for.

At one point, the commandant of the Vietnamese Air Force, Nguyen Cao Ky, took over the presidency. Inflation was out of control. Money lost much of its value. Prices were so high no one could afford to buy anything. Prices of food, fuel, and other necessities skyrocketed, creating rampant unrest among the population. Demonstrations throughout the city of Saigon were daily occurrences. Confusion was in every area of society. Following his ascension to the presidency, to stop the devastating inflation, in March 1966, President Nguyen Cao Ky sent trucks throughout Saigon with loudspeakers announcing the price of rice would be set at a specific price the next day. Anyone selling over that price would be shot in the central marketplace.

The next morning, a Chinese merchant was caught selling at the inflated price. He was arrested and taken to the plaza in front of the Ben Thanh Market in the center of downtown Saigon. General Ky sent trucks with loudspeakers throughout the city, asking the people to come to the Ben Thanh Market. This merchant was tied to a wooden stake, and when the crowd gathered, the police executed him. Merchants throughout the country stopped inflating prices.

A prominent lawyer was caught leading students in demonstrations against the government. General Ky had him arrested. He is said to have told the lawyer, "If you like the Communists so much I will take you to North Vietnam, where you will be happy." A parachute was strapped to the lawyer's back and an air force plane flew him over North Vietnam. He was forced to jump out of the plane. The demonstrations stopped for a few weeks.

***

One small evangelical church in Dalat was an outgrowth of the ministry of the Evangelical Church of Vietnam. Since there was no

Baptist presence in Dalat yet, Rachel and I often attended the Dalat Evangelical Church and enjoyed a great relationship with the pastor and church members. The pastor knew almost no English, so he helped us with Vietnamese Christian vocabulary. He frequently visited our home to encourage us. He taught us much about Vietnamese culture and the history of Vietnam. He taught us how to pray in the Vietnamese language. I learned Vietnamese hymns in the worship services. It was a great informal source of learning. The pastor believed Dalat needed more than one church. He believed we should do all we could as Baptists to lead people to the Lord and establish churches. Best of all, this fine man became our pastor.

I decided since Easter was coming, and we had built relationships with a large number of people, the time was right to hold our first Baptist worship service in Dalat. It would be totally in Vietnamese. My language teacher helped me correct my sermon and practice it until I could read it clearly. We invited our English Bible class and all of our contacts to attend.

Easter Sunday morning arrived, and thirty people came to this historical first service. None of them had ever attended an evangelical worship service, though several were Catholic. We taught some simple hymns. I preached my first sermon in the Vietnamese language. It took forty hours to prepare that sermon but only ten minutes to preach it! I had not prepared in Vietnamese an invitation to come to Christ, but in my very limited simple Vietnamese language, I invited anyone who wanted to believe in Jesus as their Lord and Savior to please come and share this with me. I was overjoyed when a man, his wife, and their two preteenage children came forward, saying they wanted to believe in Jesus. They were the first Baptist believers in the city of Dalat. This family was the Trinh Ngoc Thanh family. Mr. Thanh later became the dean of our Baptist Theological Seminary, and his wife was in charge of the seminary kitchen for many years.

We had been studying Vietnamese for fourteen months and were excited about our new house church. Almost immediately after this worship service, I was surprised when a letter came from Saigon. It read:

> Sam,
>
> We have two problems to share with you. Several believers in Saigon have expressed a call to become pastors. We are asking you to take the lead role in establishing a program of pastoral training and theological education. The other problem is that an urgent need has arisen. Lewis and Toni Myers are making preparation to return to the States for their year of furlough. The mission would like your family to move from Dalat to Saigon and assume the responsibilities carried by the Myers.

With the Myers heading for their year of furlough (later called stateside assignment), I stood at another of those forks in the road. And I needed to make a decision.

First, I came to Vietnam with my heart set on being a church planter, not a theological educator. Second, I wanted to acquire the Vietnamese language to the best of my ability, and I needed much more time in full-time language study. To learn Vietnamese well, the mission had determined all missionaries would need two years of full-time language study and another year of half-time language study. Accepting this assignment would mean moving to Saigon to begin full-time Vietnamese work with only fifteen months of language study!

In addition, I would be doing a ministry I had not planned to do. As I prayed and worked through this, I was excited that seven Vietnamese men had experienced a call from God to the ministry. Someone must begin teaching and mentoring them. With the Myers' departure, only one family was left in Saigon, and he was the business manager and treasurer. Lewis and Toni Myers were creative and effective missionaries. They had already started many significant ministries. No one was available to carry on those ministries other than Rachel and me. Reluctantly, we agreed to the move with fear and trembling and began making arrangements to move from Dalat to Saigon.

Lewis Myers was pastor of Grace Baptist Church. Grace Church was only fifteen months old, so no Vietnamese were available to pastor. The church immediately called me to be the pastor of this, our first and only organized Baptist church in Vietnam. I would be preparing and beginning from scratch our training program for church leaders. We also assumed the role of coordinating evangelism and church planting for Saigon, a city of over three million people. Lewis Myers had begun publication ministries and communications ministries, and these were given to me. I felt completely overwhelmed at the magnitude of all I was being asked to do with such minimal language study. The truth is, I did not recognize that everything I was asked to do would involve intense language study!

In addition, Toni Myers had a children's choir, which she taught every Sunday afternoon. Toni was a music major and a skilled piano player. Rachel was invited to lead this choir. Rachel is a trained nurse and never had occasion to study music. She taught herself to play some hymns on the piano in high school. Rachel would need to take her place with no experience leading a choir!

As we pursued our ministries in Saigon, I could not help but think back to my navy days when I first committed my life to carry the good news of Jesus to the world. For ten years, I had prepared carefully to arrive on the mission field and begin the ministry the Lord had called me to do. At last, I was ready to begin.

I prayed, "Lord, I know what we are about to undertake is necessary. I am willing to do it. But, Lord, please fill this vessel of Yours to overflowing with Your presence and power. I need the divine gifts these tasks will require."

Original Grace Baptist Church

Current Grace Baptist Church

CHAPTER 15

NEW BEGINNINGS

Chanh watched as the bus approached at high speed, much too fast for a bustling city street. It was time to carry out what he had planned for some time. In seconds, he would step in front of that bus and end his life.

Le Quoc Chanh was a young man from a troubled home and deeply depressed. He had lost all hope anything could change. On this evening, shortly after sunset, wandering the streets of Saigon, he paused beside a heavily traveled street. The bus rapidly approached. In just two steps, he would be directly in the path of the bus. He took the first step. Miraculously, at the very last moment, he stepped back, and the bus passed by.

He had no religious faith and knew little about God. Suddenly in that split second, he felt there was something special in his future. He determined to find out what it was.

Throughout his twenty years, Chanh had struggled through a life void of love and intimate relationships in the family. He had no source of acceptance and affirmation. His life was without meaning, without direction, and without hope for the future.

In Saigon in 1960, a small number of American consultants, advisers, and military personnel who had recently come to work in Vietnam were looking for an opportunity to worship. Around that time there were only about eight thousand Americans in the entire country. There were no chaplains or other sources in English for spiritual growth. Some of them met our new Baptist missionaries and were invited to meet in the home of Bill and Audrey Roberson, the second Baptist missionary family to arrive in Vietnam in January 1960. Herman and Dottie Hayes; Bill and Audrey Roberson; and Lewis and Toni Myers, the third family to arrive, formed a Bible study group with interested Americans. Very quickly, a few Vietnamese heard about the group and began to attend. Le Quoc Chanh was one of them. This young man, who just a short time before had almost ended his life in hopelessness, became the first Vietnamese to accept Jesus as a result of our Baptist witness in Vietnam. Just ten years later, he became the first Vietnamese pastor of Grace Baptist Church and, along with Pastor Do Vinh Thanh, became the first to be ordained to the ministry. Later, at great sacrifice, he and his family refused to flee Vietnam when the Communists took over in 1975. He led the church and kept it open through years of social upheaval, persecution, and extreme suffering. He became God's instrument to keep Grace Baptist Church open when Communists closed every other Baptist church in Vietnam. In 2007, after thirty-five years as pastor, almost blind and in failing health, he had no choice but to retire.

A number of Vietnamese in the Bible class began to believe. From this group of new Vietnamese believers, Grace Baptist church was born—organized on November 18, 1962. I count it a great privilege to have participated in the organization services of the first Baptist church in Vietnam.

The new Grace Baptist Church elected Herman Hayes as pastor. The Americans formed a separate group called the Saigon Baptist Fellowship with Lewis Myers as pastor. After six months, the Hayes family went to America on furlough. Lewis Myers became the second pastor of the church. Some of the US military personnel became volunteer English teachers as a part of an outreach program. These classes fed numerous young adults and students into the ministry of Grace Baptist Church, where they accepted Christ and joined the church.

When we moved from Dalat to Saigon in May 1964, the church

called me as its third pastor. Since the church was only about seventeen months old, everyone was new in the Christian faith. My first Sunday, I looked out on a congregation made up primarily of young adults and students with a scattering of older Vietnamese.

Preaching and pastoring in Vietnamese after only fifteen months of language study was a tremendous challenge. For six Sundays, I worked with a language teacher writing out my sermons in Vietnamese. I spent hours getting them corrected and practicing my delivery. I preached on Sunday morning, Sunday evening, and Wednesday evening prayer meeting. Using an interpreter was not an option since, at that time, so few people were fluent in English. It was a grueling schedule for a new missionary working in a foreign language!

Every Sunday, I dreaded reading those sermons. I feared I would make too many embarrassing mistakes unless I read every word. During each presentation, I felt like I was just practicing my Vietnamese, rather than preaching the gospel with the power and presence of the Holy Spirit. Each service, there was no response. I could not see the faces of the people to judge how they were responding. I was a slave to the manuscript.

On the sixth Sunday morning, seated in the pulpit area, I made a firm decision: "I am going to put this manuscript under the pulpit desk, and from now on, I will look the people in the eye, sense what they are feeling and understanding, and preach without a manuscript!" Twice before I rose to speak, fear almost changed my mind.

I stood in the pulpit, my legs weak, my hands clammy. I briefly bowed my head and prayed, "Lord, you gotta help me here!" I straightened my posture, looked into the eyes of the congregation, uttered another silent prayer for strength, and said to the congregation, "Friends, I may make every mistake that can be made in the Vietnamese language. You may understand very little I say, but I am not going to read another sermon. Please forgive me. If I make a mistake, raise your hand and help me correct my language. I will expect you to do that." With that said, I launched into my sermon.

As I spoke, I could read the faces of the congregation. I could feel a warmth and acceptance I had not felt before. I could sense when they didn't understand. There were times when people laughed. I stopped and asked, "What did I say?" They seemed to enjoy correcting me. Completing the message, I gave an invitation to accept Jesus. Two students came forward to receive Christ. From that time on, we had decisions of some kind almost every service. Gradually, pastoring Vietnamese people in the Vietnamese language became a joy. I visited in hospitals and in homes. I performed weddings and funerals, baptized new believers, and conducted all the other ceremonies of the church.

One of my first decisions as a pastor was whether to lead the church to become a large downtown organization or to develop a reproducing church that constantly encouraged its people and used its various resources to plant new groups. I decided this must become a reproducing church. I was both pastor and trainer, as I also developed a program to train men and women for ministry. Since all my students were members of Grace Church, I was able to develop a church planting ministry with them. They could study in the training program and practice what they were studying in Grace Church. As they matured, Grace Church could send them out to plant new work. One of the greatest challenges was preparing curriculum and then being able to teach it.

For years, language acquisition continued to be both my greatest frustration and my greatest joy. I knew my effectiveness over the coming years would depend on my ability to communicate with people, both in mind and heart! At the end of two years, I began to be able to think on my feet and, at times, bring in unplanned points. If I used an illustration, I had to learn any special vocabulary ahead of time. By the end of three years, I was just beginning to say what I wanted to say without any notes. My language gradually became second nature to me.

Looking back over the years, I see that so many childhood experiences prepared me for language acquisition. The Lord knew what I needed to do, and He provided everything necessary to do it. I am convinced my decisions, in the eighth grade, to beg to be allowed to study Latin and then, during high school, to study French prepared me to learn other languages. Even corresponding with my Japanese American pen pal from Hawaii planted in me a desire to know other languages. My close association with a first-generation Italian family in New York, hearing their language constantly, exposed me to another language. Majoring in Greek in the University and Hebrew in the seminary furthered that interest. Also, knowing I could never clearly share Jesus with other people without knowing their heart language was another source of motivation. I knew too, without language, I would always be drawn to the fringes of Vietnamese society made up of those few fortunate enough to be fairly fluent in the English language.

I wanted to be able to reach all the people in a truly cultural way. Without Vietnamese, I would never find my place within the culture. Also, it was apparent that becoming fluent in the Vietnamese language would open many doors to me that would otherwise be closed. This proved to be true over and over again throughout my career in Vietnam.

Toward the end of my first four-year term, I was surprised by an old friend whom I had spent hours with since my earliest days in Vietnam. He professed to be a Christian, but, in reality, he was more philosopher, historian, and anti-French revolutionary than anything else. He had gray hair, a goatee, and a slight stoop. We had many discussions about Vietnamese worldview, history, and philosophy.

"Pastor, I want to invite you to a special lunch at Van Hanh University, the largest Buddhist University in Vietnam. Will you come?" With his white goatee, he looked just like Ho Chi Minh, the Communist leader of the north. He continued, "Once a year, all the old, famous revolutionaries against the French meet for lunch and talk together. We are all old now and have many stories to tell."

"But I am an American. Are you sure they will let me in?"

"You have taken the trouble to become fluent in Vietnamese. You really are becoming Vietnamese. I have shared with them how you like to learn, and they have no problem with your coming."

I was honored by the invitation and accepted.

Seated at the table, the old revolutionary formally introduced me and said, "You need to know you are the only foreigner we have ever allowed to meet with us. We appreciate you have taken the time to learn our language, our history, our culture. You are welcome into our midst."

All afternoon we sat there. I was spellbound to hear their stories of revolution against the French. They laughed heartily as they told of being arrested, of fooling the French, of defeating them in battles with Vietnamese strategy and cunning.

To raucous laughter one man told how he had dressed as an old man and was stopped at a guard post one day. The French soldiers would not let him pass. He said, "If you do not let me walk across, then I will jump across, because I can jump higher than you can reach. If you do not let me jump across, then I will fly across, because I can fly higher than you can dream. If you do not let me fly across, then I will disappear, and you will see me on the other side on my way from my victory over you!

"The soldiers laughed at me, thinking I was a harmless old man, and let me cross," he continued. "I crossed, turned around, smiled back at them, took off my old man disguise, and disappeared into the jungle!"

I came away from that special meeting with a tremendous sense of honor at spending time with these famous heroes. My language ability and special relationships opened that door!

Serving as pastor of a Vietnamese church without adequate language was fraught with possibilities for mistakes. On one occasion, I was waiting for the music to begin as a signal for the bridegroom and me to enter the church to perform my first wedding ceremony in Vietnamese. It suddenly dawned on me I did not know the Vietnamese word for "best man." I would need to ask the "best man" to give the ring to me for the wedding vows. As I turned to go into the church, I saw one of my seminary students who knew a minimum of English. I quickly asked him, "What is the Vietnamese word for 'best man'?"

He looked puzzled, thought a moment, and said, "Người Dơi." This word did not sound right to me. During the wedding, I decided not to use it. After the service, I looked up the word "Người Dơi." He had given me the word that translates as "Batman" rather than "best man." I cringed when I thought of almost saying in front of the entire congregation, "Will Batman please give the ring to me!"

Rachel was asked to take over a children's choir. Even though she was not trained in music, she began leading the choir. It opened up great opportunities to minister to mothers of the children. One of those mothers Rachel grew to know and love was Mrs. Dieu. Her two little girls sang in the choir. Almost every week Rachel and Mrs. Dieu would pray together and then walk through the winding alleyways and paths leading to small neighborhoods crowded with people. Opportunities to share were numerous.

Mrs. Dieu was taking care of her elderly mother who was unable to walk. She simply rested on her cot through the day. When Rachel entered the home, she always knelt beside this elderly lady's cot, took her hand, and prayed with her. The two little daughters watched with great interest everything Rachel did.

When Vietnam collapsed in April 1975, Mrs. Dieu and these two little daughters were able to leave Vietnam and come to America as refugees. The two girls grew up in America, graduated from a university, and married Vietnamese young men who became pastors.

The time came when both of these two young Vietnamese couples felt called to go to the mission field. Rachel and I were seated in the auditorium the night one of the couples was appointed to serve the Lord in Taiwan.

Giving her testimony in front of several thousand people she said, "When I was a little girl, I watched Mrs. Rachel James come to my home in Saigon and pray for my grandmother. I watched my mother and Mrs. James pray together and go visiting. I said then, 'I want to grow up to become a missionary like Mrs. James.'"

Our tears ran freely. That night, we realized again that none of us ever knows when someone is watching. We cannot know what our actions at a given moment might produce in the years ahead. That night on the stage of a large auditorium—after years of praying, preparing, and waiting—this beautiful, young Vietnamese woman's childhood dream was fulfilled. She still serves on the mission field with her husband to this day.

As soon as possible, I began teaching seven students who wanted to serve the Lord. They ranged in age from about nineteen years old to one man who was sixty years old. For a few weeks, I struggled with my meager language ability. I was faced with learning and using numerous theological words and concepts. Although the Bible is translated into Vietnamese, it contains numerous religious words of Chinese origin and concepts, which are difficult to explain. With my meager Vietnamese, I could hardly read my Vietnamese Bible, much less interpret it adequately. After about three weeks, I was struggling to communicate a strategic point of doctrine. I began to tell a story that illustrated the point I wanted to make. I drew illustrations on the board. Suddenly their faces lit up with broad smiles. They began to talk excitedly with each other. I knew they had understood this point of doctrine and were excited about it. I had them explain it back to me and to each other and give their own illustrations.

Yes! They did understand.

This was a turning point in my call to teach. That night I felt the Lord opened my heart to what He wanted me to do and helped me to know how these students learn. I knew this was a great opportunity to combine my own longing to be a church planter with theological training of church planters. Together we could plant numerous churches.

The Lord wanted me to help shape these young men to be the vessels of service He wanted them to be. From that point on, I was excited to be involved in leadership development and pastoral training. I came to realize I could not—I must not—separate evangelism and church planting from the ministry of laying a biblical and basic doctrinal foundation for those who serve Him. Evangelism and discipleship are two sides of the same coin!

Every time I began planting a new work, I took a student with me to be involved in that church plant. In a brief time, that student would take over the new group of believers so I could go to another place with another student and plant a new work. I learned from experience these students must be firmly grounded in the Word of God. Then, whatever evangelism and church planting they did would focus on discipleship and build a stable group. Without someone training them and having them practice what they were learning, they would not be able to disciple and train the people they were leading to know Jesus.

As a foreigner and a missionary, I would never be able to do all a God-called, trained local believer could do to bring the gospel to his or her own people. This did not mean I left my call to be a church planter. Instead, I no longer saw theological education as an academic discipline. For me, it became a ministry of teaching and modeling sound biblical doctrine and church planting, undergirded by the practice of all the Bible teaches.

It is possible to teach theological education from a purely academic perspective, in which the student comes to know a body of material and is sound theologically. Too often, in that process, the student may become a brilliant theologian but lose the very purpose for his or her divine call which is to model the Spirit-filled life, bring people to Jesus, and gather them into churches.

I had no idea how to set up a theological education program. I asked to join the newly organized Asia Baptist Graduate Theological Seminary Board of Trustees so I could interact with the leaders of our seminaries in Asia. I wanted to learn everything I could from them, even though I knew our level of education was going to be much more elementary and practical.

One of the professors at the Taiwan Baptist Theological Seminary was Dr. Samuel Tong, a distinguished Chinese professor. He later taught for many years at Golden Gate Seminary (now Gateway Seminary) in Mill Valley, California.

"Dr. Tong, how would you go about establishing a very practical seminary in Southeast Asia?" I asked.

He studied the question carefully and then replied, "Seminaries are like a great oak tree. The oak tree begins with a small acorn and gradually grows, gaining strength with each year. Seminaries are like that. A seminary should be grown, not established."

It was this advice that captivated my thinking and guided my efforts to develop a training program. I thought of Paul's admonition to Timothy: "That which you have received from me, teach to faithful men who will be able to teach others also" II Timothy 2:12 (NIV).

Several points in that verse became guideposts for accepting students:

- Paul focuses on those who have received sound teaching and who are faithful.
- He speaks of those who will be able to teach others—that is, people who not only know but have the ability to teach others.
- He is emphasizing those who live in such a way other people are willing to learn from them.
- He speaks of choosing faithful men to teach.

These men and women are the "acorns" from which a seminary is developed. I felt we should not accept as a student anyone who was not involved in serving in an existing church or helping to start a new church. At this early point in their training, it was important for them to have opportunities to be totally involved with mind, emotions, heart, and hands in their studies. By practicing what they were learning, they knew the questions they needed to have answered as they studied.

This method would help them to discern their own level of commitment to ministry and their capabilities in ministry. It would help them discover their areas of strength and areas where they needed to grow. In this early period of becoming servants of the Lord, it would test their self-discipline and their ability under the power of the Holy Spirit to overcome the trials, disappointments, and difficulties of ministry. It would also give them that wonderful taste of God's faithfulness and the joys of Christian service. It would help them to clearly define their call to ministry at an early stage and their desire to fulfill that calling.

Other decisions also needed to be made in this beginning stage of our work. First, we were anxious to see Baptist work in Vietnam as indigenous to the Vietnamese people and culture. For years, the Communists strongly asserted, "To be Catholic is to be French; to be Protestant is to be American; to be Buddhist is to be Asian; to be Communist is to be Vietnamese!"

We did not want to simply import into Vietnam Western and American forms of Christianity. We wanted our churches, above all, to be biblical and "at home" in the Vietnamese culture. In many ways, Vietnamese culture is more akin to the New Testament culture in which Jesus lived and taught than is Western culture.

Secondly, our focus would be on people who had not believed in Jesus. We refused to "proselytize" Christians from other groups. With less than 0.5 percent of the population of Vietnam Christian, we did not want to spend our time and energy trying to entice people who were already Christian to follow us! Also, we were eager to start churches that were truly biblical and not encumbered with the historical policies and traditional practices of other churches.

Third, as far as possible, we would refrain from creating dependence upon our missionaries or upon foreign finances. So much of our various strategies and programs in the Western world are dependent on large outlays of cash and fully trained personnel. We knew the Vietnamese did not have that luxury. If we patterned our strategies and programs after Western Christianity, we would need foreign money and personnel in large numbers. If our work in Vietnam would be truly Vietnamese, then the directions we set in the beginning should be within the ability of Vietnamese believers without relying on outside funding. Our insight proved to be prophetic. As the war intensified and all foreign personnel were forced out, the church continued to exist and stand firm, because it was truly Vietnamese and their dependence was on the Lord Himself.

Grace Baptist Church became a catalyst for developing new work. One of the students, Mr. Do Vinh Thanh, began a weekly Bible study in Ngo Tung Chau, a neighborhood on the outskirts of Saigon. This group met in a small, temporary bamboo hut on a vacant piece of property. Soon after the Bible study began, I became pastor of Grace Church. I began to meet with Mr. Thanh and the group. We decided to begin regular Sunday afternoon worship services in addition to his Bible study group, and we began to see many people come to the Lord. I had to leave Grace Church right after the worship service and drive to Ngo Tung Chau to preach. During that first month, I preached two Sundays, and Thanh preached two. After another month, I preached only one Sunday, and he preached three. Thus, after two months, Thanh had complete leadership of a new church start. Soon it became our second organized Baptist church in Vietnam and the only one with a Vietnamese pastor. They named it Faith Church.

One of our students, Mr. Le Quoc Chanh, the first Vietnamese to accept Christ in our Baptist ministry, opened a Bible study in Phu Tho Hoa, a suburb of Saigon near the Saigon Race Track. Chanh was one of our first students to begin studying in our new leadership training classes. We were able to locate a vacant storefront to begin Bible studies and worship meetings right in the location where he, his stepmother, and his father lived. Mr. Chanh's father, nearly sixty years old, became a faithful member of that house church and also felt a call to the ministry. Mr. Chanh assumed leadership of this group from the beginning. This was the beginning of what came to be the Phu Tho Hoa Church, our third church in Saigon.

Another of our students began a group at a major intersection called Nga Tu Bay Hien. Missionary Sam Longbottom took another of our young students, Mr. Tot, and began a new work at a major crossroads just north of Saigon, called Thi Nghe.

Another member of Grace Church was a layman who worked with our publications department. He saw an opportunity to start a church farther out on the edge of Saigon. He and I went there on Monday nights to meet with that group. Two other students decided to go across the Saigon River to a community of fishermen. A new church was planted there. So, one by one, with the support of Grace Baptist Church, our students began developing their own Bible study groups and worship services. These grew into new house churches.

One Sunday morning, I was standing with the choir, forming a line to enter the church to begin worship. Suddenly, a strange lady with a four-year-old girl came up to me and said, "This is my daughter. I am giving her to you." She placed the little girl's hand in my hand and turned to leave.

I quickly called her back. "Wait, I must go in the church and preach now. I need to talk with you about this. Can you wait for me?"

She said she would.

I invited her to come into the church. "When the service is over, we can talk about this." I led her and the little girl into the church. They sat on the back pew.

When I finished preaching, I gave an invitation to anyone who wanted to believe in Jesus to come down the aisle and share this decision with me. I was surprised to see this lady step out from the pew, little girl in hand, and come forward. She did not know of a God who loved her so much. She said, "I want to believe in Jesus."

167

We had a wonderful visit as I helped her to understand what believing in Jesus meant. Her name was Mrs. Chieu, and her daughter's name was Be (pronounced Beh). She said to me, "Would you be willing to come to my house and share this with all of my neighbors? I am sure they have never heard about this."

"Where do you live?"

"I live in a small area off of Petrusky Street."

For a long time, I had wanted to start a church on that very street and had prayed fervently for some way to get into that area.

Petrusky Street was the street that served as a hub for buses coming from all over Vietnam. Anyone coming or going to and from Saigon by bus would stop at this place. I could see the potential for great ministry and witness there. With one student from our leadership training class and several students from Intervarsity Christian Fellowship, we began a new church in that strategic location. She never again mentioned giving her daughter away.[7]

From 1964 to 1966, Grace Church had a part in beginning eight new churches with all of our theological education students and me. Grace Church as a "church planting laboratory" worked.

I can never forget how inadequate I felt when I moved from Dalat to Saigon. At times I questioned, "Why me, Lord? This is too much for me to bear!" I felt I had so little to offer the work at this point in my missionary life. I constantly worried about my lack of language. I felt overwhelmed to try to mentor new Vietnamese pastors when I myself was so new in this culture. But God's presence and power is always sufficient. He just needs someone through whom *He* can work!

Looking back, I realize I was not much older than the students I was teaching. The beautiful thing was they were Vietnamese, absolutely fluent in their own language. Their knowledge of their own culture and value systems was ingrained. At the same time, I was trained in biblical studies and experienced in church planting. They had as much to teach me as I had to teach them. Our relationship was a perfect bond as we learned from each other.

The Lord let me begin my career with a tremendous young church, with young men and women who were capable and filled with His spirit. God used all of us together to accomplish what none of us could have done alone. This had to be the work of God!

This was the joy and satisfaction of doing what God called me to do. It was as though the Lord had carefully prepared the clay and shaped the vessel through many experiences and was now filling it and using it to accomplish that for which He made it.

This is only half of the story. Dark clouds were on the horizon!

CHAPTER 16

THE WAR IS UPON US

It was nearing Christmas 1965. I finished speaking to a joint Christmas service for three Chinese churches in the Chinese area of Saigon. I was exhilarated by the experience, preaching in Vietnamese with an interpreter translating into Chinese Cantonese. I began driving back to Saigon around 10:00 that night.

Suddenly, as I approached a stoplight, I was stunned by a terrific blast right beside my Volkswagen van. My van lurched to the left and stopped with one wheel on the tree-lined median. For a moment, I was completely stunned. I could not hear anything. I looked down and saw red on my shirt. I didn't realize it was coming from my nose because of the concussion.

For several moments, I was in shock. As I began to come out of that initial shock, I instinctively looked to my right. What once was a nightclub frequented by American servicemen was now a pile of concrete, metal, and glass. Smoke from the explosion and heavy dust from crushed cement permeated the air. People were trying to get out through the mass of concrete and glass shards.

A Viet Cong soldier had parked a bicycle loaded with plastic explosives just beside the front door of the nightclub. The bomb exploded, destroying everything in its path. As best I could tell, the terrific force of the blast had caused my nosebleed. I sat there for what seemed an eternity trying to clear my mind enough to take some action. Gradually my nose stopped bleeding. My hearing began to return.

I got out of my van to better see what the situation was. A piece of the front wall had hit my right front wheel and caused me to lurch to the left up on the median. The front windows of my car were down from the hot, humid night air. I noticed a large piece of concrete right beside me on the seat. It passed through the open window and probably hit my thigh because, when I arrived home, I had a large bruise on my right thigh. Miraculously there was little damage to my vehicle. I hurriedly moved my car off the median to get it out of the way of the many emergency vehicles and drove home. It was days before I regained my composure and recovered a semblance of peace. The war was rapidly descending on us.

In the city of Saigon, the war was now everywhere, and it was nowhere. A floating restaurant was docked on the Saigon River in the very center of downtown Saigon. One evening when the restaurant was crowded, a bomb went off on board. People ran to the gangway to get ashore. Just as the crowd was escaping down the gangway, a directional bomb with small metal projectiles aimed directly at the gangway exploded. It seemed that every day something tragic was happening. Everywhere we went, we needed to be cautious and alert. Nowhere was safe.

It was a beautiful day, March 30, 1965. Rachel and I had the day free and walked along the Saigon River enjoying watching the busy life on the river. We turned right onto Nguyen Hue Street, a major boulevard in downtown Saigon. Suddenly, a huge explosion and a powerful wave of air jarred our bodies. To our left, black smoke was towering into the sky. With a deep sense of dread, we knew the US embassy was just two blocks to the left on Ham Nghi Street.

Quickly we ran the short distance to the embassy. We picked our way through broken glass, pieces of concrete, metal, and debris of all kinds. The front of the embassy building was totally demolished. Within moments, embassy employees were beginning to stagger out of the building, Some were being led out, others carried out by employees. Within minutes, dozens of people were scattered among the rubble, dazed and trying to decide what to do next.

Rachel was the first medical person to arrive. Months earlier, she had volunteered to be one of seventeen American Red Cross volunteer nurses to be called on in case of an emergency in the area of Saigon. Instinctively she moved quickly to those needing emergency medical care. She began setting up a triage area for those most seriously wounded. Within moments, emergency personnel began to arrive from the US Army's Third Field Hospital and various Vietnamese locations.

Rachel turned to me and said, "Maybe you should go home and make sure the children are okay. I am going to stay here as long as necessary. It could be a long time."

For the next three days, she didn't come home. She worked almost nonstop at the Third Field Hospital, nursing the injured and helping to evacuate out of the country those who needed special care.

So many times, I had passed that building and stopped to look at the large American flag flying proudly above the embassy. A wave of emotion and pride always welled up within me. There is something special about seeing those stars and stripes on high, waving proudly in the breeze. On the one hand, it was comforting and assuring and on the other, inspiring. Now, the US embassy, the symbol of all America stands for, was devastated. The American flag dangled limply from a broken pole.

We learned an old car had stopped illegally in front of the embassy. A security guard had warned the driver to move, but he'd refused. Suddenly a motorbike had stopped beside the car. Shots rang out. The shooting continued as the motorbike quickly sped away with the driver of the old car seated on the back. People in the embassy, hearing the gunfire, ran to the windows to look down to see what was happening on the street below. At that moment, three hundred pounds of plastic explosives exploded, crushing the entire front of the embassy, shattering everything, sending broken windows inward.

In 1964 to 1965, threatening war clouds were gathering across the expanse of the country. Saigon was the economic engine of South Vietnam. It was also the primary target of the Communist insurgency during the early years of the Vietnam War.

We had already seen the difficulties of the war as it affected the Vietnamese people. Now the devastation was impacting Americans living in Vietnam. One American woman working with the CIA, an American man, and a Filipino serving with the US Navy were killed that day at the embassy, along with nineteen Vietnamese. One hundred eighty people were wounded. This would be just the first of many experiences in the ravages of war during the next ten years in Vietnam.

From 1964 into early 1965 became a dramatic turning point for Americans in the war that had gradually escalated since the Geneva Accords divided Vietnam in July 1954. The struggle among the Viet Cong (South Vietnam Communist soldiers), the Viet Minh (North Vietnamese Communist soldiers), and the democratic South Vietnamese army continued unabated. The situation had become so precarious our missionaries were giving thought to contingency plans should Vietnam fall to the Communists. We made a list of the most important things for us to carry out by hand should we have to leave.

On July 30, 1964, a small naval battle in the Gulf of Tonkin in North Vietnam precipitated President Lyndon Johnson's order for a massive build-up of American military. By the end of 1965, nearly five hundred thousand American troops were pouring into Vietnam. Trucks and jeeps came in by the thousands. Americans were renting everything that could be found to rent in the Saigon area. The cost of housing skyrocketed.

Many Americans brought air conditioners and other utilities with them. The supply of electricity in Saigon quickly reached its limit, and rationing was enforced. Electricity rotated between three sections of the city. Our family had electric power one day out of three. When we had electricity, we pumped water into a reservoir on the roof of the house. We filled pots and pans with water. We filled the bathtub with water. If we used it sparingly, we would have enough water for two to three days.

Saigon was always hot, and nights were extremely humid. Our house was a narrow, two-story house with windows in the front and in the back, but none on the two sides. Thus, with no fans, air circulation was difficult. At night, Rachel or I would sit on the children's beds and fan them until they went to sleep.

The streets of Saigon were not built for large military trucks and huge numbers of vehicles. Saigon in the 1960s was a city of bicycles. In the 1970s, it became a city of motorbikes. Many streets in Saigon were beautiful, old, tree-lined boulevards with a street in the center for vehicles and an additional narrow street on each side for bicycles, motorbikes, horse-drawn carts, and other vehicles. To accommodate traffic, the beautiful trees lining many of these streets had to be cut down. Saigon was known as "the Pearl of the Orient," but now it lost much of its old, distinctive beauty.

There were times every day when I would sit in a traffic jam for more than two to three hours waiting for a military convoy to pass and the roads to clear. It also became dangerous because, frequently, a Viet Cong soldier would lob a hand grenade at an American vehicle caught in a traffic jam.

My most difficult ministry was conducting funerals for young Vietnamese soldiers killed in the war. Often their families were members of Grace Baptist Church. We did everything we could to support them. I dreaded getting a notice from a family saying their loved one had been killed, and the body was being brought to Saigon. They often asked if I would conduct a Christian funeral. Conducting these funerals is still indelibly inscribed on my mind.

Just outside of Saigon was a large field. There were three spacious, temporary tin buildings. One contained dozens of bodies waiting for burial. The other two were divided into stalls approximately eight feet wide and six feet deep. Overhead on each of the buildings was a tin roof, which during the day radiated heat and humidity inside from the tropical sun. The front of each stall was completely open. Each of the stalls was just big enough to contain a small table with a crude wooden coffin on top with the body inside. There were fifteen stalls in a row in each building. Stalls were set aside for Buddhist, Catholic, and Christian funerals. A few other stalls were shared by several indigenous religions, including the large syncretistic Cao Dai religion, the militaristic Hoa Hao religion, and other indigenous religious groups. Sometimes the family and I would have to wait an hour or two until a stall opened up for a Christian funeral.

While we waited, it was heartbreaking to hear the fresh mourning and weeping of a family who had just gone into that oven-like building and identified the body of their loved one. Several times I went with families when they had to identify their loved ones. The bodies had not been cleaned, wounds were evident, and blood was matted on the clothes. Each time I hoped to never have to see that again.

These bodies had been retrieved from the field of battle, stacked on an army vehicle, and brought to this location for burial. The trip to Saigon often would take several days. The intense heat caused bodies already deteriorating to deteriorate more rapidly under the tin roof. Never can I forget conducting funerals under those conditions; each one of them was exhausting to the core of my being.

Each funeral was almost identical and equally exhausting. Join me as I conduct one of these typical funerals.

★★★

I take my place in front of the coffin, just inside the small shed. Since there is no microphone or speaker system to amplify my voice, I ask the family to come near. As I wait for the family, I am acutely conscious of the heat from the blistering sun radiating down from the tin roof, making the room almost unbearable. I need to speak loudly enough so the family can hear over the weeping and wailing of so many families gathered for funerals,

I am filled with compassion as I look out over the families, most of them have covered their nose and mouth with gauze masks in an attempt to mask the smell of so many dead bodies. I wish for one of those masks, but know I cannot speak clearly through so much gauze.

As I stand there with the coffin behind me and the crowd in front, I see the mother, father, wife, and siblings standing near, dealing with the reality of their loved one's death. This is no sterile environment with a body embalmed and waxlike in a coffin in an effort to hide the reality of death. There are no beautiful flower arrangements and wreaths expressing love and respect. There is no gathering of friends to share their heart of love for those in deep sorrow. No military representative is present to present a flag and express the sympathy of a grateful nation. Even though some in the family are Christians, hence a Christian funeral, most of the family has little to no exposure to the Christian faith, which promises life eternal with a loving heavenly Father. I feel acutely the responsibility of being the physical presence of that loving, heavenly Father who deeply cares and gives words of comfort and positive assurance of the hope we have in Christ Jesus.

As a foreigner speaking Vietnamese, I am a curiosity to other families waiting to observe a funeral. As I begin speaking in Vietnamese, a large crowd of onlookers crowds the area to hear this strange westerner speaking in their language. They are Buddhists, and in addition, almost all practice ancestor worship, two hopeless belief systems almost diametrically opposed to each other. I try to speak as loudly as possible, expressing with utmost clarity the hope we have because of the life, the death, and the resurrection of Jesus Christ, our Lord and Savior.

★★★★

Fifty years have passed since I conducted those funerals, but even now, I still have in my nostrils the smell of deteriorating flesh. I still hear and feel as acutely as then the agony of a family's hopeless weeping and moaning for a loved one who died on the field of battle. I know I can never erase the stench of death from my nostrils, but I have learned to let it remind me of the hopelessness of millions of people who die without Christ every day. They will never know the victory and eternal joy we have in Christ Jesus. I never want to lose that ache in my own soul!

Amid all of the tension and stress living in the midst of war, I was beginning to become discouraged. One morning I went to the post office to get our mail. Among the letters was one evidently written in the longhand scrawl of a young child. I quickly opened it. It read:

> Dear mishurnery,
>   We bin studying a lot about venersula lately.
> My techer gave me ur name. I prayed fer you today.
>   Ur frind, Bobby

When I read that letter, it was as if all of my tension was suddenly released. I laughed until the tears flowed. Then I wept when I thought of a little boy there in America, aware some of us were here in Vietnam, or "Venersula," going through a difficult time. That little boy will never know what his letter meant to me that day. It lifted me to a moment of joy in the midst of the tension.

We were caught between two dynamic forces. On the one hand, God was blessing in so many ways our beginning ministry in Vietnam. People were coming to Christ. New churches were being planted. On the other hand, war, with all its danger, confusion, and stress, was felt every day, and the pressure was intensifying.

In early 1965, the chief of chaplains of the US Army visited Saigon. Rachel and I took him to dinner. I told him about my six years in the navy. He approached me seriously about returning to the navy as a Naval Reserve Chaplain. Living in Vietnam, I could be of tremendous help to our Armed Forces, especially since at that time there were not yet chaplains in Vietnam. Once again, I stood at a fork in the road. Should I make that commitment? My patriotism spoke to me. Could it be I could continue ministering as I was and also be able to meet the spiritual needs of our armed forces?

My military past made chaplaincy an attractive choice. However, everything I had experienced to date brought me to the mission field to minister cross-culturally to a people who had little opportunity to know and believe in Jesus. By divine call and preparation, I was a cross-cultural church planter. Once again, past experiences and a divine call informed my decision. I could not turn away from the Vietnamese people.

CHAPTER 17

TRUST AND OBEY

In the early afternoon on the Sunday before Christmas 1965, I had almost reached my destination in the delta of Vietnam after a five-hour drive from Saigon. Just as I rounded a curve, I saw it up ahead. It was too late for me to turn around and flee. There was no escape.

Dirt was piled across the road as high as my Volkswagen van. I knew this was a roadblock put there by Viet Cong forces to stop all traffic going both directions. I knew they were lying in wait for a number of cars to line up. They would make everyone get out of their cars, take all their valuables, give a lecture on Communism, and then let everyone go. Just two weeks before, a Philippine missionary, his wife, and little baby had been stopped at a roadblock just like this. Before letting the cars go, a Viet Cong soldier had put a bullet through the baby into the Philippine missionary's heart, killing them both.

As I approached, I began trembling all over so violently my foot could scarcely put on the brakes. I was the second car in the line.

Several weeks before, I had received an invitation from a young teacher to speak to a large, rural middle school near the village of My Tho in the delta of Vietnam. I had helped this young teacher accept the Lord when I led Intervarsity Christian Fellowship students in Bible study sessions during their annual retreat. Upon graduation, the government sent her to this rural school to teach. Her letter told about how few students and faculty knew the Lord in her school. She wrote, "Would you please come and tell them the real meaning of Christmas?"

The year before, she had invited me but I did not think the road was safe enough for me to go. This year, I called both the Vietnamese and the American military police to ask about the security of the road. They both said nothing had happened on that road in several months. It should be all right, but I needed to be off of the road by 4:00 p.m. At sundown it would no longer be safe.

Rachel and I prayed about whether or not I should go. We felt I should take advantage of this opportunity. Before I left, we had our devotional from Psalm 91:

> He who dwells in the shelter of the Most High
> will rest in the shadow of the Almighty.
> I will say of the LORD,
> 'He is my refuge and my fortress,
> my God, in whom I trust.'
> Surely, he will save you from the fowler's snare,
> and from the deadly pestilence.
> He will cover you with his feathers,
> and under his wings you will find refuge;
> his faithfulness will be your shield and rampart.
> You will not fear the terror of night,
> nor the arrow that flies by day. Psalm 91:1-5 (NIV)

As I sat there, I immediately began to chastise myself for making this trip. "I should have known better. I should have declined the invitation like I did the year before. I am so stupid," I thought. "I have brought this on myself. What will happen to Rachel and the children if something happens to me?" All these thoughts pounded my mind with self-blame. The stress kept me from being able to think clearly and try to find some way out of this situation.

I don't know how long I sat there. I was paralyzed with fear. Behind me the cars were beginning to line up for a long way. It would not be long before the Viet Cong came out of hiding.

Slowly my mind turned to the scripture we had read that

morning. I had memorized most of Psalm 91 years ago when I was in the navy on Adak. Now it came flooding into my mind. The Psalm talks of abiding in the shadow of the Almighty, under His wings. This picture is like baby chickens finding refuge under their mother's wings in the midst of a storm. It speaks of trust—"in Him will I trust." The fifth verse says, "You will not fear."

I said to the Lord, "But, Lord, right now I am terrified. Help me, Lord, to find that trust in You!"

As all this flooded my mind I began to think of the sovereignty of God. He knows what is best. His plan is always perfect. I had prayed about this trip before coming. I knew I was in His will. I trusted Him; this was true. I prayed, "Lord, if tragedy strikes me today, I know through this your name will be glorified. I know whatever happens will be Your perfect will. I surrender to that will. I trust absolutely in you."

It was a moment of total trust. I felt great peace sweep over my mind and soul. I stopped trembling. My mind felt clear and alert. It was as if I was being enveloped by the very presence of God.

I looked to the right into very thick palmetto growth. I could make out the form of the guns below. There were Viet Cong, camouflaged, lying in that growth and waiting to come out. I looked to the left. Rice paddies extended to the horizon. It was the dry season, so there was no water in the paddies. The bank of the road descended at about a forty-degree angle down to a water buffalo trail running parallel to the highway like a service road. Farmers used this trail to bring in the oxen and carts to haul the rice plants to the field for planting or to take away the harvested rice straw for winnowing. Behind me, cars were continuing to line up.

I decided to risk driving down that incline and make my way forward on the water buffalo trail wherever it would lead me. Without showing my hands, I turned my wheels slowly toward the incline. Thankfully I had not turned off my engine so there was no sound of an engine starting. I used the lowest gear and eased out of line, down the incline, nearly turning over and onto the water buffalo trail. During the rainy season, the hoofs of the oxen left deep imprints in the mud. Now, those prints were dry like hardened cement, making the trail extremely rough. I drove as quickly as possible, bouncing severely, my head occasionally painfully hitting the roof of the van. I drove through a banana grove, down the trail until I was well past the line of cars. I drove up the incline onto the highway and went as fast as the van would travel the three miles to my destination.

Just before arriving at the school, I stopped on the side of the road. I was trembling again. My head was aching. I asked the Lord to help me to be calm and relax so I could speak to those middle school kids with clarity and with His power. Just as I finished praying, I heard the loud chatter of rapid gunfire, the heavy thud of grenades, and other weapons. Black smoke was billowing into the air. I knew something tragic had happened at the roadblock.

Arriving at the school, I saw the principal, several teachers, and a large number of children lined up in front of the school to welcome me. After introductions, they asked about the fighting they could hear and see in the near distance. I explained what had happened.

Speaking to those young students was a wonderful experience. When I finished. everyone exited the school auditorium to say goodbye. They were lined up all along the road.

"Pastor, please come back sometime and speak again," the principal said.

The young teacher told me as we walked to the van how this experience had opened the door for her from now on to be a witness in the school.

The principal told several young boys to ride with me back to the scene of the roadblock.

I said, "It is not necessary for these boys to go with me. It is dangerous, and I don't want them to get hurt. Also, it is about five kilometers to the site. They will have to walk that long way back."

"Don't worry about them. They face these situations all the

time. They walk everywhere. Five kilometers is no problem for them."

The boys were instructed to check and see if it was safe for me to continue on the road. Just before we reached that point, the boys left my van and walked to the site. A few minutes later, they returned.

"Oh, Pastor, it is very bad. Cars are still smoldering and many bodies have been pulled out of the cars and are lying on the side of the road. Vietnamese military are everywhere. You can pass, but you need to be careful because cars are still very hot."

I thanked the boys and drove toward the site.

I stopped and asked a Vietnamese military policeman directing traffic what had happened.

"Two truckloads of Vietnamese soldiers approached the roadblock and opened fire on the Viet Cong soldiers hidden in the field. The Viet Cong fired back, catching several cars in the middle. As you can see, cars are still smoking hot, and a number of people have been killed. Many Viet Cong soldiers are dead.

"I will let you pass," the policeman added, "but drive slowly through the wreckage. We cleared a path just wide enough for one line of traffic at a time to go through."

I could smell the hot steel of the recently fired guns and the exploded ammunition. Black acrid smoke from burning vehicles and tires lingered in the air, making it difficult to breath. As I passed by the roadblock, I could smell burning flesh as though it had just happened. I looked at the car that sat where I had been in line. Three bodies were lying just on the roadside beside the car. All three of the first cars in line were burned to a crisp. I trembled when I thought of what I would have faced had I stayed there! At least fourteen bodies had been pulled from the cars and were lying grotesquely on the shoulder of the road, the air literally filled with the smell of burned flesh.

As I made my way back to Saigon, my mind was flooded with thoughts about all that had transpired that day. Questions flooded my mind. What if I had continued sitting there, paralyzed by fear? What if I had not memorized Psalm 91 long ago? What if Rachel and I had not read it this very morning? What if I had been in this place without the presence of Christ and without the peace that flowed through me, releasing the paralyzing fear that possessed me?

Of course, I cannot answer those questions. But one truth stands out above all else. Before that experience, I thought the antidote to fear was courage. I learned that day the antidote to fear is trust. Miraculously I had come to the place of complete trust in my heavenly Father. When trust is complete, we relax our minds and emotions. Our blood pressure goes down. Our heartbeat slows. Arteries open up, and blood flows freely to the brain. Under the shelter of His wings, everything becomes clear, and we are able to take whatever action is necessary.

Complete trust does not come naturally. When we walk with Him daily and practice His presence, then as emergencies and crises come, it is easier to rest in that place of trust. If we wait until a crisis arises and then look to Him for help, it becomes more difficult to sense His presence and find that place of complete trust. It is like following a path while it is day. When night comes, it is much easier to find our way.

A second truth I learned as a result of this experience is complete trust is followed by total obedience. There are not many times I personally have had to exercise complete trust to the degree this particular experience required. "He who dwells [not moves in and out] in the shelter of the Most High [place of trust], will rest [relaxation and peace] in the shadow of the Almighty [the place of absolute obedience away from the burning hot sun or violent storms which cause us to want to turn back]."

This was the second life-or-death experience that caused me to want to make the most of every day. In some ways, I continue to struggle for balance even today because I am now driven to accomplish as much as possible. For a second time, I was spared from a violent death. Relaxation does not come easy for me anymore. I know how quickly life can be taken away, and I cannot bear to waste one day of the life God has given me! At the same time, this life God has given me is now a new life of thankfulness for each day and a desire to be obedient to His will whatever it costs.

CHAPTER 18

TESTING THE VESSEL

In summer 1966, we were due to return to the States for our first furlough. After four years on the field, we would be assigned in the States for one year. Stateside assignment is a period of time when missionaries return to America to speak in churches, tell the story of missions, and experience healing and restoration as they prepare to return for another term of service. We were returning to the States filled to overflowing with a variety of emotions from so many different experiences.

We had experienced the presence and power of the Lord working through us and His people in Vietnam to bring many to faith in Jesus. This was thrilling. At the same time, we had experienced far more death and devastation than anyone should ever experience in a lifetime. While the first term in Vietnam was extremely productive, we were leaving with a heavy heart that the Vietnam War was really just beginning, and no end could be seen.

After four years in the field, the day came for our departure to the United States. On May 3, 1966, we flew out of Saigon. We had come to Asia by ship. It was such a pleasure now to be able to fly back to America. When we left America, our daughter was three years old, and our two sons were eighteen months and eight weeks old. Now our daughter was seven, Stephen was five, and Philip four. With no memory of America, everything was a new experience for them.

We were on a train from San Diego to Los Angeles to catch our flight across the United States to our home in North Carolina. Our daughter sat beside a Chinese lady, and the two of them became friends. Two days later on the plane flying to North Carolina, Deborah kept talking about the lady who sat beside her on the train. We tried to remember which lady that was. I finally asked her "What did this lady look like?"

She replied without hesitation, "You know! The lady that looks like us."

It was fascinating that, in her mind, we were Asian people. We looked different from Americans!

During the summer in the United States, our two boys were invited to go on a Royal Ambassador camping trip. They immediately bonded with the lone African American boy their age. It was evident my boys felt somewhat alien among American boys. As the only black boy, the African American also felt alien. Immediately there was a kinship between them. The three of them decided to sleep in one tent together. This was an example of many experiences these three boys had on that overnight trip. The fascinating thing was the Asian culture of my boys was vastly different from the African American culture of this boy. However, what bonded them was all three felt acutely their differences from all the other children. Similar to my own experience as a ten-year-old encountering the beautiful music of an African American church, my boys were being sensitized for the first time to both the American and African American culture to add to their Asian culture.

It would be difficult to describe the shock of our family when we walked into a huge grocery store for the first time. We were confronted with rows of all kinds of cereal. The only kind of cereal our children had ever seen was puffed rice. A man would come down our street in Saigon pushing a cart with a machine. He would pour grains of rice into the machine. The rice was heated, and with a popping sound, it became puffed rice. In these stores, the choice of cereals was beyond belief. We walked into an ice cream shop. The only ice cream our children had ever had was homemade churned ice cream. Instead of offering a flavor or two, the questions were numerous. "We have thirty-seven flavors. Which flavor do you want?" "Do you want a sugar cone or a waffle cone?" "How many scoops do you want?" "Do you want several flavors mixed together or separate?" "Which flavors?" My children, struck with awe and overwhelmed by the choices, were speechless!

Our family went to different churches each Sunday, where Rachel and I would speak. The children were in a different Sunday school class every Sunday. Often, they were asked, "Where are you from?" They would respond rather matter-of-factly, "Vietnam." Usually the response of one of the children would be, "Is that down in Florida?" or, "Is that up in the mountains?" The kids could not believe everyone did not know where Vietnam was!

One of the boys remarked, "The only thing worse than going to a strange Sunday school class is going to a strange Sunday school class late!" After several months, they began to love America but were always asking, "When can we go home?"

The antiwar movement was growing in its intensity. Almost everywhere I went I encountered some hostility. In one state, I spoke for the Woman's Missionary Union annual meeting. After my presentation, a reporter from Associated Press asked for an interview. I met her in a back room of the church.

"We hear our air force is indiscriminately bombing innocent villages. Is this true?" she asked.

"Villages, especially in outlying areas and jungles of Vietnam, are often not mapped accurately and are difficult to identify," I told her. "I have heard that very occasionally a mistake is made, and a village may be bombed. However, when that happens, the military comes in with every kind of aid imaginable and rebuilds the village. Such action is very rare and is always a tragic mistake. It certainly is not done indiscriminately."

The next morning the headlines in the newspaper read "Missionary Tells of Indiscriminate Bombings in Vietnam." The article itself was fairly correct, but the headline was absolutely wrong! After that, I refused to give another interview to the press. I was not smart enough to overcome the prejudices of an untruthful press.

Later, on a plane to Hong Kong, I sat beside a bureau chief of the Associated Press. I told him about this experience.

He responded, "I know exactly what you are talking about. We have reporters covering the war in Vietnam from dozens of strategic locations. Our reporters try to cover the war fully and accurately. But the 'powers that be' in the States choose which stories to give to the public. It is no secret most of our press organizations are against the war in Vietnam. They choose the stories that give our involvement in Vietnam a bad name. They choose to make it look like a hopeless situation. They deliberately leave out positive stories. This happens all the time when a political agenda dictates the slant of public information. I am not just talking about the Associated Press; most press organizations also shape American opinion to match their political agenda."

To convey the progression of the antiwar movement, I'll tell of our return to the United States four years later in 1971 for our second stateside assignment. We were shocked at the intensity of the antiwar movement. I was invited to speak for World Missions Day at a seminary. When I arrived, I saw a large number of people on the campus demonstrating against the war. I was shocked when I realized they were demonstrating against me simply because I was serving in Vietnam.

Prior to going to speak, I had done some research on a rather famous church nearby, which was supporting workshops to help young adults avoid the draft. They also were promoting antiwar demonstrations. When I looked at this church's gifts to world missions, I was shocked. Out of a two-million-dollar annual budget, the previous year they had given around five thousand dollars total to local, state, home, and world mission offerings. At the same time, they were promoting Christian pacifism, which, according to their interpretation, meant one refused to go to war based on the teachings of Jesus.

My question in the message that day was, "How can you refuse to go to war based on the teaching of Jesus and at the same time refuse to be involved in the Great Commission Jesus gave to his disciples?" This is a clear teaching, basically an expectation, of Jesus: "Therefore go and make disciples of all nations, baptizing them in the name of the Father and of the Son and of the Holy Spirit, teaching them to obey everything I have commanded you. And, surely, I am with you always, to the very end of the age" Matthew 28:19-20 (NIV).

It seems impossible and illogical to promote world peace and pacifism based on the teachings of Jesus and yet not support taking the Prince of Peace to the whole world! Actually, every young adult Christian pacifist should be the first to volunteer to be a missionary to take the good news of Jesus to the world!

Rachel and I learned so much during the time in the States. Perhaps the greatest thing we learned is there are Christians all over America aware of the world's brokenness and suffering. They are solidly undergirding every effort to bring people in every nation to know Jesus and to live for Him. We learned that, while there were strong disagreements about war and peace during that era, there was strong agreement by Christian believers that the mission of bringing people to know Jesus is the greatest antidote we have against world conflict, which plunges people into war, suffering, and death. We also returned to Vietnam with a wonderful assurance that whatever the attitude of American people toward the war, we had the support and prayers of Christian people all over the United States. As is written and said in so many places, "We can descend to the dark bottom of the well when we know and trust who holds the rope!"

As we prepared to return to Vietnam for a second four-year term, we knew the situation in Vietnam was growing more threatening every day. I was returning to Vietnam to give my full time to establishing our resident seminary to train pastors and church leaders. Our children were ecstatic about returning home. Now that our children were older, Rachel and I were hoping during this term she would finally be able to fulfill her medical missionary nurse calling.

It was difficult to say goodbye to our elderly parents. My father had serious health issues—incurable cancer with one leg amputated. It was almost certain I would never see him again. Someone I highly respected asked me, "You are going to waste your life in the midst of a hopeless war, and your father is going to die. Why don't you just stay here? Your father needs you, and we need pastors in America too!" These words were stinging.

All I could do was simply share the reality of my sacred call. Every experience in my life had prepared me for this time. How could I forsake obedience to my loving Lord, who saved me, gave me my life, and called me to a people who were suffering in a war not of their own making, hurting, and lost like sheep without a shepherd?

PART IV
BREAKING, REMAKING, REFILLING THE VESSEL

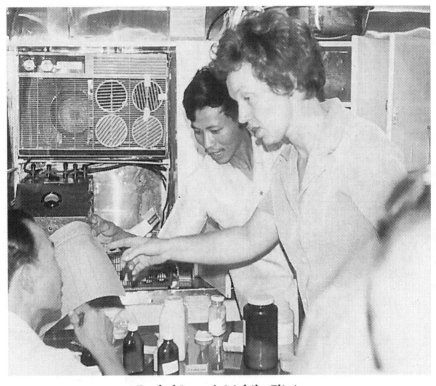

Rachel James's Mobile Clinic

CHAPTER 19
RACHEL'S "CYCLES OF PURPOSEFUL MISSIONARY LIFE"

It was early September 1967. We were settled in our home in the little village of Thu Duc. The children were in bed, and Rachel and I were having our quiet time together.

"Honey, I have some news to tell you."

"Oh, what would that be?"

"We are going to have a baby!"

"We are going to what?"

"I am pregnant, and we are going to have a baby!"

It would be difficult to describe the frenetic condition of my mind! It was in motion in a thousand different ways all at once. First, I was completely surprised. My questions came out all at once: "Are you sure? When is the baby due? Are you feeling okay? How are we feeling about this?"

Then reality began to set in. Our youngest child was five years old. It was a wonderful miracle to experience a new little life coming into our family at this point in our lives. I was excited and awed at this news.

On the other hand, I began to think about how this would change our lives, how it would affect our missionary ministry and commitments.

When we returned to Vietnam in June 1967 from our stateside assignment, we moved to the village of Thu Duc to establish our resident Baptist seminary. Rachel and I were praying intensely about her missionary role in this next term of service. At this point, she was the mother of three children ranging from five years old to eight years old. She was a highly trained nurse, with excellent practical experience. The main reason she was on the mission field was because of her divine call to go to the field as a nurse. As a wife learning language, adjusting to a new culture, and mothering our children, she had not yet found the opportunities to use her nursing skills possible. Her only medical involvement was to give advice and counsel to our friends and treat the missionary kids for their minor bumps and scratches. In fact, years later at a meeting of retired missionaries, one of these grown missionary children said to Rachel, "Aunt Rachel, I wish I had a boo-boo for you to make well!"

It was not that she was not doing mission work; she did plenty of that. She just couldn't do the medical ministry she loved and wanted to do. As her husband, I knew how important it was for her to be able to fulfill that part of her missionary calling even as she performed her role as wife and mother. With our youngest son turning six years old and beginning school, she would finally be free to be the nurse God had called her to be. Now, though, we were going back into small-baby mode!

When we talked from time to time about how much I wanted her to be able to fulfill that "nurse calling," she reminded me of her philosophy of the life of a wife and missionary mother. Rachel said, "A missionary wife goes through cycles of life and ministering. There are times when she is free to do what she wants to do. Then she may enter a cycle where she is busy almost full-time carrying out the responsibilities that come naturally to a wife and mother. Then after a time, circumstances may change, and she is free to do other things God calls her to do. Then she may enter into another cycle of life, which requires different time commitments and responsibilities, especially as the children grow and are involved in various endeavors. It requires patience to move in and out of these cycles, but each one can be fulfilling. All of this is the Lord's work and in His will and timing. He opens the door to the specifics that He desires me to be and to do."

With our youngest child starting school, we had begun to pray with great intensity the Lord would open up some avenue of medical ministry for Rachel. She was entering a new cycle of missionary life and ministry.

Then, it happened. Rachel was going to have another baby! We had not planned in any way to have another baby! Once again, we turned to the Lord. By now we knew not to ask, "Why, Lord? Why is this happening to us?" We had learned from experience there is usually no answer to that question. We also learned from experience God would reveal His plan to us in His timing. We trusted Him absolutely for that!

As we prayed, we remembered our one-year delay coming to the mission field and how disappointing that had been and yet how valuable and rewarding the following year was as we planted a new church. We remembered being called out of language study before we were finished and how disappointing that was. Yet, God had used the opportunity to make us even more fluent in language than we would have been by staying in language study. I remembered my time in the navy, as a new believer, when I was sent to Adak in the Aleutian Islands. I was so disappointed on that cold, isolated island, thinking I would not have a chance to grow in the Lord. Yet that was my greatest year of spiritual growth. Continuing to trust in the Lord, any feelings of disappointment at the news of a new baby became a year of great excitement about what God had in store for us as a result of this new little person coming into our family! On May 30, 1968, little Michael David James was born.

What we did not know was at the time we were praying for Rachel's nursing ministry, there was a young Christian medical doctor down in Birmingham, Alabama. At that very moment in the summer of 1967, he was receiving notice he was being drafted into the United States Army. Dr. Leo Record fought this draft every way possible but could not avoid it. He was drafted, closed his medical practice, and began his military training. In October 1968, he landed at Bien Hoa Air Base in Vietnam to take up his station in the field hospital at Long Binh Army Base, very near our village.

Within weeks, he received a letter from the commanding general of the Armed Forces in Vietnam. "The war is not going to be won by bullets and bombs. We are going to have to win the hearts of the people. We want all medical personnel in Vietnam to begin medical clinics in villages across Vietnam to give aid to the sick and help to the poverty-stricken people in an effort to win their hearts and allegiance. No money is to be spared carrying out this order."

In his unpublished manuscript, *Not by Chance*, Dr. Record tells how he consulted with his best friend, Chaplain Bert Yancey, about his problems with this order. Without language, how would he ever understand the people's medical condition? He had no interpreters to help him communicate. Chaplain Yancey told Dr. Record he knew a Baptist missionary who lived nearby in the village of Thu Duc who had a seminary there. Perhaps the seminary students could be available to help interpret and guide the medical team in this work. He told about going to the missionary's home several times. On one occasion, he brought with him a number of military guys for Christian fellowship.

Chaplain Yancey and Dr. Record came to the seminary to meet with me. When I finished speaking for the morning chapel service, I found them waiting in my office. In the process of introductions, I discovered Dr. Record was from Kernersville, North Carolina, just a few miles from my hometown. He was a layman in his Wesleyan Church. We knew some of the same people in the Wesleyan Church in my hometown. We felt like we were neighbors twelve thousand miles from home! The two men explained to me about Dr. Record's desire to conduct medical clinics among people who had great medical need. He was going to need some help with interpreters and coordinating the ministry.

I said, "Dr. Record, my wife, Rachel, is a graduate of Duke University School of Nursing with a bachelor's of science in nursing degree. She is fluent in the Vietnamese language. We have prayed for a long time for Rachel to have an opportunity to be able to fulfill her calling as a missionary nurse. By law, we must have a medical doctor to be responsible for the medical practice. Rachel will provide the nursing skills. We have been praying intensely for someone to come and help us. You've already shared that when we were praying for help, you were being drafted to serve in the army and were assigned to Vietnam!

"This is too great to be a coincidence! Dr. Record, you are an answered prayer! We need to go to my home now and let you meet Rachel, and the two of you can make plans."

Within minutes, we were introducing Dr. Record to Rachel. As soon as we began talking, Dr. Record suggested he would be available one afternoon a week to bring medicines and whatever else was needed to hold a clinic. Rachel could find the right places for a clinic and serve with him in seeing and treating patients. The more Rachel and he talked about this possibility, the more excited she became. We began to talk about all of our house churches and meeting points around the city. Many of them were in poor areas where people had no available medical care.

"Dr. Record, in the midst of this war, almost every medical doctor is in the military," Rachel said. "Statistics show there is now one medical doctor for every three hundred thousand civilian people in Vietnam. Most people will live all their life and may never have an opportunity to even see the face of a medical doctor!"

I added, "We have a number of seminary students who could be freed up to go to these clinics and help manage the crowds. They could also talk with the patients while they wait to be seen, give them tracts, and help them to know about Jesus and the reason you are giving this medical care to them."

This was one of those exciting times that began with prayer, and with almost lightning speed, God answered. Ideas and plans began flowing fast and furious so the only thing left was to go and do it!

During the next week, we chose a strategic location. The pastor agreed, the time was set, and all the details of notifying the community were worked out. The pastor and his wife and a couple of students were assigned to meet the medical team.

Rachel arrived first and made sure everything was set up. The doctor and his driver arrived in an army jeep with a load of medicines. The clinic opened. Every Friday afternoon, the clinic was held at some location where the need was greatest. Each Friday afternoon, Rachel and Dr. Record would see around one hundred patients.

Skin problems, parasites, upper respiratory issues, and gastric problems were common among the people at every location. Children had numerous sores on their body, which could easily be healed with the right treatment. Parasites were very common, and with the appropriate medicine these could be taken care of.

"Come here, Rachel, and look at this ear. Do you see the ear drum? This is what an infected ear looks like, and here is what we need to do about this."

Another time: "See these sores on this child's head? Here is what we need to do to get them to a point where they can heal."

Dr. Record would then take the necessary action with Rachel assisting with the operation and learning how to do it. Again and again, the doctor would find issues frequently seen in Vietnam, show them to Rachel, and teach her what needed to be done and how to do it. Each clinic became a learning process for Rachel and a healing time for the patient.

On another occasion, a young man came in with a huge goiter on his neck. They recognized it was a malignant tumor. It was so huge it was almost bigger than his head. Both Dr. Record and Rachel realized this cancer had gone too far for medical help. There was nowhere to refer him for any kind of treatment.

This was the most disheartening thing about the clinics. So many problems required continuing care by skilled doctors in adequate medical facilities. But in Vietnam in the midst of war, these were not available. It was heartbreaking to see so many illnesses that could be healed anywhere except the current circumstances in Vietnam.

In 1973, the American armed forces began to withdraw from Vietnam. Within a few months, they were all gone. The succession of military doctors was no longer there to provide for our clinics.

Our social ministries missionary, Gene Tunnell, learned the American military was selling some of its equipment rather than transport it back to the States. He learned that a military canteen vehicle was available. This was a truck fitted with stainless steel inside. It was equipped with a simple kitchen and would take meals out into the field for army troops. We purchased this vehicle and remodeled it inside to make a mobile clinic. The mobile clinic was equipped with an examining room, a treatment room, a medicine room, and other facilities. Rachel administered the mobile clinic. For several years, Rachel had been studying under the teaching of the US Army medical doctors. She had become thoroughly knowledgeable about the most prevalent diseases and ailments of the Vietnamese people and the best ways to bring healing.

In 1971, when we went on our stateside assignment, she studied again at Duke University and the University of North Carolina at Greensboro, North Carolina, to become a nurse practitioner so she could increase her nursing capabilities. She knew the Vietnamese government would require her to be accompanied by a licensed medical doctor when the clinic was in operation. With such a shortage of Vietnamese doctors, where would we ever find a medical doctor? This became a matter of earnest prayer for the Lord to intervene.

One day, Rachel was attending a meeting of medical nongovernmental relief agencies and social workers in Saigon. A number of Vietnamese medical personnel were there. She met a Vietnamese woman who was a medical doctor. As she shared about our mobile clinic, this doctor showed great interest.

Rachel said, "Tell me something about your background and medical training."

The doctor responded, "I interned at the Bowman Gray School of Medicine of Wake Forest University in Winston Salem, North Carolina. This medical school is affiliated with the North Carolina Baptist Hospital. I understand that you and your mobile clinic are affiliated with Baptists. I was excited when I heard that."

Rachel exclaimed, "You cannot know how thrilled I am we have a mutual connection!"

In the conversation, the doctor asked, "Would it be possible for me to begin going with you in the mobile clinic?"

Rachel could hardly contain her excitement. She said, "We have been praying for a medical doctor to go with us to give legitimacy and increased skilled medical care to the patients. Please, please, come with us."

As they were preparing to go on the road for the first clinic, the doctor asked, "Should we wear a cross on our white coat to let people know that the clinic is Christian? I am a Catholic, but I am not sure how Baptists identify themselves."

"We have a large sign on the side of the mobile clinic revealing we are Christian," Rachel said.

Once a week, Rachel and the doctor traveled to various sites where the need was greatest. Our seminary students always met them at these places to give a gospel witness and help with the crowds of people.

In 1974, the situation in South Vietnam was growing more dangerous by the day. Word came the Viet Cong Communists were offering a reward of twenty-five thousand dollars for any Western medical personnel kidnapped and brought to them. The Viet Cong were desperate for medical assistance. With her blond hair and white skin, Rachel was easily recognized as a westerner. Wearing the white coat of medical personnel, and traveling in a mobile clinic clearly marked Christian was now extremely dangerous.

We had to make a decision. Should Rachel continue to be

involved in the mobile clinic? It was her decision to make. After much prayer and discussion, Rachel made her decision.

"Sam, I just can't give up the ministry God has placed in my care. The need is just too great. I have decided I will take every precaution possible. We will change locations every week. We will travel different streets every time we go out. I will no longer ride in the mobile van. I will drive a good distance behind the van and, at times, drive a different route to our destination. We will choose our destinations carefully. We will not dress as medical people. We will make whatever changes need to be made. I simply cannot, I will not quit."

With that decision, she continued the mobile clinic until the day she left Vietnam.

On a trip back to Vietnam fourteen years after the collapse of Saigon, we had the privilege of meeting this wonderful doctor who had accompanied Rachel those years. We learned on the day Vietnam collapsed, she was on the road in the mobile clinic, bringing needed help to desperate people.

Our philosophy as a missionary couple on the field has always been to make sure we are both missionaries. I have always been just as concerned about Rachel's fulfillment of her divine call as she is concerned about my fulfillment of my call. For this reason, we both acquired Vietnamese language and cultural understanding equally. I shared in the maintenance of our home and family so Rachel would have time to acquire language. We shared in my work as much as possible so she would make relationships and learn culture. Our entire family became a bicultural and a bilingual family, at peace whether in an American setting or in a Vietnamese setting. We both have seen our call as husband and wife and mother and father to our children just as much a sacred calling as our vocational call. This means we are both equally committed to both of these callings. I confess I disagree with those who believe a missionary wife's role is only in the home, having the babies and taking care of her husband and family. Missionary wives are divinely called to missions even as they are divinely called to their marriage. Her calling is as valid as my calling.

I have often thought about the fact that Rachel could never have fulfilled that opportunity as a nurse had she not received her call to be a nurse and trained to that end. Nor could she fulfill her call unless she became fluent in the Vietnamese language. She also spared no effort learning Vietnamese culture and ways of living. I watched as she related to her patients, as she took medical histories and explored aches and pains with them. Hers was not just a physical healing ministry. She listened to their life struggles and to their marriage and family problems, and she helped them "bleed off" their struggles, grief, and depression. Her relationship with her patients was almost miraculous, as she gradually opened their hearts up with a loving touch so they could see the difference Christ makes in a person's life. Once again, I was reminded that the Lord knew what our life was going to be like. He put us together to meet the needs He wanted met among people who live in dark places around the world where they don't yet know Him. We both were clay in the Potter's hands, each molded into the unique vessel to do what He wanted done.

CHAPTER 20

THE NIGHT I BECAME A MISSIONARY

A few weeks after our return to Vietnam in May 1967, I was walking to the seminary one morning. A crowd of Vietnamese was gathered at a small intersection three blocks from my house. I decided to see what had attracted so many people.

In the middle of this crowd was an American soldier lying in a veritable pool of mud, wet from his blood. His face was unrecognizable, and his twisted helmet lay nearby, torn from his head. He had been riding a motorcycle. Just as he'd reached the intersection, someone had opened fire, hitting him in the face and upper torso. He had fallen from the speeding motorcycle and lay there, dead and alone, on the side of the road. I looked down into the contorted face of a young blond-headed soldier who would not return home alive, and my heart was broken. I had seen dead Vietnamese soldiers, even enemy soldiers, but this was my first time seeing an American soldier up close, dead from a Communist attack. Somehow, he did not deserve to die all alone, lying in the dirt on the side of a road in a strange country with no one around to identify him and take some kind of action. It was as if he was my brother, and I cared deeply, even though I had no idea who he was or why he had been riding a motorcycle on that dangerous road.

The crowd was just standing around, staring at this grotesque spectacle. At first, anger welled up in me, as I saw no one was even trying to do anything but stare. Immediately, compassion flooded my soul. I yearned to hold him, to protect him, to wipe his face. I wanted to let him know he was not alone and that I cared. There were no cell phones in that day; nor was there even a telephone available. I can never forget the helplessness I felt. Seeing an American military truck approaching, I ran out on the road and waved the truck over. The driver said he would contact the military police. Within fifteen minutes, an emergency vehicle arrived.

The death of this soldier on the side of the road was a stark reminder that American military were all over the country now. All of our soldiers were in danger in the midst of a war that could break out anywhere at any time. Life was totally unpredictable. It was a shock to see one of my own countrymen die this way. Somehow, I knew this was what I would see over and over again in the coming years.

We had just moved to Thu Duc and opened our Baptist seminary there. On our last stateside assignment in 1967, I completed my master's of theology studies, except for writing my thesis. I planned to extend a few months to complete it. The mission wrote asking me to return urgently to Vietnam to open our residential seminary. I was hesitant. I felt those coming for training were in need of a lot more spiritual maturity before we began uprooting them, bringing them to a seminary in a full-time residency program. However, due to the urgent need, I agreed to do this, provided we could continue our distance education. I also realized it would be another four years before I could take another stateside assignment and complete my thesis.

We had decided to locate our new seminary in Thu Duc, a small village about seven miles northeast of Saigon. Locating there would be preferable to locating students in Saigon. where there would be a myriad of things to distract them from their studies. From Thu Duc, it would be easy for them to go the seven miles into Saigon for ministry. Our family also moved just a few blocks from the seminary.

The road from Saigon to Thu Duc was the main highway leading north to the demilitarized zone separating North Vietnam from South Vietnam. It was also the road to Long Binh, the largest American military base in the world. Thu Duc was halfway between Long Binh and Saigon. Military supply convoys of all kinds were constantly traveling that road. We lived just one block off of the highway.

During the years in Thu Duc, we often had groups of military men in our home. Sometimes an Army chaplain would come to our house with a group of men and several gallons of ice cream. We would sing, worship, tell stories, and just "chill out" for a few hours. Thanksgiving and Christmas, we would have our table filled with military guys. This was a great ministry but also a source of great grief. Too often, a chaplain would come to our house and remind us of one of the men who had been in our home and had been killed.

One Saturday, a jeep pulled into our yard. A lieutenant colonel stepped out.

"Sam, I haven't been able to go to church in Saigon for several weeks, and it looks like it will be several weeks more. I'm on my way now to a fire-support base for an extended time and thought I'd just drop in for a few minutes. Actually, I have not been able to give my tithe at church, and I was wondering if you could get it to the International Baptist Church in Saigon. I just don't know when I'll be back."

"Sure, I'll be glad to take it for you. I sure hope everything'll be okay out there where you are going."

"Well, there are always surprises in places like that. Things are really heating up out there for my guys."

Three days later, a chaplain came to our front door, removed his helmet, and looked at me with a tense but unusually stolid face. I knew immediately something was wrong. I invited him in. He evidently had been in the field. His combat clothes were sweaty and dusty. He sat on our tile floor rather than get our furniture dirty. He did not say anything for a while. I just let him sit there quietly. He then looked at me, tears brimming over his eyes. "Do you remember the lieutenant colonel who came to see you the other day?"

"Yes, he was here just three days ago. Left his tithe for me to take to church for him."

"Well, he and his driver just hit a land mine." His voice trailed off, he swallowed hard, and almost in a hush, he said, "Both of them were killed."

We were both overwhelmed with emotion. It seemed to help both of us to talk about him and what a wonderful Christian model he was to the men under his command.

On another occasion, a chaplain entered our home, looked at me without even speaking a greeting, and burst into tears. He slumped down on our tile floor, leaned against the wall, and sobbed.

When he was finally able to talk, he said, "I went off base into the field to conduct services for several groups of our men, something I often do when they are in the field for an extended time. My chaplain's assistant went with me. Suddenly, we were caught in a firefight with Viet Cong soldiers. My assistant was moving ahead of me. I saw him go down. I knew he was hit, and it was bad. He never said a word. I sat down beside him there in the bushes. I cradled him in my arms while his life slipped away, and there was nothing, nothing I could do. No one could save him." He paused for a few moments, just looking at the floor. Then, "I just needed a quiet place where I could, kind of, open up my emotions. You know, I can't do that in front of our men."

One after another of these grief experiences gradually built up a powerful force of emotion within me. This was especially true when I wrote letters to widows or parents in America. The pain of so much grief over the years was more than I wanted to admit to.

Slowly through constant warfare, the country was descending into a survival-of-the-fittest atmosphere. The struggle to survive in the general population caused a breakdown of law and order. With husbands away in the military and so many war widows, it became increasingly difficult for Vietnamese families to stay together and maintain a standard of living. To survive, people began to do things that, under normal circumstances, they would never do. Prostitution, robbery, petty theft, and other activities became the normal course of living. A simple act like going to the market required constant alert. This was not characteristic of the Vietnamese culture, but the society was gradually becoming a war culture.

Unconsciously, my method of handling all the death and deterioration of life in society was to stuff my feelings inside. Unconsciously, I had to control my feelings, lest they explode in unacceptable ways. After a time, all my emotions became wooden and unfeeling. Worst of all, I was not feeling love as I had once felt it. Anger was always just under the surface and ready to emerge at the least little happening. My life had become a cauldron of emotions, most of them negative. I had to struggle to keep them inside.

In a way, these emotions were like knots in a rope that extended all the way to my heart. These knots completely blocked positive emotions of love and compassion. They began affecting my behavior in ways I did not even recognize. Deep down, I knew someday, if I wanted to reclaim a life of joy and continue to serve my Lord, I would have to face this reality and deal with it

On December 31, 1968—Western New Year's Eve—our family stayed up until midnight playing games, singing, and having prayer. Together, we enjoyed welcoming in the New Year. We all went to bed shortly after midnight. For some reason, at around five in the morning, I awoke and was conscious of a strange uneasiness. I decided to check around the house to see if anything was wrong. The scene that greeted me in the living room told me why I had woken up.

We had been robbed. Everything was gone. The thieves had taken the children's new bicycles they'd received for Christmas, my sound equipment, cassette tapes, records, and even things in the kitchen—everything was gone. The back door was leaning at an angle, wide open.

I quickly ran outside to see if anyone might still be around. The streets were deserted. First, I felt a deep sense of disappointment and regret. Then anger began to take over. I seethed for days. I reported the robbery to the local police, but they did not seem interested.

About a week later, I needed to go into Saigon. I turned the key to start my engine, and there was no sound. I knew my battery must be dead. I went around to the back of my Volkswagen Microbus to check the battery and discovered, to my dismay, that someone had stolen my battery!

Two weeks later, several seminary students awakened me early in the morning. They said, "Pastor, come quick. Someone has broken into the seminary and stolen almost everything we have."

When I arrived at the seminary, I saw in the kitchen that someone had stolen bags of rice, kitchen appliances, bowls, chopsticks, and about everything else they could possibly carry off. The thieves had broken into my office and taken all our new office equipment. With this third robbery in such a short time, I was furious. I literally seethed with anger. I thought to myself, "I have come twelve thousand miles to Vietnam to help people and minister to them. What do I get for it? They steal me blind."

We began a search to find out if any of the students were involved, but nothing turned up. We went to the police station in the nearby village. The police were no help at all. I began to keep a watch at night to see if I could see anything unusual happening. One night, I saw a strange sight. Around 1:00 a.m., a police jeep stopped about fifty yards up the road from our house. Two police officers got out, carrying what looked to be empty sacks. I continued to watch. About ten minutes later, the police jeep blinked its lights twice. Two men stepped out of the shadows and walked to the jeep. They threw two filled sacks into the jeep. They left without turning on any headlights. The next morning, I heard another house had been robbed.

I went to the police station and asked to see the director of the police. He welcomed me into his office and asked what he could do for me. I told him what I had seen and that I suspected those men in a police jeep dressed like police were the people who had just broken into my home and the seminary and stolen all of our possessions. I expressed my belief that, as the director of the police, he would want to know this since the people doing this were posing as police officers. I said surely no police officers would do something like this. I did not want to accuse him of running a crooked police force. I noticed in the back of the police station a number of boxes of television sets stacked up unopened, as though they had just come off of a truck. He was polite and said he would look into the matter.

Two nights later, a young police officer dressed in civilian clothes visited our home. He seemed nervous. "I have known your family for a long time. I know something about the Christian faith, but I am not a Christian yet. I have learned to greatly respect your family and the seminary students. I am so sorry you have been robbed.

"I am here on my own volition to help you understand something very important. Thu Duc doesn't have much police protection. I advise you not to investigate this robbery any more. The story you told our police director disturbs all of us. If you continue your investigation, something bad will happen to you. I want to warn you and try to prevent that from happening. No one knows I have visited here tonight, but I assure you I know what I am talking about. Please leave it alone. Go on with your work."

The young police officer left our house. I did not pursue the matter any further, but it simply increased the anger and helplessness. I had absolutely nowhere I could turn for help.

Weeks later, one of the Protestant chaplains in the US Air Force at the large military base in Cam Ranh Bay called. He said, "The Protestant men of the chapel have decided to open an orphanage here in Cam Ranh Bay. They are concerned about all the war orphans in this area. They have nowhere to go, and no one seems to take care of them. We want to help those whose parents have been killed in the war by opening a very good orphanage. We have tried every way possible to get permission, but the government will not respond. Would you be willing to go to the government and be a liaison for us to get Vietnamese government permission to set up the orphanage?"

I agreed to help.

I went to the appropriate ministry of government and asked what we needed to do to get permission to open an orphanage. The young woman gave me a stack of forms to fill out. The stack was at least three inches high. I filled out the forms in duplicate and returned them to the ministry. She looked through them and said, 'You should have filled these out in triplicate." With that, she gave me additional forms. I took them home, filled them out in triplicate and returned them to the ministry. I waited while she looked through them. She then said, "You are short one form." I asked her for the form, took the entire file home, filled that form in triplicate and took it back. By now, my attitude was less than honorable! The young woman gave me a receipt and suggested I wait for her to contact me.

Six weeks later, a person in the air force called and asked about the progress of the application. I went to the ministry and inquired. A young woman went to look for the file. After almost an hour she returned and said, "What application is this? What are you asking me to do?" I showed her my receipt. She took it, and about one hour later, she returned to say, "I am sorry. I can't locate your file. I think we have lost it."

I was furious. Never had I seen such inefficiency. I asked for the forms again, took them home, and filled them out in triplicate. I returned them to the ministry and asked for a receipt. I tried my best to smile and be polite. Inside I was filled with anger. This, added to the recent events of being robbed, intensified a growing sense of frustration, helplessness, and anger.

A few days later on Saturday afternoon, I was in Saigon for the day. When I got in my Volkswagen van to return home, it would not start. No matter what I did, I could not fix it. Often ambushes occurred on the road between Thu Duc and Saigon after dark. I needed to be home by sunset. I asked several taxis before I could find one willing to take me out to Thu Duc. No one wanted to drive that road in the late afternoon. We began the trip weaving in and out through the maze of pedestrians, bicycles, trucks, army jeeps, horses and wagons, motorcycles, ox carts, and every other imaginable vehicle.

The taxi driver asked me politely, "You have been in Vietnam a long time, haven't you?"

"Yes, for many years."

"Then you must like the Vietnamese people?"

At that point in my life, answering this question was difficult given all that had happened recently. My house had been robbed. My car battery, stolen. The seminary, robbed. Even the effort to help war babies by starting an orphanage had become a nightmare. I thought about the fact that I was a Christian, a missionary, a pastor, and a seminary president. I replied in a manner appropriate to all of these titles, if not a bit hypocritically. "Oh, yes. I love the Vietnamese people."

In the midst of all of the traffic, he turned his face toward me. He looked straight in my eyes and said, "What do you love about us?"

It was not a good time to ask me a question like that! I wanted to say to him, "Don't push it, brother! I don't want to talk about it!" Given all that had happened over previous weeks, this was not a good time.

I braced myself and tried my best to answer his question. Whatever I said in reply could not have been significant.

Arriving home, I paid him the exorbitant fare he exacted of me. I went into the house dejected. Rachel had dinner on the table. I tried to eat, but I had a huge lump in my throat. I was deeply concerned about my state of mind and attitude. I realized acutely my love for the Vietnamese people was gone.

I have always believed, if you could take the Christian faith, put it in a pot on the stove, and boil away all the excess, what you would have left in its purest essence would be love. That purest essence of the Christian faith is God's unconditional love. I realized I no longer possessed that kind of love. I wondered if it had ever really been there. At any rate, it was gone. I had allowed the circumstances of life to destroy it.

I went to bed but couldn't sleep. After tossing and turning for hours, I went into our living room, knelt down, and began to pour out my heart to the Lord. I confessed my lack of love for the very people to whom I was divinely called to be God's servant. I confessed disappointment in myself because I had allowed the negative events of life to take away my love for the people.

During my prayer, I realized I had a big decision to make. I had failed as a missionary. I had failed as a true servant of the Lord. How could I stay on the mission field if I did not have the very essence of the Christian faith I was offering to others? I decided the best thing for me to do was to begin the process of packing up our few remaining belongings and return to the States. "I am through as a missionary," I thought.

No matter how much I tried to go back to bed, the Lord would not let me go. I struggled in prayer all night.

Sometime in the wee hours of the morning, God spoke to me. There are times when our backs are completely against the wall, and our strength is gone. That is when God steps in and intervenes. I have no doubt that God Himself intervened in my life in that moment of total defeat. His words welled up in my heart. They penetrated my consciousness with unmistakable clarity. It was a feeling of absolute oneness and intimacy with God.

"My son, you are not in Vietnam because you love the Vietnamese people. You are here because I love them, and I want to love them through you."

God loves all the people of the world, including Vietnamese people, and has even from the foundation of the world. Throughout history, God has been in the process of communicating His love. He communicated His love by becoming flesh and blood in Jesus Christ, dying on the cross, being raised again from the dead, and dwelling in us. Now we are the channels by which God wants to communicate His love. Among Jesus's last words to His disciples uttered in the upper room following his resurrection was, "Peace be with you. As the Father has sent me, I am sending you" John 20:21 (NIV).

We often confuse our human love with His eternal love. Human love is so fragile. One word can destroy human love. One gesture or facial expression can take away our human love. But God's love is eternal. Nothing can separate us from the love of God. God's love knows no condition. His love is freely given.

When I received my divine call to go to Vietnam, I did not know one Vietnamese person. I did not know one word in the Vietnamese language. I knew nothing of the people of Vietnam, their customs, or their culture. I only knew that God was calling me there. How could I love them when I did not even know them? Why did God choose Rachel and me to go there to those people? Now I know God had something of ultimate importance He wanted to communicate to them through our lives.

I gave my life to the Lord to be used by Him. For a long time in Vietnam, my love for the people seemed to grow. My interest and absorption into the life of the people and their culture was exciting. I was excited to learn their language. I enjoyed their food. My commitment to them was unquestionable. Humanly speaking, I really loved them. But human love is too fragile to weather the tests and trials of cross-cultural living. I have no doubt God Himself called me and engendered in me the interest and love for the Vietnamese people. Why? Because He needed someone to go to them and embody His great love for them and to communicate His desire that they be saved. The problem was I saw that call as my call more than His call to me. I saw that love as my love, not His love. I was trying to fulfill a divine calling in my own human power, not His power.

Vietnam, like most cultures around the world, is a non-Christian culture. Therefore, the people conduct themselves by a value system not informed by God's love and Christian teachings. Vietnam at this time became a culture torn apart by war. Every day of their lives carried a threat to their continued existence. The Vietnamese people learned to survive. To survive in that hostile society, they had to become tough. They found every way possible to provide the necessities of life. The one thing they had no chance of finding was the peace and contentment derived from experiencing God's unconditional love. Thus, the behavior destroying my human love was natural for them because they had never known anything else.

I went to Vietnam as a Christian and a missionary because the Vietnamese people are lost without Christ. They deserve the opportunity to know Jesus and to be saved. I had no right to expect them to live their lives and conduct themselves as Christians. When they robbed or acted as though they had little care or concern for even their own people, I had no right to become angry and condemn them. This kind of behavior was the very reason God had placed me in their midst to show them a better way and a more eternal way.

Why would I cease to be a Christian simply because people acted less than Christian? Why should I cease my missionary calling simply because the people acted like people who do not know Jesus? My very purpose in life was to help them know Christ and have a new life in Him!

What I did not realize was that my human love was so weak it could not take the stress of that environment. I would have to be emptied of myself, my own strength, and my own love or lack of it and then filled to overflowing with His power, His eternal love, and the very presence of God Himself.

There, in the early hours of that morning, I realized in a fresh new way what the apostle Paul was saying in his letter to the Galatian Christians. He said, "I have been crucified with Christ; and it is no longer I who live, but Christ lives in me; and the life that

I now live in the flesh I live by faith in the Son of God who loved me and delivered Himself up for me" Galatians 2:20 (NIV).

Clearly, I had to lay myself on the altar and die so that He could live through me. My only choice was to surrender my life totally to the Lord and allow Him to empty me completely and refill me with His presence. I would become one with Him in a way I had never experienced before. My love, or lack of it, would have to give way to His eternal, unconditional love. My strength would have to become His strength.

That moment in my life was a miraculous time experiencing the ministry of the Lord—breaking, remolding, and remaking me into a new person and a new instrument in God's hands, one with complete trust and absolute obedience to Him.

The following morning, I was walking through a market area. I had walked through there many times before. A woman with leprosy sat at the entrance to the market. She had pads of ragged material wrapped around her arms and knees as she pulled herself along the ground into the market entryway. She sat on a bamboo mat day after day with a small bowl in front of her. She hoped someone would drop in a coin. Leprosy had almost completed its work of deforming her body. A gaping hole was where her nose used to be. Huge holes were on each side of her head where her ears had been. One tooth protruded at an angle from her mouth. Her fingers and toes were completely gone. Her face was so deformed it was hardly recognizable as a face.

Up to now, when I walked by her, I had turned my face away to keep from looking at her. This morning, I looked at her as though I was seeing her through Jesus's eyes. I was filled with feelings of compassion. My first thought was probably no person in the world loves this woman in this condition. Surely no one ever touches her, talks with her, or shows any kind of love for her. I could not resist sitting down on the edge of her mat.

I began to talk to her. "Chị ôi, I want you to know there is a God who loves you. He is always with you. You are never alone.

He wants you to know He loves you with an unfailing love. He does not look at the outside, at how beautiful or how bad we look. He looks at your heart, and He wants to love you unconditionally.

"This body gets old and frail, and sometimes it gets sick. This body is just temporary. It will deteriorate and rot away. But someday, God wants to replace this old body with a new body, a spiritual body, a heavenly body. He wants you to come home with Him. He created you, loves you, and wants you to be with him, healthy and whole forever."

I talked to her about Jesus and how she had hope and eternal life in Him. I searched her face to see if she had some faint flicker of recognition of what I was saying. The disease had so ravaged her body that most likely the muscles in her face could not allow a response.

Every morning I stopped to see her. Knowing how sometimes we long for a soft, healing touch, I would place my hand on her shoulder or touch her gnarled nub where her fingers once were. I always looked for some response. Some weeks later, as I talked to her one morning, I am sure I saw a tear in her eye and watched it roll slowly down her cheek.

Much later, I began to realize this was a picture of how God relates to us. We are sinners—far from what God created us to be. Sin ravages our life and utterly distorts the image of God in us. God keeps approaching us in His great eternal love. Even though our behavior reflects no response to that love, He never gives up or ceases to love us. No doubt our behavior and attitudes often are so abhorrent that normal bounds of human reasoning would expect Him to turn His face away from us. But His love is eternal and keeps reaching out regardless of our sin. God does not want anyone to perish without knowing His eternal love, which He has given to us in Christ Jesus.

I often have thought how loving an old leper woman, as physically deformed as she was, may be easier than loving someone who is spiritually or emotionally unlovely. Often, we know those in the same household or in the same church or in the same class or workplace who are so very difficult to love. They hurt us. They reject us. Perhaps they consciously or unconsciously do things that threaten our good name or our sense of well-being. I, myself, was living in the midst of an entire society that, in many ways, was very much like this. We have every reason to turn away from them.

Our fragile, human love cannot possibly survive. The apostle Paul states it so clearly: "For I am convinced that neither death nor life, neither angels nor demons, neither the present nor the future, nor any powers, neither height nor depth, nor anything else in all creation, will be able to separate us from the love of God that is in Christ Jesus our Lord" Romans 8:38-39 (NIV).

Love requires no response but the response of genuine love returned. It demands no reward. It is love purely for the sake of love. The only way changes can occur in them or in us is when we fall in love with our Lord. We focus on Him and become one with Him, and then He is able to love through us when we no longer can. He takes our eyes, our hands, our feet, our voice, our gifts, and our talents. He fills them with His ministering presence.

This is the night I became a missionary after spending six years in the field. My life was never the same after this experience. At the very core of my staying fifty-four years in the mission field is what I learned and experienced that early morning in the little village of Thu Duc. God intervened in my life, transforming anger into love, despair into hope, and surrender into victory.

CHAPTER 21

THE WEIGHT OF GRIEF, THE JOY OF BIRTH

Lunar New Year, January 30, 1968, it was two o'clock in the morning. We were awakened by the sound of guns in the distance. Immediately, we knew this was not fireworks for the Lunar New Year. This was not a small skirmish such as we had become accustomed to hearing. This was prolonged firing with heavy explosions.

Our family stayed up late to see the New Year begin. In Vietnam, the Lunar New Year is the biggest celebration of the entire year. It is like Thanksgiving, Christmas, New Year, and the Fourth of July all rolled up into one big celebration. The fireworks we'd heard at midnight had been loud, but these sounds were not fireworks.

I looked at my clock. It was 2:00 a.m. The sound was now deafening. We were moments from being impacted. "Rachel, we better get the children on the floor and cover them up." Moments later, something ripped through the tile on our roof. My heart was beating rapidly, my breathing shallow. I was almost paralyzed with fear. Crawling from window to window as cautiously as possible, I tried to see what was happening. Furtive figures darted in and out of the shadows. Even if we could sneak out in the darkness, there was no possibility of escape.

Some days previous to this when we were not at home, an American contractor had left a .38 caliber pistol and ammunition wrapped in a shoe box. A note was taped to the box, saying, "This is my gun. I will not need it anymore, but you may." I did not want that gun in my home. I didn't want anyone to suspect I was anything other than a missionary. Not sure how I could safely get rid of it, I had temporarily hidden it in a bottom drawer of our desk and locked it. I could not picture myself using a gun under any circumstances. I had done enough of that during my military service in the Korean War. In fact, I saw myself laying down my gun, which brings death, and taking up the Word of God, which brings life. This was my mission in life now.

As I saw the proximity of enemy soldiers, my first thought was they just might begin searching house to house. I knew at times like this, many of them were given drugs to allay any feelings of sympathy or guilt that would hinder their effectiveness at killing. They could be wild and uncontrollable. I simply could not allow them to come in unhindered and bring death and destruction to our family. In the darkness, I went to my desk and pulled the pistol with ammunition out of the drawer. I loaded it and waited for whatever was about to happen. The enemy was gradually taking over our village.

At about 3:00 a.m., the firing ceased. Everything was deathly quiet. I sat there looking at the gun in my hand. What had happened to me? I'd never dreamed I would have a gun in my hand again. My guilt almost overwhelmed me. I took the gun back to my desk, unloaded it, and put it back in the drawer. I asked the Lord to forgive me for my weakness in those moments. I crawled back to the windows and waited.

There was no way to know what all of this meant. Was it over? What were they after? Why were they attacking our sleepy little village?

Suddenly, the firing broke out again, closer than ever. With no hesitation, I ran back to the desk, loaded the gun, and again crawled from window to window. I determined, guilt or not, if anyone tried to come into our home, I would not hesitate to use it. When my wife and my children were threatened with death, I decided with all of my being, I would do everything in my power to keep my family safe. In spite of my misgivings, I was glad I had a gun. To this day, I am convinced that, on that night, I did the right thing under the circumstances. I have no feelings of guilt.

It was not until the next morning, as we listened intently to the radio, that we learned the attack on our village was just a small part of a nationwide invasion by Communist forces in a concerted effort to take over South Vietnam. This event was popularly known as the Tet Offensive. They attacked every area of Saigon and every major city in Vietnam. Days before, they brought weapons and ammunition secretly into the Saigon Racetrack and concealed the weapons there. This became a rendezvous point for literally hundreds of troops. From there, they spread out over the city attacking preplanned targets in a wild night of terror. During the next day, Communist soldiers were found wandering around the city in a daze as the effects of the drugs they were given began to wear off. Many could not even remember what had happened that night.

The Communists had control of our village for five days. We remained in our house, lest they see foreigners lived there. At night, we could sneak outside in the dark and see the war raging around us. Helicopters and American AC-130 gunships circled our house and poured fire down into the village marketplace. Every third bullet was a tracer bullet glowing red with heat. It looked like hot lava was being poured down out of heaven. During the day, jet planes dived right over our house and released their bombs. We could see the bombs twisting in the air, falling with a tremendous jarring sound into areas five hundred to seven hundred yards away. Many nights, the B-52 bombers would drop a huge number of bombs in areas not far from our home. The entire house would shake like an earthquake. In the morning when Rachel and I got out of bed, the only place the pillow was white was where our heads lay. The rest was covered with fine dust falling from the ceiling from the tremor of the bombings.

We were fortunate to live slightly downhill from the village water tower. Electricity had been cut off for days, disabling the water pumps. Since we lived downhill from the tower, we could open a spigot and get a small amount of water, which had leaked into the pipes and flowed down toward our house. Within a minute, the water in the pipe was exhausted. We were so blessed we lived there in that spot, or we would have been without water the entire time. We always kept a good supply of food for occasions like this, so by being careful, we had food the entire time.

On the fifth day, the Vietnamese Army drove the enemy forces out of the village. It was a great feeling to realize we had been through all of that and were still alive and free.

Our family was standing together on our porch, enjoying being out in the sunlight in peace and quiet. Two American armed personnel carriers were passing by our house. Seeing us, they slammed on their brakes. A lieutenant colonel came to our porch.

"Where did we evacuate you these past few days?"

"Colonel, we were not evacuated anywhere. We have been here the entire time."

"No, you couldn't have been," he said. "We sent in armed troops and evacuated all Americans out of this area!"

"I'm sorry, Colonel, but I beg to differ. Our family has been here in this house for the past five days. We knew nothing about an evacuation!"

"What kind of weapon do you have?"

"I just happened to have a .38 caliber pistol."

"Man, that would do nothing but make them mad. I'm going to leave you an M16 rifle. You need something to defend yourself."

"Please forgive me, but I can't accept that. We are missionaries here, and we have no guards or protection. You see, we cannot afford for the people around us to suspect we are military or have some other occupation. Our life depends on that. Everyone around here knows we are here only to minister to the people. I really thank you for the offer."

With that, he bade us farewell, and they went on their way.

Our family drove around the city to see the conditions. Thu Duc was a disaster area. Blocks of houses were totally destroyed. The central market no longer existed. The evangelical church building in Thu Duc was almost destroyed. Outside walls had collapsed, and most of the ceiling was gone. I noted the pulpit area especially. The Lord's Supper Table sat in front of where the pulpit used to be. It was totally untouched. The pastor told me later he and his family had crowded under that Lord's Supper table at the height of the attack to find safety. It was a miracle they did not sustain even the slightest scratch, even as the church building fell around them.

At one point, we had to stop to let traffic go by. I looked to the right, and at the foot of a tree was a dead body minus one of its legs. As I looked up the trunk of the tree, I was shaken to see a foot, severed, sandal still on it, caught between the tree trunk and a large tree limb. I hoped the children did not see this and have it inscribed indelibly on their minds. However, years later when our oldest son, Stephen, was studying at Golden Gate Baptist Theological Seminary (now Gateway Seminary), he wrote a very moving poem about that foot dismembered from its body, hanging in the crotch of a tree. That was the first I knew he had seen it.

In the days following, there was real question whether more attacks would follow. Those of us in the Saigon area decided it would be best if our wives and children went out of the country for a while until things settled down. Six families were living in the Saigon area. The board gave permission for wives and children to evacuate to Bangkok, Thailand. They would allow one husband to go each week so one husband would be there all the time to take care of any needs the families might have. This meant every sixth week I could go and spend a week with my family. The mission in Thailand provided temporary apartments in various high-rise apartment buildings for the families.

One reason it was good for Rachel to go is because she was six months pregnant. If another attack occurred and anything happened to the bridge over the river between our house and

Saigon, we would not be able to get to the hospital. Because she was six months pregnant already, she would not be permitted to fly at a later date if the need arose.

We realized she would have to give birth in Bangkok. This meant at least three months away from home. As we thought about the meaning of this, we realized we were entering one of those really tough times in life. We had made it through the Tet Offensive, a very tense time for our family. Now we would add a time of separation, during which Rachel would have the care of our three children during the last three months of pregnancy. I was living alone in a highly volatile location in Vietnam. We had faced many tough times, but this would take more faith and trust in the Lord than we had ever needed. It would be too difficult to describe how Rachel and I felt as we hugged, looked deeply into each other's eyes, and said goodbye. I almost lost my composure when my little nine-year-old daughter looked at me with concern and said, "Dad, are you going to be okay?" My family boarded the plane for Bangkok. It was a lonely drive home to Thu Duc.

I was living alone in our home, trying to keep the seminary going. It was difficult because the main highway between Saigon and Long Binh was unsafe. We lived just a block off of that highway and very near a major intersection. Almost every night, there was an ambush of military vehicles on that highway. Sometimes the ambushes would occur just a block from our house. The first time it happened, I jumped out of bed, dressed, and tried to get a look at what was happening. The second time I woke up, dressed quickly, and just waited. The third time I woke up, lay there for a while, and then went back to sleep. The fourth night, I woke up, turned over, and went back to sleep.

That was the way with the war. While we never got accustomed to living in the midst of war, with each passing event, there was less visceral reaction. I sometimes likened it to the proverbial frog that sits in a pot of water. As the fire beneath slowly heats the water, the frog becomes adjusted to the increasing heat. Finally, even though the water boils and the frog is going to die, he still does not jump out because he has adjusted. I was at times afraid I was becoming like that. This would mean my alertness and caution would not be intense enough to be aware of danger. My natural reaction for self-preservation would be weakened.

In May, a second offensive began, as Communist insurgents again tried to take over large segments of the country. This was not as serious and disastrous as the Tet Offensive. The area where I was living was not significantly affected, but unexpectedly, an event happened that very much affected me personally.

It was Saturday morning, and I had to go into Saigon. Mornings were always safe on the highway, so I was somewhat relaxed as I drove toward Saigon. I did wonder why there was no traffic on the highway. About halfway to Saigon, a bridge crossed a large branch of the Saigon River. As I approached, I noticed the highway was closed. A Vietnamese military policeman was crouching in the ditch at the side of the road. He motioned for me to stop. I stopped and waited for a minute. He continued to kneel and concentrate on the tree line at the end of the rice paddy.

I walked over to him and asked, "Do you have any idea when the road might be open?"

His response was quick. "Get down, now! There was an attack at the bridge, and the large right span of the bridge has collapsed into the river. Snipers are all around here. I have been telling cars to turn around and leave because it is dangerous. Get back in your car and leave as fast as you can."

Just as I turned toward my car, I heard the burst of fire from an AK-47 rifle some distance away. Simultaneously, the asphalt between me and the military policeman exploded in a cloud of dirt and asphalt. The asphalt hit my pants legs, and a piece hit my hand, shallowly puncturing the skin. The military policeman opened fire in the direction of the shooting. He waved me back to my van yelling "Mau di, mau di" (Go, go quickly)! He kept firing as though covering my retreat. I turned the van around and headed back home. I estimated the bullets from the AK-47 hit within about six inches of my feet and legs. It wasn't until I arrived home to an empty house, all alone, cleaning my slight wound, that I realized how close I had come to losing my life.

This was one of those moments when everything about life was called into question. I thought of the night not long before when the bomb had gone off beside my van in the Chinese area of Saigon and how the piece of cement had been lying so close beside my body. I thought of the roadblock on the road to My Tho. I was miraculously delivered from that disastrous roadblock. Fresh on my mind was the Tet Offensive and trying to keep the Communist rebels from coming into our house. Now, again a miracle! I owe my life to a Viet Cong soldier, who was evidently a poor shooter.

Our family had now been in Vietnam for six years, much of that time in the midst of a war that was totally unpredictable in its location and timing. My first emotional reaction to what had just happened was fear and fatigue. It was one of those weak points in life when it would be easy to just quit. How long should we continue to take this risk? Was there a point when enough is enough? Was the Lord trying to say something to me through all this? What was going to happen next time? How many more times would I get?

My second reaction was an overwhelming thanksgiving to the Lord for His protection. I thought of Rachel in Bangkok with our three children, expecting our fourth within two to three weeks. I thought about how much I loved her and our children. My heart almost broke when I thought about what might have happened to our family if I had lost my life. I am not ashamed of the tears that flowed. Never had I longed to be with Rachel and our children more than at that moment. Never had our house seemed so void of life.

As I processed all that had happened, I began to realize this was the third time the Lord had given me another life. I easily could have lost this one.

"He must have much more for me to do," I thought. "From

this point on in life, I cannot, I will not, I must not waste another day. Life is too short. I am going to make every day count for something." I determined to never again put off until tomorrow what could be done today! I became an even more driven person—driven by a burning desire for the Lord to show me what He wanted me to be and to do. "I will not rest until I have followed His perfect will, whatever it is and wherever He leads." Increasingly, my life was being filled with absolute trust in God's perfect will.

One morning in late May, I received a call from an air force chaplain at Cam Ranh Bay. He thanked me that the papers I had submitted for government permission to open the orphanage had been approved. The board of directors was meeting to set up the procedures and organization for the orphanage. They were going to develop a job description for a director for the orphanage. They wanted my advice and counsel.

On the morning of May 28, 1968, I flew on Air Vietnam to Nhatrang. From there, I needed to get to the small village of Ba Ngoi, and transportation would be provided into the Cam Ranh Bay Air Force Base. Missionary Bob Compher, who was working in Nhatrang, met me at the airport. I asked him about the best way to get to Cam Ranh Bay. He said the best way would have been to catch a military plane from Saigon directly to Cam Ranh. Since I did not do that, I could either go by bus or by train almost to Ba Ngoi. Then I could get a taxi or motorbike to the base. He advised against going by bus because the road was not safe. I took the train.

The train to Ba Ngoi was a very old train. It pushed a heavy, metal platform in front of the engine to protect the engine should it hit an explosive on the tracks. The seats in the cars were actually wooden benches running along the side of the car. You sat with your back to the windows and faced toward the center of the car. I noticed the sides of the passenger cars were very thin, easily punctured by anything. The floor was made of plywood. There were three passenger cars and eight or ten freight cars with military equipment. I was the only foreigner on the train. Riding on top of the front car and the rear car was a contingent of Vietnamese military, serving to guard against an attack. Nothing looked safe to me, but I was there, and I might as well keep going.

We were halfway to Ba Ngoi when shots rang out. All of us fell prostrate on the floor. The train began to slowly grind to a halt. The troops on top of the train dropped to the ground and returned fire with heavy shooting and a number of grenades.

The firing died down as quickly as it had started. We sat there for several minutes, and then the train slowly began to move forward again. Everyone quietly resumed his or her seat. No one spoke, cried, screamed, or made any reaction. It was as though this kind of thing happened every day so why worry!

The meeting began the next morning, May 29, 1968. I made my report. When I finished, I began to have an urgent desire to go to Bangkok to see my family. I felt like I would die if I did not go immediately. I prayed while the meeting was going on. The more I prayed, the more urgent my desire became. At midmorning, I told the group I would have to leave to go to Bangkok. "Please forgive me," I said. "Can you get me a seat on a plane for Saigon?"

The chaplains were very gracious and within an hour I was on my way to Saigon. I went directly to the Foreign Ministry to get an exit visa. Normally, this would take three working days. I told them it was urgent I go to Bangkok today. They said to return at three o'clock, and they would try to have the visa ready. I purchased my ticket. At four o'clock, I was on a plane to Bangkok.

It was dark when I arrived at our apartment. In those days, there were no cell phones or email to relay messages, so the family had no idea I was coming. Our reunion was one to remember forever. The joy was unspeakable.

After the children were in bed, Rachel shared with me that all the missionaries in Bangkok were on the coast of Thailand in a retreat. There were no families left in the city. She said, "I knew you were coming sometime soon, but I was praying about what I would do if our baby were to arrive early. There would be no one but a

Thai helper to take care of the children. Not one of our missionaries is in the city to take me to the hospital. I was wondering how I could get in touch with you to let you know. I knew if our baby came, I would have to take a taxi alone to the hospital. How did you know to come right now at this crucial moment?"

I told her of my meeting in Cam Ranh and how I was positive the Lord had prompted me and opened the way for me to come. I told her how I'd thought that, if I didn't come immediately, I would die!

She said, "I have an appointment with the obstetrician tomorrow morning. She is going on vacation, and this is the last time I can meet with her before our baby comes. If everything is ready, I think our baby is going to be born tomorrow."

Though I was utterly exhausted from the emergency travel, I could not sleep. All I wanted to do was just to hold Rachel in my arms as securely as I could. I thought of this servant of the Lord whom I loved so much going through all of that uncertainty alone. I could sense her concern about the care of our children in her absence, about having a baby alone in Bangkok, and a myriad of other things. Not once did she complain about the situation we were in. I was reminded again how God had given me someone who was uniquely equipped to handle monumental problems with an unshakeable faith. I could not keep from thanking the Lord over and over that He had miraculously communicated with me the urgency of my coming to Bangkok to be with her!

The next morning, May 30, we went to the Seventh Day Adventist Hospital. At two thirty that afternoon, Michael David James was born. We named him Michael because of the very critical time when he was born. We had just come through the Tet Offensive, and we were somehow protected from harm. These were some of the darkest days we had experienced in our life together. Michael was the archangel in the Old Testament who was the "protector and defender of Israel" in their darkest hour. Early Christianity considered Michael to be the healing angel. This little life, which we named Michael, came to us in a very dark hour, giving us new joy, hope, and life as a family in difficult times.

Michael's birth is just one of many, many times when God prompted, we followed, and miracles occurred.

I remained in Bangkok while Rachel was healing, and we were all adjusting to a new baby in our family. One morning, a postman came to our door with a telegram addressed to me. The telegram had been delivered to Saigon several days before, but I was not there to receive it. It was then forwarded to me in Bangkok. It was from the International Mission Board. I opened it. It informed me my father had died. I knew he was ill with cancer. When we left the States on our last visit, I knew I was saying goodbye to him for the last time. His death now was a shock. He had already been dead for four days. I did not know it. I made an appointment at the post office to call my family in the United States. I was given a six o'clock reservation. That would be 6:00 a.m. in North Carolina.

When I called home, my older brother answered. I explained why I had not called before now. His response was, "The funeral was yesterday. We were wondering why we hadn't heard from you." My heart ached to be there with my family. That was impossible; it would have been even if I had been notified earlier. The cost of flying to the States was more than we could bear. Also, the policy of the board at that time was we were not allowed to return to the States in the middle of a term of service.

As I became busy with so many things in Vietnam, I gradually adjusted to my father's death. However, since I was not there when he died and did not get to participate in the funeral, I did not have a chance to grieve. The grief was stuffed inside with all the rest of the grief from living in the midst of the suffering and death occurring all around us.

When we were preparing for stateside assignment after this second four-year term in Vietnam, my mind turned to how I could best prepare myself for future ministry in Vietnam. I originally was scheduled to finish my master's of theology thesis and to do my PhD in New Testament studies. This would give me all the credentials necessary to operate our Baptist seminary. Several things happened that changed those plans.

Due to so many Vietnamese husbands away or killed in the war, women were forced to work outside the home to support their families. There was no childcare available anywhere. Masses of children wandered and played in the streets of the city. They were unable to go to school. They had little teaching at home. I personally became concerned about this situation. We decided to open a preschool/kindergarten teacher training program at the seminary. There were many young Christian women who could study necessary parts of the seminary curriculum and also study a full teacher training program. A female missionary in her last years on the field in Bangkok was a specialist in preschool education. She agreed to come to Saigon and design the curriculum for this program. She would stay at the seminary and train these teachers until she retired.

We admitted ten of these young women. One of the women was Chinese, a member of our Chinese church in Cholon, the Chinese section of the city. During Miss Binh's second year of study, a young, unmarried Chinese missionary came from Hong Kong to pastor the Chinese church. She fell in love with this young pastor. Something happened to that relationship. She was devastated. One day, I looked out of my office window and saw her walking in a heavy downpour of rain. She had no raincoat, shoes, or hat of any kind. She walked back and forth on the street. I called her in. She was soaking wet. I sent her to dry off, change clothes, and return to my office.

We talked for over two hours. "Pastor, I need to confess to you, I have fallen in love with the pastor of the Chinese church where I am starting a preschool program. I thought he loved me, but he doesn't. He told me so. I don't want to live anymore. I was walking in the rain hoping I would get sick and die!

"I also have so many problems with my family. My father

drinks whiskey all the time, and we have no money to live on. He is crippled and can't get out and work. My mother gambles every time she gets any money. They let me study here thinking I will be able to support our family when I graduate. They don't care about me. They only see me as money for them to live on. My hope was he would marry me and take me to Hong Kong with him. That is the only way I can escape my future here."

There was no doubt she was extremely depressed. We prayed together. She promised me she would come back tomorrow to talk further with me.

Early the next morning, our doorbell was ringing incessantly. A young Chinese man rushed into our house wringing his hands and shouting, "Miss Binh's dead. Miss Binh's dead! Last night, Miss Binh drank a whole bottle of green oil" (a Chinese/Vietnamese ointment). He went on to tell us that the family had rushed her to the hospital, but she could not be saved. "She is dead!" he concluded.

It would be difficult to describe the feeling that swept over me. I had just spent two hours with her, promising I would be available to talk some more. I had encouraged her, telling her we would get through this difficult time. I knew, sadly, in Vietnam there was no hope of a counselor or a psychologist and certainly no psychiatrist available. Psychology and psychiatry were basically nonexistent! I knew she needed medical help, but I had nowhere to send her. The question I kept dealing with in my mind was, "Why could I not help her? What could I have done differently?" For days, I lived in grief and self-doubt.

Foremost in my mind was the fact that getting all this theological education and knowledge was good, but were we at the stage in our work where all this detailed study was really needed? I knew nothing about people. People were the vessels in which the gospel lived and moved and had its being. I needed to commit myself to learning about people—how they thought, why they hurt and needed healing, why they behaved as they did. What kept them from turning to Jesus? These thoughts took root in my mind and heart. I made a decision. I would forego my current plans and pursue future higher education in the field of pastoral care and counseling. Little did I know, this would be a life-shaping experience and open a new horizon of ministry.

If we could just teach these young pastors how to minister to hurting people in the midst of war, with all its grief and suffering, it would be a tremendous contribution. All around us and in every church, house church, and Bible study group were people who dealt every day with brokenness, anguish, grief, hopelessness, discouragement, and depression, and living in the midst of war intensified all of these things! In my own life, I knew more about the Bible, theology, doctrine, church history, and other things I learned in the university and seminary than I would ever be able to teach. But I knew nothing about the clay vessels in which the gospel resides. In seminary I learned to talk, but I did not learn to listen. Too often I helped people to know Jesus with their mind, but what they needed even more was to bring Jesus into their lives where they hurt, into their heart where they felt, and let Jesus meet their need for healing. Too often, people were taking Jesus about skin deep. At the least little problem, they turned back to their old lives.

The more I prayed about this, the more I felt the Lord leading me in this direction. The gift of counseling was there all the time. I just needed to be trained and to know how to teach others. Pastors in a country in protracted war affecting every area of life needed a different kind of training than those serving in other countries that do not experience war.

What I did not acknowledge was I myself was in need of healing. For almost ten years I had lived in the midst of war. I was carrying so much grief, which for years I held inside, afraid to face for fear of what it would do to me if I let it out. I didn't know how much my father's death had affected me, and I had no way of dealing with it in Vietnam. It was not until I began my graduate studies that I realized, above all, I was the one who needed healing.

We left Vietnam for our second stateside assignment in June

1971. This time, I was prepared to stay in the States until I finished my training.

I completed writing my master's of theology thesis in record time. While researching and writing the thesis, I applied to the PhD program in Pastoral Care and Counseling at Southern Seminary in Louisville, Kentucky. I was accepted into the program but learned it was going to take about five years to complete this degree. Immediately I realized I could not be away from Vietnam that long.

I applied to Southeastern Seminary in Wake Forest, North Carolina, and was accepted into their new doctor of ministry program, which was designed as a practical terminal degree rather than a research degree. Many of my courses I could take at Duke University, the University of North Carolina, and the seminary. It was exactly the degree I needed.

In 1971, during my doctoral studies at Southeastern Baptist Theological Seminary and at the University of North Carolina in the pastoral care department at North Carolina Memorial Hospital, Jim Rentz was my very wise counselor and supervisor. Jim was a Vietnam veteran. He recognized the grief I was carrying from my years in Vietnam. He was not only sensitive to my grief about my father's death, but he also knew the heavy load of grief at seeing so many of my military brothers die. He could sense my deep feelings for the Vietnamese people in their suffering. As he worked with me, I relived my acute grief conducting the funerals of Vietnamese soldiers and the American men visiting our home one day and killed the next. I was forced to share about the dead bodies I had seen as though it had all happened just yesterday. I recalled and rewrote again the letters I had written to wives and parents of fallen soldiers.

Jim knew I had stuffed these feelings until I could no longer feel anything! He could see all the symptoms. Where he noticed this load of grief most was as he watched me deal with very sick and dying people in the hospital. In addition, he sensed I had never really dealt with my father's death. All this load of grief was affecting me in ways even I did not recognize. He skillfully led me through these raging emotions hidden within me.

It was the most painful thing I had ever done. It was as if my whole being was being torn apart and then remade into something so much better. It was as if the vessel God had made was being broken so He could remake it into something far more beautiful and useable! This experience became a turning point of healing in my life for which I will always be grateful. Day by day, my life was gradually being cleansed of all the clutter that had gathered. I began to experience the Lord's presence in a fresh new way. Sometimes I felt all around me the underbrush of life was so thick I could no longer see God. Cleaning out that underbrush opened up a whole new vista of our Lord.

Each knot that blocked my emotions so tightly was being untied until love, compassion, and all of those positive feelings were freed and released. The most beautiful part of the healing was I recovered my ability to love and accept love from the most important two people in the world to me—my wife, Rachel, and my Lord, Jesus.

When we returned to Vietnam in 1973, after I had graduated from my studies in pastoral care and counseling, I led more people to the Lord in the next two years than in all of my previous years in Vietnam! I am convinced what I received most in all of my studies were the gifts of personal cleansing and the gift of listening!

CHAPTER 22

THE LAST DAYS

I went into our children's bedrooms early that morning in January 1975. I looked down at my three boys and my daughter sound asleep and softly kissed each one of them. There was something different about leaving this time.

I was accustomed to flying to various places in Vietnam, where we had students studying in our extension seminary. These past few years, the war had become more and more intense. With each trip, my anxiety increased. Air Vietnam was actually a very safe airline, but in time of war, especially this kind of war, anything could happen, anywhere, at any time. I silently wondered if all would be well, and I would return in a few days with no problems. I became somewhat emotional as I looked at their sleeping faces.

I arrived in Danang and went directly to Hope Baptist Church to teach seven extension students. When I arrived, I was surprised to find the church filled. One of the leaders told me it would be good if I could teach everyone rather than just those seven students. As I taught and interacted with the congregation, I sensed an unusual level of anxiety among them. Some said they didn't know why, but they just felt compelled to come and listen.

Late that afternoon after teaching, I flew to Qui Nhon, just south of Danang. Missionary Bob Compher met my plane. We went straight to the Qui Nhon church, where six students were waiting to study a course on relational evangelism. When we arrived, we found twelve students in the class. Six of them were not believers.

As I taught, I divided them into groups of two and let them practice what I was teaching. The six seminary students led all six of the nonbelievers to the Lord.

The next day I was taken out to a rural village location, where a new church was being planted. Several hundred people were gathered in a field. I was asked to preach rather than teach a class. It was strange to have that many people come in spite of little advertisement and preparation. Again, I sensed a high level of anxiety among those who had gathered and a hunger to hear the gospel. There was an overwhelming response.

In the afternoon, I flew to Nhatrang to teach. I was expecting a small extension class. However, when I arrived, it was filled with people. Missionary Walter Routh and I were to take turns teaching two days. After dinner, I was to teach the evening class. The atmosphere in the church was filled with anxiety and also a spiritual hunger. I finished teaching, but no one moved. Everyone continued to sit quietly and prayerfully. It was as though the Holy Spirit had descended on everyone in the room. One man stood to pray and prayed with great intensity, weeping as he prayed. Others began to weep and pray. There was confession of sin, deep remorse, and hunger for God's forgiveness. Soon everyone was praying aloud at the same time. It sounded like a great symphony of prayer as voices rose and fell. Most fell to their knees praying. Occasionally someone led in a hymn. Sometimes there was just silence or a time of testimony. The hours passed, and no one left. We sang and prayed all night.

As the sun came up, breakfast was being prepared. Just before the blessing for the meal, a group of people came flooding into the church. They had been walking all night and immediately fell to the floor exhausted. Through their deep grief, they began speaking through tears and growing anger.

"The Northern Army is attacking throughout the mountain areas and the central coast. Our army is dropping their weapons and fleeing. At any moment, Nhatrang is going to be filled with people fleeing these attacks," they said.

Walter Routh and I watched as masses of people began entering the city, carrying on their back whatever they could save. I learned the entire country was under attack by the Communist armies. If I was going to get back to Saigon to my family, I needed to leave immediately.

Fortunately, I got a seat on the first plane leaving for Saigon.

On the plane, I heard everyone talking about what had happened in the past twelve hours. Evidently this was the major thrust of the Communist forces in their efforts to finally conquer the Republic of South Vietnam. The American military had pulled out of Vietnam completely in 1973. The Vietnamese Army was left alone to defend its country. They had lost their will to fight and fled, as the overwhelming force overran villages and towns. Vietnam was rapidly falling.

I arrived home and began listening to news reports. The movement of Communist forces was taking place throughout the country. The Vietnamese government was giving assurances the military was standing strong and would resist this campaign successfully. It was difficult to know what exactly was happening and who to believe. The war raged from the end of January to April. By the first of April, Saigon was flooded with refugees from all over the country. There was nowhere left for them to go.

March 31, 1975, Bob Davis and Gene Tunnell were in Danang to help with the large number of refugees that had flooded the city. They had to force their way from Hope Church to a ship, which had been commandeered by the South Vietnamese Army and hundreds of refugees fleeing to Saigon. Just as the ship was departing the wharf, Communist forces moved en masse into the city. Within the hour, Danang, the second largest city in Vietnam, surrendered to the invading forces.

On Wednesday, April 2, 1975, most of the wives living in the Saigon area independently made the decision it was time to depart Vietnam. Since our daughter was in high school at Morrison Academy in Taiwan, Rachel decided she and our three boys would go to Taiwan. There were already crowds at the airport looking for opportunities to leave. We were able to get tickets on Cathay Pacific Airways. On the afternoon of April 4, Rachel and the children boarded the plane for Taiwan. I waited until the family boarded the aircraft and then left to go to my office at the seminary.

I was halfway to my office from the airport when I noticed black smoke towering in the sky in the direction of Tan Son Nhat Airport. I knew it was a plane crash, and my family had just taken off for Taiwan. In a panic, I returned to the airport and began making inquiry about the crash. The airport was in great turmoil. I asked numerous people, including various officials, yet no one seemed to know or be able to tell which plane had crashed.

After at least an hour of waiting, I finally learned that a US Air Force C5 Galaxy had taken off just behind the Cathay Pacific plane my family was on. This plane was a part of Operation Babylift, which was designed to take selected nonessential American civilian personnel and their families and a large number of Vietnamese orphans out of Vietnam. Reports later revealed the rear door of the plane did not close securely. An explosive depressurization occurred, blowing the rear doors open, causing structural failures, and cutting most of the hydraulic systems in the tail of the plane. The pilots struggled to turn back to the airport for an emergency landing. In rice paddies, several miles short of the runway, the plane, with 311 people on board crashed, killing 153 people, most of them orphans.

It would be difficult to express my own feelings when I discovered this was not the aircraft my family was on. However, I knew the family of our next-door neighbor, Mr. Ron Drye, an American contractor, was on that C5 Galaxy. The family had visited us the night before their departure and shared that they did not want to leave, but the US government had ordered them out. Mrs. Drye was employed by the government, and they had to follow orders. Their daughter was just sixteen years old, a little older than my daughter. Their son was the age of one of my sons.

They had spent many hours playing with my children at our home. The bodies of mother and son were found in the wreckage. Their daughter's body was not found. I spent many hours with Mr. Drye as we waited for word about his daughter. He was holding on to the very slim hope she would be found alive somewhere, somehow.

Three days later, the Air Force called from the Philippines saying Mr. Drye's daughter had just been identified in a hospital at Clark Air Force Base near Manila. She had evidently been sucked out of the plane by the depressurization and had fallen into a rice paddy. Evidently, she had taken her place on the lower deck of the plane to help take care of the orphans. She was found unconscious, much of her hair gone, completely without clothing, lying in a rice paddy not far from the crash. She was transported unidentified and unresponsive to the hospital at Clark Air Force base. It took several days before they could identify her. She was not only alive but would fully recover.

So much death had a profound effect on me. All around us there seemed to be a constant encounter with death. Unconsciously, as a means of survival, I often tried not to feel anything. Now and then, someone close and intimate died, and all the grief bottled up inside came flooding back like an unstoppable river. There in the gloom of grief was a small ray of sunshine when we learned of the survival of that young sixteen-year-old girl with flaming red hair and a cute freckled face.

★★★

With each passing day, the challenges intensified. There was the need to stabilize our work, minister to refugees, and make plans for our own departure from the country if it became necessary. I was chairman of the school board for the Phoenix Study Group, which was essentially the American school for dependent children of Americans and other nationalities still living in Vietnam. On April 6, the school board decided we should take necessary steps to close the school and dispose of finances, libraries, and equipment. The American embassy was trying to keep secret the fact that American families were leaving Vietnam. They were afraid of starting a panic, resulting in a stampede of families leaving, which would indicate all hope was gone for saving Vietnam.

The American ambassador was absolutely convinced the US government would not allow Vietnam to fall to the Communists. He was ignoring every clear proof the country was going to fall. The embassy was trying to continue operating as though everything was normal.

I was asked to go to the American embassy for advice regarding preservation of the school records and disposal of assets. Upon arrival at the embassy, I learned the American ambassador, Mr. Graham Martin, could not see me because he was in Bangkok. I found out later he had given orders not to look favorably on any kind of evacuation of Americans.

A State Department officer met me. I had the feeling this man was pretty far down in the echelon of staff. He was unfriendly and emotionally distant, as though I was some nondescript Vietnamese coming in for a favor.

"I am with the school board of the American school here in Saigon. We are going to close the American school and need some advice about the best way to preserve the children's academic records and disposal of assets. Would it be possible for the embassy to preserve our records along with other records you have here?"

His response was, "Well, first, you need to know we will never allow Vietnam to be taken over. The last thing we need is for a bunch of Americans to panic and begin to flood out of the country. Vietnam will not fall. Now, you should continue the school as usual."

I was furious he would think we would be so foolish as to believe something like that. I felt thoroughly patronized by this man. I knew he was trying to avoid creating a panic among Americans, but being talked to like a child naive enough to believe him was beyond my comprehension.

I immediately left the American embassy and went to the Canadian embassy. I knew there were Canadian children in the school. I met with the deputy ambassador, who informed me forthrightly Vietnam would collapse within days.

"My advice to you is to close the school now, immediately! Dispose of the assets. If you wait until the last minute there will be mass confusion, and you will not be able to do anything. If we can be of any help to you, just let us know."

With that advice, we proceeded to close the school. The entire school library and other assets were given to Vietnamese schools and distributed in an orderly fashion.

With Rachel and our children already in Taiwan, I was living alone in our house. Saigon was now surrounded by Communist forces. During the day, the city was eerily quiet. At night, there was random firing in the streets of Saigon and periodic heavier firing could be heard on the outskirts of the city. Living in the house alone, nights were very unsettling. Each night as I lay on my bed, I determined to leave Vietnam the next morning. Then the morning would dawn, and the birds would be singing. Life seemed to return to normal. I would say to myself, "Okay, one more day!" Making the decision to leave Vietnam was just too difficult.

On Friday, April 11, I turned the seminary leadership over to Rev. Dao Van Chinh, who was serving as dean of the seminary. Since my own future in Vietnam was so uncertain, I gave him the president's office, and I moved my office into an apartment on the second floor of a small building behind the main seminary building. Rev. Chinh had gone away that afternoon. I was in my office when several strange Vietnamese men in civilian clothes came into the building. They were heavily armed. They spoke roughly to the seminary receptionist. "Where is the American president?"

"He is not here, and the American is no longer president."

"He is here because his car is parked outside."

One of the men forced his way past the receptionist and kicked open the president's office door. Of course, there was no one there.

They hit her in the face and told her they would return. She came to my office, weeping and frightened.

She said "They spoke with a North Vietnamese accent. I know they would have killed you!"

I was forced to acknowledge that staying in Vietnam was both dangerous to our seminary staff and students and a threat to my own life. I climbed over the back wall and spent the rest of the afternoon at home.

Every day, a large number of people were gathered outside my gate. I asked several people one morning why they were there. They said, "We know you are an American pastor. When you leave, we know Vietnam is falling. It might be you can take some of us with you. This is our hope." I tried to assure them this was not a possibility.

One morning as I was about to open my gate to go to the seminary, a woman tossed her little child over the fence toward me. Fortunately, I caught the child. The mother was turning to run away when I ran through my gate to catch her. I put the child down, took her hand and placed the child's hand in hers, turned, and walked back to my car. Tears were welling up in my eyes so I could not speak to her. I could hardly see to drive. All day long, my heart was breaking at the plight of the people I had grown to know and love so much. Even though they were not Christians, they all called me Pastor. Their desperation and my helplessness overwhelmed me!

On Wednesday, April 16, we called a meeting of the six career missionary men remaining in Vietnam. There was agreement around the table that the fall of Vietnam was drawing very near. All of us expressed hope that just maybe a miracle might occur, and we could return to Vietnam in the near future. It was difficult to acknowledge we might never return to Vietnam. The main discussion had to do with how we would wrap things up and when would be the right time to leave, if we had to go. We reiterated to one another the FMB's position that all decisions regarding staying or leaving should be made by those of us who were present in the field. The policy of the board was workers on the ground would know the local situation and make decisions better than someone twelve thousand miles away in Richmond, Virginia.

I hasten to add, this was before the day of CNN and Fox News, reporting crisis situations on a continuing basis all over the world. That means that people outside of the country may know the overall situation better than people living in the midst of the circumstances. Several weeks prior to this, we had advised all short-term personnel and nonessential personnel to leave Vietnam as soon as possible. One volunteer couple had refused to go.

As a group, we decided that of those of us who remained, each individual, should make his or her own decision when and whether to leave. No one would feel guilty for leaving or be made to feel guilty by someone else because of the decision to leave. However, we all felt, by staying too long, we were endangering our local Christians and specifically those who worked for our mission organization. The new government would, without doubt, consider people in any way associated with Americans as traitors. We also agreed that, after the Communists assumed control, there would be no way they would allow us, as foreigners, to be active in any way. We might stay a few days, but we could do nothing. Consolidating their authority, they would get rid of foreigners.

The awesome struggle and deep sadness among our missionaries at the possibility of leaving was palpable. Our feelings were much deeper than I could have ever imagined they could be. We agonized as we thought of our wives and children and our inability to communicate with them. We knew the stress level of our children would be high, not knowing how bad the situation was in Vietnam and whether or not their fathers were safe. No one wanted to leave, but at the same time, it was difficult to know our children were so far away and unable to communicate with us. We knew our wives would fully understand, but our children had no way of knowing.

In the midst of this deep soul searching, praying, and seeking

God's guidance, there was a knock at the door. An elderly volunteer couple who had been in Vietnam for a few months asked to speak with us.

"We have decided my wife and I will remain in Vietnam even if and when the Communists take over," the man said. "We are not going to be cowards and run home at the least sign of danger. Frankly, I am surprised and disappointed at your lack of spiritual commitment. At the least sign of danger, you are willing to put your tail between your legs, abandon your call, and run."

Whatever he intended by his words, it was like an electric shock to those of us seated around that table. Everyone was a veteran missionary. All had seen the suffering of our Vietnamese people during the past few weeks. Everyone around the table had taken enormous risks for so many years during the war and especially in those last days. We were all working around the clock to provide food for the people who were destitute. The more he spoke, the angrier we became. The word *coward* was especially intolerable coming from someone so new in the country and who knew so little about the situation.

One of the rather mild-mannered missionaries suddenly stood up, reached across the table, and grabbed this man by the collar. He pulled him across the table and said directly, not even an inch from his face, "Don't you ever use the word *coward* about anyone at this table or imply we are not being spiritual!" His fist was drawn back, and he was ready to punch the volunteer in the face.

There was a mad scramble to separate the two.

Later, reflecting on this event, I remembered the story about the disciples in the Garden of Gethsemane the night Jesus was betrayed by Judas. The chief priest and the soldiers were confronting Jesus to arrest him. The disciple, Peter, feeling the intensity of the situation and overwhelmed by his emotions, pulled a sword and cut off the ear of one of the soldiers. For the first time, I really understood that story. At that moment, any one of us could very easily have been Peter.

The truth is, we are all human, and everyone at the table had been affected by the long days of stress and concern. This elderly volunteer and his wife had not been a part of our discussion. They had not experienced the years and years of war and brutality of the Communists. They had no children. They were not separated from a family, with children constantly concerned for the safety of their fathers. They had not experienced the deep spiritual atmosphere in which we were earnestly seeking God's guidance and making decisions.

On the other hand, all of us were dealing with deep sorrow that possibly we might have to leave the people whom we had loved dearly. We all knew deep within us what Communism was like, as we had seen and were seeing it expressed in Vietnam. We knew when the Communists assumed control, there would be nothing we as foreigners could do to help our believers or to minister to the people. In fact, the slightest contact with our believers inevitably would bring on them suspicion and punishment. Though we hated to admit it, the truth was there was no other decision we could make. This experience reminded me of how human all of us really are and how crises can reveal our humanity in ways none of us can even imagine.

Thursday, April 17, I was leaving my home very early in the morning. The main street leading downtown was eerily empty. As I began turning onto the street, a policeman stopped me. A moment later, I observed three American-type jeeps with a small Communist flag passing by at high speed. The military men in the jeep all had on the helmet and green uniforms of Communist forces. There were no guns visible. They were heading in the direction of the presidential palace with a heavy escort of South Vietnamese police. It was strange the escort was not sounding its sirens and no lights were flashing as was almost always the case when they were escorting someone. Even now, I am still puzzled by this sight, since such a visit or meeting as far as I know was never mentioned in the press or talked about elsewhere. Some may question if I was mistaken in what I saw that morning, but I know beyond any doubt what I saw. In my own mind at that moment, I wondered if plans were being made for an imminent surrender, perhaps even that morning? The pressing question every day was, "Is this the last day of freedom for Vietnam?"

By April 18, it was impossible to continue operating the seminary. The classrooms and grounds were filled with refugees. Some students were beginning to find their own way out of the country. Most were going back home to their families. Others were looking for a place to live to try to weather the coming storm. There was no longer a need for our staff to work. My work as president of the seminary was finished.

On April 25, I decided it was time to leave. Missionaries Bob Davis, Peyton Moore, and I made the decision to join our wives and children in Taiwan, where the children were in school at Morrison Academy. Herman Hayes, Gene Tunnell, and Earl Bengs remained for a few days and then left the country for Southeast Asia.

Several days later, it was a sad morning when I toured every room in my house. I went in the children's bedroom and could hear their happy voices. I could see their prized possessions lying around just as they had left them. I looked at mine and Rachel's bedroom. I saw all the little things that represented our years of marriage and the beautiful moments of conversation and relationship Rachel and I had enjoyed. I stood at the front door looking over our living room, and with tears in my eyes and a small bag in hand, I closed the door, turned around, and walked away.

I made my way through throngs of people, all milling aimlessly around the airport grounds, confused, wondering what they could do. I found Bob Davis and Peyton Moore in the midst of the thousands of people. We had no idea how we would leave Vietnam. In all that crowd, I saw a man whom I had led to know Jesus and baptized at Grace Church. He had a very high position with the Airport Authority. He spotted the three of us in the crowd. Making his way to us, he asked if we were leaving Vietnam.

We said, "Yes. We don't want to, but we have little choice."

"I understand that," he said. "Where are you going?"

There was just one plane, a small DC-3 belonging to Cathay Pacific, sitting on the tarmac. I asked, "Where is that plane going?"

He replied, "It's going to Manila."

I said, "We are going to Manila."

"Wait here," he said. "I will see what I can do."

A while later, he returned with three tickets in hand. He told us the price of the tickets in US dollars. It was reasonable. Bob Davis had a briefcase filled with Vietnamese money. The man immediately stopped him and said, "We are only allowed to accept American money." None of us had enough American cash to pay. We told him we just did not have that many dollars. "Then," he said, "I am so sorry but I cannot get you on that plane."

Quickly I said, "I have an American Express credit card."

His eyes lit up. "Give it to me. I can process that. Wait here."

Within a few minutes, he returned with a receipt, which I signed. He gave us the tickets. Evidently the credit card was never processed because I never received a bill from American Express.

He then directed us to follow him. He took us to a room on the side of the terminal and told us to stay there. Gradually, a few others were brought into the room.

Everyone was strangely quiet. No one felt like talking. Midafternoon, a mortar round hit the main part of the terminal building. We all took refuge wherever we could find it. I ran just outside and lay in a culvert under the road. The scene was chaotic— sirens wailing, people shouting and crying, Vietnamese military and policemen swarming the terminal. When it seemed safe, I found a place to look inside the terminal. The dead, dying, and wounded lay scattered everywhere. With hundreds of thousands of people crowded on the grounds of the terminal, it was mass bedlam. Thankfully, no more mortars were fired.

We waited in the small room until around ten o'clock that night. We were warned the least light could be spotted by Viet Cong and a mortar could be directed toward that light.

A Vietnamese employee came into the room and said, "Follow

me. It is dark, and no lights are allowed. Form a line, and each person put your hand on the shoulder of the person in front and follow carefully." The small light in the room was turned off so no light would be seen when the door opened. We left the room and walked into total darkness. It was so dark we could not even see the person in front of us. We climbed the steps into the DC-3 and found a seat. Almost immediately, the two propeller engines roared to life; the plane began to move quickly. How the pilot could see where to take the plane, I have no idea. We gained speed down a darkened runway with no lights and lifted slowly into the night sky.

Seated by a window, I looked down at the city that had been my home for almost fourteen years. There were fires burning here and there. The tears flowed freely as I felt the full weight of emotion at leaving the people I had learned to love so dearly and to whom God had called me so many years ago.

I began to second guess my decision to leave. Questions flooded my mind. "Did I really have to leave?" "What will happen to our Christian families?" "Am I abandoning the people God called me to serve in this their darkest hour?" The question that haunted me most and continued to haunt me for years to come was, "What will our Christians think of me leaving them in such an hour as this?" It was not that I thought I could do anything for them, but I thought at least I could suffer with them. "If I can ever return to Vietnam, what will they think of me? Will I still have their love and respect?"

I turned on the overhead light, took out my New Testament with the Psalms in the back. It just happened I opened to Psalm 137, which reads in part, "By the Rivers of Babylon we sat and wept when we remembered Zion ... for there our captors asked us for songs, our tormentors demanded songs of joy; they said 'Sing us one of the songs of Zion!' How can we sing the songs of the Lord while in a foreign land?" Psalm 137:1-4 (NIV). This Psalm is about the fall of Jerusalem, the sacred city, the location of the temple of God. To the Jewish people, their whole identity as a people was wrapped up in the Holy City. Now, their enemy was carrying them away from everything they held dear. They were being taken as captives into Babylonia. It was as though they were being taken away from God Himself!

As I reflected on this Psalm, I thought to myself, "Sam, now who are you?" "What is your identity now?" For years, I was proud of being a missionary to the people of the Republic of Vietnam. People, Christians and nonbelievers alike, who passed by my house would greet me with, "Hello, Pastor." I was pastor of Faith Baptist Church, which I had helped plant. When their Vietnamese pastor died, they asked me to be their pastor until another could be found. I was president of the Vietnam Baptist Theological Seminary. My students called me Teacher. This was my identity. At that moment, however, all of that was gone. I had been stripped naked of every identity I held precious. I no longer lived in that house among neighbors who knew me as Pastor. I was no longer pastor of anything. I was no longer president of a seminary. It no longer existed. If someone asked me who I was, I could not reply with pride, "I am a missionary to the people of South Vietnam." Nothing was left!

Then, it hit me with great force, and I said to myself with determination, "Sam, you are a child of God. This is your identity! No matter what the circumstance or geographical location or ministry opportunity, no matter what position or power, this is an identity no one can ever take from me. The only way I will lose this identity is if I personally deny it." I determined never again would I allow geography, position, authority, power, or anything else to determine who I was. "I belong to the Lord! I am His child!"

I wish I could say this realization gave me great peace and joy, but my pain was too real to so easily go away. I had no way of knowing that, in the coming years in other circumstances, I would have to come back to this insight over and over again!

The truth is our true identity is never found in what we do but in who we are. Being comes before doing!

We landed in Manila and caught the next plane to Hong Kong.

Carter and Agnes Morgan, long-term missionaries in Hong Kong, took me into their home. I was dirty, dead tired, and emotionally drained. Never did a bath feel so good after all those hours in intense stress, anxiety, and sleeplessness.

My arrival in Taiwan was a joyful reunion with family and fellow missionaries. The mission opened its arms to us and provided everything we needed. We stayed on the campus of Morrison Christian Academy. Our families moved into small cottage duplexes built in the old days for workers who were hired to help a missionary family in their home. These were located conveniently behind the local missionary houses. Communication from Southeast Asia Area Director Dr. Keith Parks told us he would soon be there to visit. He encouraged us to rest and recover from the past events and to be in no hurry to think about another assignment.

The day after I arrived in Taichung, Taiwan, I went to the local market to get a few things for us to eat. Cheerfully and without thinking, I went to a lady selling bananas and asked in Vietnamese to buy some bananas. She did not understand. I tried again in Vietnamese. Suddenly I realized I was speaking Vietnamese. I was now in Taiwan, where Chinese is the language. I tried to ask her in English. She did not understand English. I picked up a hand of bananas and asked her, "How much?" She responded in Chinese, which I did not understand. Finally, I took a piece of paper from my pocket and a pen and gave them to her to write the price. She wrote it in Chinese characters. I wrote a suggested price in English. She did not understand. Suddenly all the weeks of frustration, tension, emotions, and even anger flooded me. I felt as though I was now starting my missionary career all over again, unable to communicate, feeling helpless beyond words. I quickly put the bananas down and walked away without saying or doing anything foolish.

For the first time in my life, I was in real "culture shock." I felt like I would die if I had to begin a new language, learn a new culture, and find a new ministry! I found a quiet place on the side of a road and sat down, my head in my hands. I poured out my heart to the Lord. I acknowledged I was physically exhausted, but more than that, I was emotionally fatigued and spiritually drained. My fear was I was no longer able to control my emotions. For the first time in years, I no longer had a vision, goals, or expectations. I was going to have to learn to relax and just trust as I put myself in the Lord's hands.

Within two weeks, Dr. Parks arrived in Taiwan. He told us around five hundred thousand Vietnamese refugees were on the island of Guam. There was a great need for Vietnamese speakers to help with the care of this huge number of people. Would we be interested in going to Guam to minister to refugees? All three of us immediately responded, "Yes!"

He said, "Go ahead and make preparations. I will notify our missionaries on Guam you are coming."

Bob Davis, Peyton Moore, and I were elated by this opportunity. It was one of the most healing things that could happen to us. We would be separated again from our families, but this time, there would not be the uncertainty and stress.

On Guam, I served as an interpreter for the naval hospital, working with doctors treating the many different illnesses among the refugees. I was assigned to spend the majority of my time with refugees who were extremely depressed and some who were catatonic.

One day, I was sitting in a tent with a mother whose young son had been lying on his cot for days without speaking. Doctors had determined his problem was not physical but emotional. His mother told of fighting through a crowd to board a boat thinking her husband was right behind her. "I turned to look for him, shots suddenly rang out, the boat quickly cast off, and we were moving toward the sea. I searched the crowd on the shore, but it was getting dark—so many people, and I could not see him. I am sure he must have been killed. I know he would have done anything to get on the boat with us. Now, I am here, all alone. I don't know what to do or where to go. I wish I could go back to Vietnam. I did not want to leave, but my husband said it was best for us as a family and especially for our son."

One day as we sat talking, a bus filled with newly arrived refugees who had been picked up at sea stopped at a bus stop near her tent. She was watching as refugees were getting out of the bus. Suddenly she jumped up and exclaimed, "My husband, my husband," and broke into tears. She ran out, threw both arms around him, and the two broke into tears. She brought him into the tent. He knelt beside his son's bed, spoke softly and gently to him, and hugged him close. The little boy's eyes fluttered open. He looked at his father, burst into tears, and began trying to talk through his sobs, "Ba ôi, Ba ôi, Ba ôi" (Father, Father, Father)! What a miraculous, moving reunion!

After around six weeks working nonstop long hours day and night, I received a call from Richmond, Virginia. Dr. Winston Crawley, director of IMB's overseas division, was calling, asking me to come to Richmond to do some research projects. Longing to reunite my family once again, I accepted, and we flew to Richmond for an undetermined amount of time.

The New Bridge Baptist Church in Highland Springs, Virginia, had recently outfitted a house especially for a stateside-assigned missionary. We were privileged to be the first to live in this home.

I was used extensively during the fall and spring orientation programs, sharing and interacting with new missionaries going to the field. This helped me process past events so that healing could begin. Gradually healing came.

CHAPTER 23

NEW CHALLENGE, NEW COMMITMENT

In April 1976, Rachel and I began looking at the myriad of opportunities for service around the world. The truth is nothing seemed appealing. The grief over our loss of Vietnam still held us back from committing to another people and another task.

As Rachel and I prayed about our future, we did not want our choice to be like choosing an ice cream flavor. That is, what tastes good! We were almost desperate for a word from the Lord. We needed a new and fresh call from Him.

Dr. George Hays, area director for East Asia, called me to his office. The IMB had instituted a new position for each area of the world. He asked if I would like to accept a position called field representative. Since the area director was located at the board headquarters in Richmond, he would like to have someone on the field to serve as an advisor/pastor to the 550 missionaries in East Asia (Korea, Japan, Taiwan, Hong Kong, and Macau). He needed someone to live in East Asia. The job called for someone with experience in the field, church planting, and evangelism, and someone who would be available to advise. He needed someone who could walk with our missionaries on a regular basis and counsel those who were going through difficult times. He wanted someone to formulate opportunities for personal growth, marriage and family counseling, leadership development, and other needs. He felt my years of ministry in Vietnam, education credentials, pastoral care and counseling training, and knowledge of life and ministry overseas was greatly needed, especially for new missionaries coming to the field. He also felt that Rachel, with her nurse and nurse practitioner training, and seminary education would relate ideally to missionary families. We were excited for the first time since leaving Vietnam.

I remembered what Dr. T. B. Maston, longtime professor of ethics at Southwestern Baptist Theological Seminary, told me several years ago. He said, "Sam, if you have to make a decision, and it is a question of mind's reasoning or heart's desire, always follow your heart." I thought about East Asia, especially Hong Kong, where we had worked and learned to love Chinese people while waiting for Vietnam visas. I thought of Japan, where I was saved and surrendered to missions. I thought about Korea, where I had served in the navy during the Korean War and where a great spiritual awakening was occurring among the Korean people. In those countries were 550 missionaries with nearly 300 missionary children of all ages. My love, appreciation, and respect for my fellow missionaries and my knowledge of their needs were major deciding factors. I simply could not turn away from that. Every experience and decision we had made in the past had prepared us for this job. The following morning, I told Dr. Hays I would accept this position and would be ready at any time to move to the field.

That afternoon, I received a letter from Taiwan. It was from Dr. Carl Hunker, president of the Taiwan Baptist Theological Seminary. He informed me that, in a few years, he would retire. The seminary trustees wanted to know if I would consider coming to Taiwan, studying Chinese, and following him as president of the seminary. This was another of those forks in the road. Rachel and I prayed earnestly about the decision we now faced. It became clear I should move ahead with the field representative position.

Thus, in April 1976, I was elected field representative for East Asia and decided to set up my office in Taipei, Taiwan. This began what may be four of the most satisfying, meaningful years of my life.

Coming from Southeast Asia, I realized I would have to win my way into the heart of East Asian missionaries! I also knew you couldn't just walk in among a lot of people and say, "Hi, everyone! I'm here to be your friendly counselor!" and expect everyone to line up to bare his or her soul to you. This new assignment was going to be a challenge! I determined to visit every family in the area.

How can I forget the time I visited a missionary family in an isolated community on an island several kilometers from the coast? The missionary and his wife had lived there for not quite a year. When I arrived, the words of this husband and wife tumbled over each other almost too rapidly to understand—so hungry was their desire for company. Late that night, he shared with me that his assignment was to work with the one local church and its pastor to plant several churches in the area. He and the pastor had a good but distant relationship. They met together but always in a public location. Sometimes they met at the church building. He was never invited into the pastor's home. Also, "I have not felt any support from him for starting a new church. We have not even talked about it, and this is what I was sent here to do."

On Sunday mornings, the pastor's wife was never at church, so he did not get to know her. He said, almost in tears, "I just don't know what to do to have a good relationship with him."

As he was laying out the problem, I began to think of all of my years relating to Asian people, their psychology and communication patterns. I seemed to have a special feeling about this pastor. My studies and experience as a pastoral counselor began to come to the forefront of my thinking.

I suggested to him, "Tomorrow morning, I want you to go to his home. When he comes to the door, tell him you need to meet with him about something important. Begin to take your shoes off at the door as though you are coming into the house. As an Asian, and also a pastor, it will be difficult for him to ask you not to come in. Sit down and share with him how much you appreciate him and are growing to love him in Christ. Share with him how you are praying for him and his wife. Tell him how much you want to have an easy relationship where the two of you can share together. Wait for him to respond."

I was so proud of him for accepting this challenge.

At noon, he returned home glowing with excitement. He said, "It worked!"

He shared with me how the pastor invited him in. "I told him how much I love him and his wife and want so much to have a good, loving relationship with them. When he responded to me, I noticed tears in his eyes."

I asked him about his feelings and if I had hurt him in some way.

Suddenly he burst into tears and began sharing. "Please forgive me," the pastor said. "Eighteen months ago my wife gave birth to our only little son. When the doctor put him in my wife's arms, she saw that he has a severe deformity."

With that, the pastor wiped fresh tears from his face. "My wife wants to keep this a secret from the church family. She never goes anywhere. She just stays at home with our baby."

To the people in that culture, a birth like this meant they were being punished for some sin they had committed. The baby was reaping the punishment for their sin. The pastor called his wife to come in and sit with him as he shared with the missionary. She wept bitterly. The missionary said, "I wept with them."

Then, the missionary said, "I took their hands in mine and poured my heart out to the Lord in prayer. Then I told them how much this meant to me and how much it made me love them. We sat and talked almost all morning. I did not try to teach them theology or give them advice. I just listened to them. After a while, the pastor's wife went into the bedroom, picked the baby up, and brought out him for me to see."

Choking back tears, the missionary continued, "I got to hold that baby close and just love him. It was a miracle to see them relax and enjoy watching me with their baby. I really think this is the beginning of a new freedom for them to open up and fellowship with the church members. They will be a great witness for the Lord."

As I think back on this one opportunity among so many others for ministry to a fellow missionary, my heart overflows with thanksgiving to the Lord for giving me this opportunity to serve Him. The Lord had guided me through those dark, difficult days in Vietnam and led me to get training, so I could relate to people in almost any situation and see the Lord bring them through whatever they were going through.

I often think of missionary couples on the verge of divorce who had the courage to call and ask for help. So many of them not only saved their marriage but went on to serve the Lord until retirement or until the Lord called them to another ministry.

In 1979, the timing was right for a trip into the People's Republic of China. No one from the IMB had visited in China since the last missionary departed twenty-eight years before, when the Communists assumed control of China. A small group of select missionaries and I boarded a ferry in Hong Kong to make the trip up the Pearl River to Quangzhou (Canton) for a four-day stay. On the way up the Pearl River, we remembered how, in the 1800s and early 1900s, missionaries to China would have taken a boat up this same river to Quangzhou, at that time the most prominent city in China next to Beijing. It was not far from that river and near Macau that Sun Yat Sen was born and raised. He was the Chinese revolutionary who led the overthrow of the last emperor of China and became the first president and founding father of the Republic of China (1912–1949).

Dr. Jaxie Short was among the last Baptist missionaries to leave China in 1952. Though it had been twenty-eight years since she had served in Quangzhou, she knew exactly where to take us and how to get there. The first morning in Quangzhou, she said, "We'll take bus number one and get off shortly after we pass some railroad tracks. We'll walk up the hill, and there will be Pui Ching School with the former Baptist seminary and Dongsan Baptist Church nearby."

This was exactly what happened. We walked by a house on the school grounds, and she affectionately patted the outside wall of the house and said, "This was my room where I lived." She remembered everything as though it was yesterday.

On Sunday morning, we went to the Dongsan Baptist Church near the grounds of the former Baptist Seminary. It had only been open for three weeks. Every seat was taken. Overflow crowds were gathered outside the church. There were no pews or chairs in the balcony yet, but it was filled with people sitting on the floor or standing.

I asked a young man standing outside the church, "Why are you here this morning?"

He responded, "I remember stories about my grandmother and grandfather coming to this church before the Communists came into power. I want to follow their example now that we can go to church."

Rev. Mathew Thong preached on Mathew 18:19–20. After the service, Rev. Thong took us to his office and told us, in recent weeks, three protestant churches had been allowed to open in China. The Dongsan Church was one of the three.

He shared the story: "One day, Communist commissars came to the factory, where I was forced to work as a common laborer for the past thirty-five years. They ordered me to get into their vehicle. I had no idea where they were taking me. Only after nearing Quangzhou did they tell me I was being brought back to reopen the Dongsan Baptist Church, where I had been pastor when the Communists took over. I had no prior warning of this and was taken immediately to the church.

"I was faced with repairing and painting the church auditorium, locating pews or chairs, furnishing the pulpit, and readying the choir loft. I had to locate people to help with all of the work. After much searching, we found the church's piano at the old YMCA building covered with dust and sitting under a stairwell."

With a glint in his eye and a hint of a smile, he said, "One day, the government sent Communist cadres to the church with portraits of Dung Xiao Peng and Hua Guofeng, the leaders of China. They ordered me to install these in the pulpit area where a huge cross hung. I thought about this for a few moments. I did not want to have to refuse this request, but I did not want those portraits hanging in such a prominent place with the cross. I said to them, 'You must remember, when Jesus was crucified, there was a thief crucified on each side of him. I don't think it is good to place these two portraits on each side of the cross!'

"They did not insist, so we hung the portraits in the vestibule beside the front doors leading into the church. Of course, when the front doors swing open, the pictures hang behind the doors!"

After church, three laymen went with us to lunch in a crowded restaurant. The three men wanted to sit at a table in the middle of the restaurant.

One of the men said, "We need to sit in a noisy, crowded area in case a bug has been placed near us and our conversation recorded." They proceeded to talk about many things that had happened over the years. They were extremely cautious in their conversation and careful not to criticize the Communist regime.

I was deeply moved by this visit to China. Since this was the first trip by anyone from our FMB since the Communist revolution, it was important to write a report. My report to Dr. Keith Parks, president of the board in 1979, stated there could be creative ways to place people in China. They could work in secular capacities but also would have opportunities to quietly minister to people.

Six years later, in the spring of 1985, an organization was set up to reach people groups around the world who were closed off from a "missionary" presence.

On one of my visits to Hong Kong, I was told by a medical doctor friend who worked with Vietnamese refugees in a camp in Kowloon of the tremendous medical need there. He desperately needed a nurse who spoke Vietnamese. As I left that day, I knew Rachel would want to know about this. She was a nurse completely qualified to do what he needed. Her mobile clinic in Vietnam had uniquely prepared her for this kind of medical work.

Sharing with her about the refugee camp in Hong Kong, I asked, "Could we possibly move for the next few months to Hong Kong so you can help in the refugee camp?"

Rachel was immediately interested in this opportunity. We spent time praying about it. We felt some concern; our son, Michael, would be uprooted from his elementary school in Taipei and would need to go to a strange school in Hong Kong. Our other two sons were in boarding school in Taichung, Taiwan, just two hours away by train. We would be leaving them. It seemed the complications were just too many for our family.

But the tremendous need of those refugees gripped our hearts. Within days, we were on our way to Hong Kong.

With little advanced notice, the Hong Kong Mission provided an empty apartment and as many basic needs as possible, especially in the kitchen so we could prepare meals. We slept on a mattress on the floor. When Christmas came, we found a potted plant almost dead from lack of water that someone had left in the apartment. We decorated it with lights and tinsel. We had many good laughs as we saw how the lights made it lean far to the left. We put Christmas gifts around the pot. We called it our "Charlie Brown Christmas tree."

Rachel began her work in the refugee clinic immediately. Her fluent Vietnamese changed the climate of the clinic. She provided nursing for the physical needs, and when she spoke Vietnamese, the refugees poured out their hearts to her. They had arrived in Hong Kong by small boats, with only the clothes on their body and no possessions. There were children of all ages, most sick from days at sea. We came in response to the physical need, but Rachel's presence in the camp was far more needed spiritually and mentally. Despair, depression, homesickness, anxiety, and all of the related feelings poured out uncontrollably as soon as the refugees met a Vietnamese-speaking missionary woman who cared deeply for them. This was the real ministry!

One day, an elderly Vietnamese man came running into the clinic holding up a tract in Vietnamese about salvation in Jesus. He brought it straight to show to Rachel. He was laughing and speaking excitedly about this tract. At first, Rachel had difficulty understanding him, and then she realized he had a heavy North Vietnamese accent. She heard him almost shouting at her, "There is a God!" It says right here, "He has come to us to bring hope where there is no hope, joy where there is only sorrow, peace where there is worry and anxiety, and salvation for those who are lost." He continued excitedly, "This God has come into the world in Jesus! We can know him!" He could hardly contain his emotions at finding this. Knowing of the American woman who spoke Vietnamese, he wanted her to know what he had found.

Rachel confesses that, during all of our years in Vietnam, North Vietnamese were the enemy. Now, she was treating their illnesses and relating to them for the first time in her life. In the midst of trying to overcome her longstanding feelings of animosity toward the north, she was suddenly confronted by this North Vietnamese man! She was flooded with compassion. She realized afresh that, under Communism, people like this man had never had an opportunity to hear the good news about Jesus. He had no exposure to the Bible, tracts, or literature. No radio or television brought the good news. So quickly, in all the darkness, the brokenness, the hopelessness a light broke through, bringing hope, joy, and healing both to these Vietnamese refugees and especially to Rachel's own heart and mind. Love poured out of her for these people who had once been enemies. Up to this point, the masses of people in the camp were just names and numbers on a list of refugees. Now, they had an identity! They were children of God, who needed to know Him.

Who could have anticipated that our decision so long ago that she become fluent in the Vietnamese language would someday put her in an intimate relationship with North Vietnamese refugees in Hong Kong!

Serving in East Asia for those four years, working with our missionaries throughout the area required all our education, training, skills, and everything else we had ever learned in life. At the same time, we had an opportunity to learn from our fellow missionaries and local brothers and sisters. It was a life-shaping experience from which Rachel and I would glean knowledge and strength to serve the Lord through all our next years of service no matter what we did or where we served. I was beginning to feel we had found our niche for the rest of our lives. The Lord had other plans.

Upon finishing that term of service, I was asked to stay in Richmond, Virginia, to lead the design of programs for orienting new missionaries and constructing a new Missionary Learning Center. Thus, we began a new challenge in missionary life.

CHAPTER 24 _____

A NEW MOUNTAIN TO CLIMB

"**S**am, if you could go back to East Asia again, what would you like to see happen out there?" the trustee of the FMB asked me in my office during the January 1985 trustee meeting.

"Wow," I responded, "it has been three and a half years since I was assigned to East Asia." My mind immediately turned to 1980 and my call back to Richmond to lead the design of the field orientation programs and work with the architects to design the Missionary Learning Center (now International Learning Center). "I have been totally immersed in designing this learning center and getting it going well. I would have to think about this."

Suddenly, ideas began to flow. I shared the many changes that needed to be made. He left with no further comments.

I welcomed the challenge to think about these things, but it stirred the ache in my heart to return to a ministry overseas. During my years as field representative, I was intimately involved in the life and ministry of all our missionaries in East Asia. Sharing some of my concerns with this trustee inspired new ideas and brought memories of all of the changes urgently needed. Even though I had no relationship at all with the area, I felt compelled to begin defining the needs. The words and ideas tumbled over themselves to get on paper. I was expressing several years of pent-up concerns. I thought maybe someday I might be in a position to address these needs.

In March, Dr. Charles Bryan, director of overseas operations, came to my office. "Sam, the current area director for East Asia has decided to retire. The trustees have expressed an interest in your serving as area director for East Asia. I am considering several people to nominate for that office, and with your permission, you would be one of them."

Dr. Keith Parks, president of the Foreign Mission Board called me in for a "talk."

"Sam," he began, "what do you know about East Asia?"

"Dr. Parks, a trustee came into my office two months ago and asked me a similar question. My four years as field representative all came back to me. There was so much that needed to be done out there, but I was not in a position to change things. This motivated me to write a paper on what I believe are the greatest needs and challenges in East Asia. I had no idea I would ever get to share this."

I gave him the paper I had written. He drilled me with questions. The interview focused on some of my own areas of need—areas in which both he and I knew I needed personal growth. He bored into my sensitive areas of weakness. It was a tough interview but extremely helpful. In the end, I had no idea whether he felt good about the interview or not.

At the June 1985, meeting of the FMB trustees, I was elected area director for East Asia.

Addressing the trustees, I remember sharing lessons learned from my three previous area directors. Dr. Winston Crawley, secretary for the Orient, taught me the importance of concise, clear communication. Dr. Keith Parks, area director for Southeast Asia, taught me the importance of visioning, planning, and setting clear directions. Dr. George Hays, area director for East Asia, taught me how to ask questions, to probe, and to gain a clear understanding before making decisions. I set my own direction based on General Dwight Eisenhower's definition of leadership: "Leadership is getting other people to do something you want them to do because they want to do it." This would require developing and communicating vision in such a way that personnel caught the vision, were inspired, and made it their own. The influence of these men continued to shape the vessel God was forming for His purposes.

I stressed there were many problems in East Asia that need to be addressed. My challenge would be to work toward change in such a way the changes would be supported and effected by personnel in the area.

At my first meeting with missionaries in Hong Kong, I remember the response of Dr. George Wilson, president of the Hong Kong seminary, to my election. He welcomed me as area director and then said, "The Chinese have a proverb that says, 'A known evil is better than an unknown good.'" He was glad the trustees had elected someone everyone already knew!

The challenges were many! In the 1950s, following the World War II, property value was cheap in Japan, Korea, and Taiwan. The missions in these countries had wisely bought properties for several thousand dollars that had appreciated over the years and were now worth tens of millions of dollars. The best stewardship of our property would have to be considered. Very wise mission leadership was already considering alternatives for the use of these properties, so these alternatives were considered strategically, and the process for using them sped up.

Another problem revolved around the rapidly changing times and economic conditions in the highly developed countries of East Asia. Modern societies with rapid urban development demanded mission strategies be examined and radically changed.

As the leader responsible for strategy, I began to think in simple terms such as: What are we doing that we need to keep doing? What are we doing that we need to stop doing? What are we doing that needs significant change to keep moving forward?

In an Orient Missions Conference in Hong Kong in 1965, Dr. Winston Crawley made a statement: "Southern Baptist missionaries up to now are largely from the rural, agrarian south. We are accustomed to single-family dwellings with front and backyards for the children to play. We are accustomed to privacy where we can exercise our individualism. Across all of Asia, the need is urgent for Southern Baptist missionaries to live and minister in the large, rapidly growing urban centers. Asia is moving from a primarily agrarian society to huge urban complexes. I am not sure our missionaries who come largely from the rural settings of the southern United States will ever be able to adapt to living and working in the large urban areas of the world. We can no longer afford the luxury of single-family dwellings such as we have enjoyed in the past. We may not be able to adjust to the style of living in multifamily dwellings and the high-rise apartments." (I have taken these words from personal notes taken at the conference.)

We were now twenty years beyond that statement, and his words were prophetic. The question I asked increasingly was, "Are we ready and willing to make the changes necessary to effectively reach these urban centers of the world?"

An elderly missionary lady who served faithfully for years in China paid a visit to Taiwan at the age of ninety. She visited one of our missionary families in the city of Kaohsiung living on an upper floor of a high-rise apartment building. Her remark to this missionary church planter was, "You need to move out to the villages where the people are, instead of living cooped up in this building!" She may not have known that five thousand people were living in that one building. All around that building, in walking distance, were other buildings similarly populated.

Another strategic question that had to be answered was, "What is the difference between doing evangelism in a 'vertical society' versus in a 'horizontal society'?" I often heard missionaries living in high-rise apartment buildings say, "The only people in my building I can get to know are the ones I meet regularly in the elevator. People who live on my floor seem reluctant to get too acquainted with people who live on the other side of a thin wall!" Wives in high-rise apartment buildings say the only way they have found to meet and develop relationships is by taking their children to the common playground, where children can meet and play together. There they meet other mothers, many of whom are dealing with common issues and problems.

Developing relationships in these vertical societies can be very different from the relationships developed with a neighborhood spirit between next-door neighbors living on the same street. There are inevitably various concerns, even fear, of relating to people living in the same building versus those who live in open space, just a fence and a garden away.

As I assumed my work as director for East Asia, I became aware that a vast majority of our missionaries were involved in administrative and management positions either in the mission context or in local convention contexts. They were involved in numerous committees and responsibilities requiring considerable time, which met organizational needs but did little to affect the life and progress of the gospel among the people of the country. Relatively few were actually involved in giving quality time to planting new churches. It was not because they did not want to. It was largely because of traditional and historic roles. Something drastic would have to be done to awaken us to new administrative structures and strategies to communicate the gospel.

Some missionaries had settled into a ministry for years and had lost their freshness and enthusiasm for God's work. Because there was no challenge to change or mechanism to move to a more exciting, fruitful role, they simply continued where they were. One veteran missionary couple had served in a city, isolated in the far south of the country for more than twenty years. They went there to help a national pastor plant new churches in that area. The pastor never evidenced a vision for planting other churches. He asked the missionaries to attract people to his church by teaching English. The missionaries had faithfully done this for twenty years, with little to no results. Even though they were depressed at the results of their work, they simply settled for this, because they had been placed there by the mission. We needed to discover situations like this and make necessary moves to help personnel gain fresh perspectives and vision in a new area of service.

In some countries, social ministry-type programs were initially instituted to help people come to know and understand the good news of Christ. In the beginning, there was a strong witness to the gospel. However, over many years, the programs gradually adapted to the people attending who had little interest in learning about Jesus but great interest in the activities of the program. Such programs continued with considerable outlay of funds and numerous personnel. Though these programs had lost their original purpose, they continued because personnel were assigned to them and numbers of people were participating in the activities.

These various problems had been engrained for years and would not be changed without drastic action of some kind. In order to attack many of these problems, each mission organization entered into an eighteen-month strategy study to examine what we were doing, why we were doing it, what was it costing us, and what had been the results.

The resulting change was dramatic but not without opposition. The East Asia area was an extremely traditional area. It had been heavily influenced by the great spiritual giants of the China mission era. For some, change was almost sacrilegious. Everyone realized East Asia had changed dramatically in every way. Almost everyone realized change had to take place if we were to make progress, but change was painful to say the least.

People began to catch the vision of what could happen in East Asia. This vision was supported by research, facts, and evident realities. Everything was presented to local national leadership so these leaders could give their input. Each mission, in its annual meeting attended by all the missionaries in the country, had opportunity to discuss, debate, make alternative proposals, and accept recommendations.

The missions dealt with the recommendations of the strategy studies, and their decisions to make significant changes revealed a maturity reflecting deep spiritual values and commitment. Interpersonal relationships guided by the indwelling spirit of God were evident in the debates and decision making. A burning desire to see people brought to a saving knowledge of Jesus motivated people to make decisions. Everything was conducted with the highest standards. In the end, every mission organization in East Asia stood strong before the task, accepted the challenges, made changes where necessary, and embraced the final recommendations. The area was dramatically changed. It had been like a great ship, wallowing in the water, unable to turn until it began moving forward. Only then could a new direction be set.

As a leader, primarily responsible for the area's strategy, I often found myself deeply conflicted during the process. On the one hand, my pastor's heart was moved when I talked with people who were significantly impacted by the study. At times, I wept with them as they faced the painful loss of an assignment that had become a part of their very identity over many years of faithful service. On the other hand, my commitment as a visionary leader strengthened me to stay strong with what was essential to progress. Giving in to emotional appeals would mean we would become a dinosaur in a rapidly changing world.

There is a fine balance between meeting our own needs and meeting the Lord's needs. People across the United States sacrifice to give mission offerings, trusting us to make the best possible decisions in using their gifts. We can do no less as we use their sacrifices to accomplish God's work!

During this significant period of leadership, the Lord was refining the vessel he had formed. I learned so many valuable lessons. I learned we have to be before we can do. That is, it is who we are that causes us to do what has to be done. Influence never comes from position, power, or delegated authority. It comes through the relationships of trust built over time between leader and fellow wayfarers in the journey of work, ministry, and daily living. My deep love and respect for our missionaries grew by leaps and bounds as I saw them make painful decisions to effect the changes needed. To the person, they put reaching their people for Christ first. Everything else was secondary. This was especially true when they themselves captured a clear vision to which they could commit their lives.

I learned people called of God to serve Him in difficult times and circumstances are among the most resilient people in the world. The Chinese speak of the chrysanthemum as the flower that, when the winds blow and storms rage, bends and bows before the forces of nature but will always return to stand straight and tall. The Vietnamese who suffered literally hundreds of years of war and threats to their existence liken themselves to the bamboo, which bends but never breaks. Missionaries often threatened by hostile culture, political strife, religious fanaticism, and sometimes just inertia, may bend, but they never give in to the threatening forces that challenge their very existence.

After many years leading fellow missionaries, I stand amazed and in wonder at the faithfulness and determined commitment of these servants of God who stand firm day after day, adapting and changing as necessary before so many varied threats from so many different directions.

It is one thing to serve as an international volunteer for a few days or even weeks, however valuable and important that may be; it is another thing to go under the divine call of a Holy God to plant one's life among a people where God wants His name to be known and His will to be done. These are the servants of God who willingly answer the call of God to forsake their former being in order to become the incarnational presence of Christ. They place their lives in the midst of a culture, a people who otherwise would never come to know and experience the glory of God through our Lord Jesus Christ. God forbid we should ever neglect a life of total commitment for a life of modern cultural trends, which bring short-term satisfaction but are like a pebble dropping in the water, making waves briefly but leaving no evidence it was ever there.

People have often asked me, "Sam, you have lived through so much war, so many organizational changes, and through so many controversies. How have you been able to remain in the field and at the task through all these times of unrest and confusion?"

My reply, "I have kept my focus steadfastly on Jesus. He is my reason for being and the source of my call. If ever I allow that focus to wander to other things or to people, I am through as a missionary. I am so glad to say after fifty-four years of missionary service with more than nineteen years in global leadership positions, mostly overseas, my love and respect for missionaries is greater today than it has ever been.

CHAPTER 25

A HEART-WRENCHING DECISION

most severe test of this vessel God formed to be a servant came as suddenly and unexpected as a hard freeze in the midst of a beautiful springtime! All the years of careful formation and preparation saw a most serious test during a time of great joy and satisfaction.

In Kowloon, Hong Kong, March 1992, I literally trembled with excitement at the possibility of opening a presence in the People's Republic of China. In 1949, Chairman Mao Tse Tung had declared the People's Republic of China a strict Marxist/Communist nation. By 1952, the last Baptist missionaries had been forced out of China. This new opening could be a historic event!

Mr. and Mrs. Dick Lusk, missionaries in Hong Kong, had made the contact with the China Christian Council in Quanzhou and received a tentative invitation to teach English. We were scheduled for an appointment with the China Christian Council to confer about this possibility.

It was late afternoon when I was leaving my home to catch the train to Quanzhou, China. On my way out, the phone rang. Dr. Keith Parks, was calling from Richmond, Virginia.

"Sam, you are aware of the controversy we are facing in Europe regarding the Ruschlikon Seminary. Our trustees have defunded the seminary, and the European Federation is extremely disturbed by this. Almost all countries in Western Europe have broken relations with us. We have had resignations of almost all our regional and area staff, along with a large number of missionaries. The future involvement and direction of our work in Europe is seriously in question. The need for leadership in Europe is urgent. The search committee of the board of trustees met and would like to interview you regarding the possibility of being named regional vice president for Europe, the Middle East, and North Africa. They would like you to respond whether you would consider this or not. Don't mention this to anyone since this is a tentative inquiry regarding your interest."

"Dr. Parks, I am on my way even this minute into China to discuss with officials about placing personnel in Quangzhou. I would need to pray about this."

"Pray about it, and I will call you tomorrow night when you return from Quangzhou."

My excitement about this significant trip into China was now torn. In my mind, I reasoned with a thrill that, finally, we would have a physical presence in China after a forty-year absence! In my heart, I was moved emotionally, knowing our missionaries in Europe must be hurting with broken relationships and no leadership. Such a loss of experienced leadership and missionaries was unprecedented.

I was also torn, tormented by another perspective. Our missionaries were in the midst of all this inward turmoil in Western Europe with little to no leadership. At the same time, they were facing challenging and unprecedented new opportunities in Eastern Europe after the collapse of the Berlin Wall on November 9, 1989. How could I decide between East Asia, ready to take on exciting new directions in China and elsewhere, and Europe, facing historic new opportunities but burdened and severely hindered by conflict? I was at another of the forks in the road, which demanded a difficult decision and a dramatic change in direction.

The situation in Europe seemed impossible to reconcile. Everything in me said, "Don't take this position in Europe!" Yet, my heart was speaking loud and clear that our missionaries were like sheep, deeply wounded, with no shepherd to lead them through this critical time.

My heart was telling me I must allow the Lord to work through me to bring back the peace and excitement that our missionaries had enjoyed with our European brothers and sisters in Christ for so many years. I could not ignore the fact that resolving this would demand everything I had ever learned and experienced. If God was calling, I could not refuse to allow the Lord to use me to accomplish His will.

The decision some years before to do my doctoral work in pastoral care and counseling uniquely equipped me to deal with these kinds of conflicts. "If the Lord formed this vessel to be used for a purpose like this, then why would I refuse to let Him use me?"

Just as I entered my home in Kowloon, the phone rang. Dr. Parks asked for my response. I remember saying, "Dr. Parks, this is like moving into a hornets' nest. I need to have my sanity examined if I deliberately place myself in this position!" I explained my thinking and finally said, "I am willing to make myself available."

On June 24, 1992, in San Antonio, Texas, I was elected vice president for Europe, the Middle East, and North Africa by the IMB trustees.

Departure from Asia after thirty years of service was emotional and heartrending. It was another of those times when I stood at a fork in the road, and all my past experience informed my decision. Yet all my past experiences and years of preparation gave me the assurance that, where God's finger points, His hand will make the way. We may not always have all we want, but He always gives us what we need.

I slowly began to be aware of being filled with the Holy Spirit. I began to think of possibilities of recovering a new and more effective relationship with our Western European friends and the exciting challenges in a new Eastern Europe.

At one very low point in the beginning of my work toward reconciliation, I was on my knees deeply in prayer. The Lord reminded me of my experience in Vietnam when He had spoken to me those words that had transformed my life as a missionary: "My son, you are not in Vietnam because you love the Vietnamese people. You are in Vietnam because I love them, and I want to love them through you." That was when Galatians 2:20 became the verse for my life. "I have been crucified with Christ and I no longer live, but Christ lives in me. The life I live in the body, I live by faith in the Son of God who loved me and gave himself for me" Galatians 2:20 (NIV).

My task now was to be so filled with the presence of Christ that my mind, eyes, heart, hands, and feet were no longer mine but His. My continuing prayer became, "Above all, I am now following your leading, Lord, and I trust you for the courage to exert the leadership necessary to accomplish what You want to happen in all of Europe." Seldom had I felt more dependent on the presence of the Lord. During that time in prayer, I knew beyond any shadow of doubt that God's desire for Europe would be accomplished! Complete trust leads to radical obedience!

After months of visits and key meetings with European leadership, what is known as The Hamburg Agreement[8] was signed and presented to the European Baptist Federation Council annual meeting just outside of London, England, on September 28 to October 2, 1992. It was approved with only one negative vote. It was presented to the IMB trustee meeting on October 12 to 14, 1992, and was unanimously approved.

When I was elected regional vice president, I predicted it might take years before trust and relationships could be restored. That was before I came to know both sides were filled with Christian men and women of good faith, committed ultimately to what is good for the purposes of God as He works through us to bring a lost world to Christ.

I can see the hand of God gently yet firmly continuing to shape my life for moments like this. What seemed so impossible, He formed and worked through His human vessels to bring about His perfect will.

In 2002, at the age of seventy, we felt God was leading me to retire. In talking it over with Dr. Avery Willis, overseas vice president of the International Mission Board, he asked me, "What would you like to do now?"

My immediate response was, "I would like to go home to Vietnam to serve."

He responded, "I can make that happen."

Shortly after my retirement, I was given International Service Corp status and assigned officially to Vietnam. It would be difficult to describe the sense of peace and excitement at returning to the work of teaching pastors and church planters even though I was not able to do this openly because of the Communist regime in that country.

After years of overseas administrative assignments, I was finally returning to my original call fifty years before, when I stood on the flight deck of my aircraft carrier and committed to sharing Jesus and planting churches in those areas of the world where the name of Jesus was not yet known.

In January 2003, the Second Gulf War in Iraq was about to begin. The regional leader for the Middle East and North Africa approached us about coming to his region to serve among the personnel as an encourager and "member care" person during the coming second Iraq war. With my training in pastoral care and counseling and past experience in three wars, I could not decline this invitation.

We transferred once again from Vietnam to the Middle East and North Africa region. Rachel and I began our work immediately. Much happened during our five years of service there, much of which I cannot write about yet, but one experience stands above all others.

In a country in the Middle East and North Africa, I arrived at a missionary's home just before dark. He had invited me to come for a very key meeting at his home. The location was very inconspicuous on a narrow, dirt street away from the main streets. Upon entering, I saw twenty-seven men talking excitedly together. I knew these men belonged to a people group of over two million people scattered through several countries. Research showed there was not even one Christian among this people group. One of our personnel had made contacts, and as a result, these twenty-seven men had become believers.

They were meeting in very small groups. Each group did not know the other groups existed because utmost secrecy was required. Conversion from Islam to Christianity meant a sentence of death. This country did not hesitate to exact that punishment on such "infidels." This night, they were meeting secretly for the first time together and realizing there were more Christians than they had imagined. There was excitement and joy as they met each other for the first time as believers.

Suddenly, outside there was a loud commotion. A woman was demanding to be allowed to enter the meeting. The men were refusing to let her in because, in Muslim culture, women are not allowed to meet in a room with men. My colleague who set up the meeting explained patiently that they were now Christians. We do not discriminate against women that way. God loves them equally with men, and they are welcome to worship with us. She entered and took her seat in the back of the room.

Our person in charge whispered to me that two of the men were not yet believers but were relatives of one of the men. He assured me their presence would be no problem.

The time came for me to bring the message for the evening. My message emphasized that God is a God of love. I shared with them how much God loved us by coming to us in the person of Jesus Christ. God revealed who He is to us through Jesus. Jesus became the sacrifice for our sins. We need to accept God's great love and His forgiveness and receive a new life in Him.

After the sermon, we served the Lord's Supper. Since these

were very new believers they had never heard about the Lord's Supper. We went into great detail to explain what we are doing when we partake of the elements. As we drink the grape juice, it represents the blood of Jesus poured out on the cross for our sins. As we eat the bread, it is the symbol of His body, which was broken for us. We do this to remember Him and the great work of salvation, which has come to us through Jesus's death on the cross and His resurrection.

I sat quietly as the elements were served, looking at each man, wondering, "Do they really understand what is taking place? Is it possible with such little knowledge and background for them to comprehend what is happening?"

An old man was seated near me. I noticed his eyes began to shine with tears brimming over, running down his weather-beaten face. I then noticed the young man seated next to him. He, too, with head bowed, was beginning to shed tears. Here and there across the room, men were wiping the tears from their eyes. Seldom have I been so deeply moved as in those moments, experiencing the new faith and emotions of these men. For the very first time in their life, they were worshipping together the one true God and partaking of the Lord's Supper.

The service over, a young man asked, "May I sit beside you?" His English was very good. He began, "All my life, I have been a Muslim. As a child, I never learned there existed any other religion. In recent years, I have heard of other religions, but I paid little attention. I have watched as Islam has become more and more violent. I know about the beheading of people, the destruction of families, the persecution of anyone not a Muslim or not the right kind of Muslim. They are vicious and unfeeling. Also, I learned Christians are evil and are infidels who deserve to be punished.

"I have read the Koran many times and memorized most of it as a child. Never have I ever heard that Allah is a God of Love. The word *love* seldom occurs anywhere in my religion. Tonight, I heard about a God who loves with such great compassion and sacrifice. I have come to understand for the first time who Jesus is and why he came into the world. I want to tell you I have waited all of my life to hear this. For years, I have not wanted to be a Muslim. Tonight, I want to ask Jesus to come into my life. I want to receive the love of this great God."

Needless to say, I was overcome by the testimony of this young man who had waited for so many years to find what his heart yearned for. Questions flooded my mind. What if he had not come into contact with these Christian men? What if he had not come to this meeting? What if he had not heard a message about how much God loves him? What if this missionary had not had such a compassion and call to minister to the people of this people group? He may never have heard and found the peace and joy in Christ Jesus.

I made my way home that night filled with thanksgiving for what had just happened in the lives of these men. I knelt by my bed and poured out my heart to the Lord, grateful for the way He works in the world. There is nowhere I would rather be than in the center of His will. To follow where God is leading transcends geography, position, power, and specific ministries. It may or may not be where we want to be. And it may or may not be doing what we want to do, but it is always exciting, challenging, learning, growing, and rewarding.

There is no doubt, the source of my own deep sense of peace and joy in service, whether in Asia, dealing with crisis in Europe, or serving in the Middle East and North Africa, is because God created this vessel, formed it, and filled it according to His desire, because He used it according to the purpose for which I was made.

CHAPTER 26

THE FINAL DECISION—FOR NOW

At midnight, I was in a deep sleep. From somewhere in the distance I was suddenly awakened by a voice, "Sam, Sam!" It was coming from near our bathroom. I immediately noticed Rachel was not in bed. She was on the floor and could not move. Her legs were too weak to even attempt to stand.

For the next hour, she and I struggled to get her back into bed. When it was over, I lay in the darkness pondering all that had happened. My foremost thought was, "What if I was not at home? What if I had been in Vietnam?" The answer was clear. It would have been disastrous.

I was due to leave for Vietnam in two days to accompany a group of Vietnamese American pastors to Vietnam to assess some projects they were going to undertake. I also was scheduled to teach. There was no question in my mind what I must do. I canceled the trip.

My mind immediately turned to the future. For some time, I had contemplated my future service in Vietnam. My assignment called for me to be in Vietnam one to two months out of every three. In just a few weeks, I would reach my eighty-second birthday. I thought about my teaching schedule in Vietnam. Every day, I begin teaching Tuesday through Friday at 9:00 a.m. and continue until 5:00 p.m., with brief breaks in the morning, afternoon, and lunch. I always teach in Vietnamese, which is a stress preparing lectures, materials, and dialoguing with students. It was beginning to take every ounce of energy to finish the four full days of teaching each week. There were many other responsibilities I would also perform. Could it be my age was catching up with me? Was it time to retire again? This question echoed constantly in my mind. I did not want to reach a point where others made that decision for me.

I faced the reality that Rachel was now no longer young. Her health was not as strong as it had been over the years. Arthritis was ravaging her spine with spinal stenosis in three strategic locations. This had weakened her legs and feet, so walking and standing had become more and more difficult. Was it fair for me to leave her alone at home while I was absent weeks at a time in Vietnam? I had been afraid to make this a matter of prayer because I did not want to face the answer. Now I had to face it.

Considering all the angles of our situation, it was time for me to retire from my service in Vietnam. On the one hand, this was a traumatic decision and, on the other, a relief; I was finally making the decision I needed to make.

One of my strengths but also a great weakness has always been my refusal to acknowledge age. When I was having my annual physical examination, I shared with the doctor that something may be wrong because I seemed to be somewhat weaker physically than before. He pulled his chair close to me, took me by both arms, and spoke right into my face. "Have you ever heard of aging?" He said, "Sam, there is nothing wrong with you. You just have to admit you are getting older and certain limitations are becoming real to you. Accept it."

When I went to my car to go home, I was suddenly overwhelmed with grief. It dawned on me, with great force, my life as I had known it was over. The tears poured from my eyes. I thought of how I had always been consumed with climbing the next mountain. I'd never asked for those mountains, but they were always there one after the other. Three times, I had almost lost my life, which had made me driven, never wasting a moment of my life. I cried out to the Lord, "What can I do now, Lord, that it is all over!"

It was good for me to cry it out. I began to experience the gentle presence of the Lord, calming my soul. He did not say anything momentous to me. He did not resolve the conflict raging within me. What He did was make me acutely conscious of His loving presence while he allowed me to work through this. Somehow, I knew He was in the process of breaking the pride I always battled. It was always my temptation to find my meaning in life in what I did rather than who I am in Him. I had always struggled with the pride of thinking accomplishing great things for the Lord would bring me self-esteem and the esteem of others.

When we lost Vietnam, I had to deal with my pride, and the Lord taught me my true identity is never found in geography, position, authority, or power. My one true identity is I am a child of God. This identity can never be taken away; nor can I lose it. I am a child of God.

When my work in Europe was completed, and I returned to Vietnam to teach, I had to be reminded again that my identity and true meaning in life was not tied to physical, mental, or spiritual accomplishments. It was simply that I was and always would be a child of God with all that means, as I lived my life for Him. Was it so preposterous that I had to keep learning this over and over again?

What I have never faced is, unavoidably, there will come a day when age robs me of all of those things my pride taught me brings self-esteem and fullness of life.

I believed and taught that there are three essentials to self-esteem. One is a sense of belonging. Everyone has to feel he or she belongs somewhere or to something. If not, we feel isolated. We wonder what is wrong with us that we are rejected or don't seem to be able to feel a sense of belonging. Unable to be accepted by good people, we still search for a belonging, usually among the wrong kind of people. We naturally hunger to belong.

The second essential to having a healthy self-esteem is to have a sense of competence. Everyone has to feel they at least have a sense they can do something well. Otherwise, they wonder what is wrong with them. They can't seem to do anything! Self-esteem suffers.

A third essential is to have a sense of meaning or worth in life. Everyone wants to feel they have meaning or at least a sense they are worth something to someone. Now I needed to listen to my own teaching!

It became evident, with arthritis affecting every area of Rachel's spine, she would not be able to stand more than a few minutes at a time. This meant she could no longer shop for groceries, prepare meals, and perform other chores around the house. My new task lay starkly before me.

I remember the morning I stood by myself in the kitchen looking over my new "kingdom." I had seldom prepared meals before. I knew nothing about cooking. I was raised in the old school of life, which said the kitchen belonged to women. Women had a natural inborn ability to cook and make food appetizing. Men did not belong in the kitchen. Here I was, in the kitchen. If we were going to eat, I was going to have to prepare the food! My sense of belonging never depended on working in the kitchen! I had zero sense of competence in this place! If I had to judge my sense of worth, it would never include the kitchen. I remember thinking, rather jokingly, as I looked over the kitchen, "Surely I have not actually died and gone on to that other existence. If so, this must be that other place where lost souls go and suffer pain and agony, with gnashing of teeth and a hopeless eternity."

I asked, "Lord, is this my reward for all of those years of faithful service? If so, I really was not counting on this. I was really counting on going out in a blaze of glory with a fanfare from the heavens. I know, You don't have to remind me that I followed Your perfect will with absolute trust, but this is not exactly what I envisioned. You're gonna have to help me here!" Thankfully, I know God has a sense of humor!

So it was that my new divine call came to me. I still have the burden to reach a very lost and broken world. I will find ways to do that. But now, instead of God using me to minister to countless people of the world, He is calling me to serve that special one he gave me sixty years ago when He placed a never-ending love for each other in our hearts. He joined us in a holy union to become one flesh, together to go wherever He leads. We committed together as the old hymn so beautifully says, "It may not be on the mountain's height or over the stormy sea, it may not be at the battle front our Lord will have need of [us] but if by a still small voice He calls to paths [we] do not know, [we'll] answer dear Lord with [our] hand in Thine, [we'll] go where you want [us] to go."⁹

With that renewed call of God, I launched into the task He had given me to do. It did not take long to discover my sense of belonging in the kitchen. My sense of competence in household matters began to soar. My meaning in life and sense of worth reached a height I never dreamed possible as Rachel and I began working together to meet not only her needs but mine and our family's. I remember well the first time I prepared a meal for several of our children and grandchildren who came for a visit. I was bursting with pride when my young granddaughter, Ana, finished her plate and said, "That's the best spaghetti I have ever eaten!" I also remember Rachel telling someone on the phone, "Since Sam has been cooking, I have lost eight pounds!" I told her she needed to explain that just a bit. I do cook healthy food!

For so many years, I traveled across the world in response to various challenges and needs. In those years, people in jobs with area or regional responsibilities were not allowed to use board resources to enable wives to travel with husbands. This meant Rachel had to take care of our family, especially the needs of our children, in my absence. She had to become mother, disciplinarian, and "walking encyclopedia" to answer all the kids' questions. She became the nerve center for our family.

Now, in these latter years of our relationship, it is my turn to take care of her. I often think how, for 61 years, she has taken care of me and enabled me to serve the Lord in so many different capacities.

She did it as a part of her calling and because of her love and support of me. Now it is my privilege to serve her as increasingly she has needs only I can meet. God has given me this unique call at this point in life. Just as He gave me that unique call to serve, God gave me a unique love for Rachel that has endured the ups and downs of life together. Only the Lord and my love for Rachel could give such joy and peace in leaving what had to be the most rewarding and challenging life anyone could ever live to take up another life, radically different and alien, in an entirely different world.

I know exactly what Paul meant when he said, "I am not saying this because I am in need, for I have learned to be content whatever the circumstances. I know what it is to be in need, and I know what it is to have plenty. I have learned the secret of being content in any and every situation, whether well fed or hungry, whether living in plenty or in want. I can do everything through Him who gives me strength" Philippians 4:11-13 (NIV).

And so it is a little boy, ten years old, from a small rural town in North Carolina heard an African American church choir and, through this first cross-cultural experience, began a journey that led to the divine call of a loving God to serve peoples of countless colors and cultures around the world. Rachel and I, together, in whose hearts He placed an unconditional love so many years ago, are now serving each other. But our hearts are still burdened for and our eyes are still looking out toward a broken and wounded world, which so desperately needs healing. Who will take our place ...out there?

EPILOGUE

Following my retirement at the age of 70, I engaged in 15 more years of service overseas, including five years in North Africa and The Middle East and 10 years in Vietnam. The story of serving in Vietnam in the years following the Vietnam war is a story that should be told! I yearn to be able to share how it was to be a servant of the Lord there and how God has worked under difficult circumstances, but the nature of the government makes it risky to tell these stories, lest they bring harm to our Lord's work.

These stories will become a sequel to this book in the very near future, when it is safe and acceptable to share in publication.

NOTES

INTRODUCTION

1 Lewis Carol, "Pig and Pepper," chapter VI, in *Alice in Wonderland* (New York: Barnes and Noble Classics, 2003), 73.

2 John Ortberg, *Everybody's Normal Till You Get to Know Them* (Grand Rapids: Zondervan, 2003), 18.

3 Augustine in "The Confessions and Letters of St. Augustine," vol. 1, chapter 1, in *A Select Library of the Nicene and Post-Nicene Fathers of the Christian Church*, ed. Philip Schaff, LLD, 14 vols., (Grand Rapids: Wm Eerdmans Publishing Company, 1953), 45.

CHAPTER 1

4 Philip Bliss, "Let the Lower Lights Be Burning" in *Baptist Hymnal* (Nashville, Tennessee: Convention Press, 22nd printing, 1956), 300.

CHAPTER 3

5 Booker T. Washington, *Up from Slavery* (New York: First Signet Classics Printing, Norrell afterword, New American Library, Penguin Books, 2010).

6 Ibid., 154.

CHAPTER 15

7 This story is told in more detail in Sam James, *Servant on the Edge of History* (Garland, Texas: Hannibal Books, 2005), 119–130.

CHAPTER 25

8   "The Hamburg Agreement," located in IMB Archives.

CHAPTER 26

9   Mary Brown and Charles Paxton, "I'll Go Where You Want Me to Go," (Nashville, Tennessee: Baptist Hymnal, Convention Press, 22nd printing, 1953), 425.

Printed in the United States
By Bookmasters